ZAGATSURVEY®

2001

DALLAS FORT WORTH RESTAURANTS

Editor: Benjamin Schmerler

Local Editors: Suzanne Hough and Kay Winzenried

Local Coordinator: Michele Axley

Published and distributed by
ZAGAT SURVEY, LLC
4 Columbus Circle
New York, New York 10019
Tel: 212 977 6000
E-mail: dallas@zagat.com
Web site: www.zagat.com

Acknowledgments

We are particularly grateful to Katharyn Casey, John Forsythe and Gil Stotler. Special thanks to Gisella Bottiglieri and Diane Steele for their clerical assistance. Their dependability, tireless efforts and accuracy were priceless. Susan Thomas also contributed to this effort.

In addition, we are grateful for the input of the helpful diners who responded so quickly and enthusiastically to the *Survey*.

This guide would not have been possible without the exacting work of our staff:

Phil Cardone, Anne Cole, Erica Curtis, Liz Daleske, Carol Diuguid, Jessica Fields, Jeff Freier, Shelley Gallagher, Sarah Kagan, Natalie Lebert, Mike Liao, Dave Makulec, Jefferson Martin, Laura Mitchell, Andrew O'Neill, Robert Seixas, Zamira Skalkottas, Troy Segal and LaShana Smith.

The reviews published in this guide are based on public opinion surveys, with numerical ratings reflecting the average scores given by all survey participants who voted on each establishment and text based on direct quotes from, or fair paraphrasings of, participants' comments. Phone numbers, addresses, and other factual information were correct to the best of our knowledge when published in this guide; any subsequent changes may not be reflected.

© 2001 Zagat Survey, LLC
ISBN 1-57006-284-6

Contents

About This Survey	5
What's New	6
Dining Tips	7
Key to Ratings/Symbols	9
Map	10
Most Popular	11
Top Ratings	
• Food, Cuisine and Special Feature	12
• Decor, Outdoor, Romantic, Room, View	15
• Service	16
Best Buys	17
ALPHABETICAL DIRECTORY,	
RATINGS AND REVIEWS	
• Dallas	20
• Fort Worth/Mid-Cities	86
INDEXES	
• **Cuisines**	118
• **Locations**	125
• Breakfast	133
• Brunch	133
• Buffet Served	133
• Business Dining	134
• BYO	134
• Caters	134
• Cigar Friendly	136
• Dancing/Entertainment	136
• Delivers/Takeout	137
• Dessert/Ice Cream	139
• Dining Alone	139
• Expense Account	140
• Family Appeal	140
• Fireplace	141
• Game in Season	142
• Happy Hour	142
• Historic Interest	142
• Hotel Dining	143
• "In" Places	143
• Jacket Required	143
• Late Late – After 12:30	143
• Meet for a Drink	144
• Noteworthy Newcomers	144
• Offbeat	145
• Outdoor Dining	145
• Parties & Private Rooms	146
• People-Watching	148
• Power Scene	148
• Pre-Theater/Early Bird Menu	148

- Post-Theater/Late Supper Menu 148
- Prix Fixe Menu. 149
- Pub/Bar/Microbrewery 149
- Quiet Conversation 149
- Raw Bar 149
- Reservations Essential 150
- Romantic 150
- Senior Appeal 150
- Singles Scene 151
- Sleepers 151
- Teenagers & Other Youthful Spirits 152
- Theme Restaurant. 152
- Wine/Beer Only 153
- Winning Wine List. 153
- Young Children 154

Wine Chart 156

About This Survey

Here are the results of our *2001 Dallas/Fort Worth Restaurant Survey* covering nearly 900 restaurants in the Dallas/Fort Worth area.

By regularly surveying large numbers of local restaurant-goers, we have achieved a uniquely current and reliable guide. Nearly 1,000 people participated. Since the participants dined out an average of 4.1 times per week, this *Survey* is based on about 213,200 meals per year.

We want to thank each of our participants. They are a widely diverse group in all respects but one – they are food lovers all. This book is really "theirs."

Of the surveyors, 60% are women, 40% are men; the breakdown by age is 10% in their 20s, 20% in their 30s, 26% in their 40s, 31% in their 50s and 13% in their 60s or above.

To help guide our readers to Dallas/Fort Worth's best meals and best buys, we have prepared a number of lists. See, for example, Dallas/Fort Worth's Most Popular Restaurants (page 11), Top Ratings (pages 12–16) and Best Buys (page 17). On the assumption that most people want a quick fix on the places at which they are considering eating, we have provided handy indexes.

We are particularly grateful to our editors, Suzanne Hough, whose restaurant reviews and food-related stories have appeared in *D Magazine*, *The Orange County Register* and *The Dallas Morning News*, and Kay Winzenried, a restaurant and travel writer for *Dallas Market Center*, *American Way* and *Where Dallas* magazines, America Online's Digital City, as well as Fodor's national & international guide books, and our coordinator, Michele Axley, a food, wine and travel journalist in Dallas.

We invite you to be a reviewer in our next *Survey*. To do so, simply send a stamped, self-addressed, business-size envelope to ZAGAT SURVEY, 4 Columbus Circle, New York, NY 10019, or e-mail us at dallas@zagat.com, so that we will be able to contact you. Each participant will receive a free copy of the next *Dallas/Fort Worth Restaurant Survey* when it is published.

Your comments, suggestions and even criticisms of this *Survey* are also solicited. There is always room for improvement with your help.

New York, New York
February 27, 2001

Nina and Tim Zagat

What's New

Texans like to herd around what's new and hot, so they're stampeding to Salve!, a Mi Piaci Ristorante sibling, which offers Tuscan tastes in an oh-so-smart Uptown Dallas setting. Right around the corner opened We Oui, a brightly colored French-American with whimsical bistro creations and an active bar crowd. In nearby Oak Lawn, Monica Greene is generating an authentic buzz with Ciudad, which specializes in the cuisines of Mexico City and the Yucatán.

'Nosebleed' territory, as city dwellers call the far northern suburbs, is also active. As housing developments and business parks sprout up in these areas, upscale chains such as the Cheesecake Factory in Frisco, as well as ambitious newcomers like Plano's Mignon, a French steakhouse, and Taqueria Cañonita, which serves 'Mexico City Soul Food', have opened to feed the populace.

There's also been a whirlwind of celebrity chef activity: superstar Stephan Pyles turned in his toque at Star Canyon; Tom Fleming set sail from The Riviera's kitchen and came ashore at Lombardi Mare; he, in turn, was replaced by the Hôtel St. Germain's beloved Michael Marshall, whose clogs were then filled by Salve!'s opening chef Sharon Hage; lastly, Laurels' culinary wizard Danielle Custer returned to her native Northwest, despite legions of fans.

In Fort Worth, popular Reata reopened after a devastating tornado but soon lost chef Grady Spears. In other news, the Forest Park neighborhood is being rejuvenated thanks to The Pegasus, a meze-style global eatery, as well as Sapristi!, a casual French bistro/wine bar from Saint-Emilion owner Bernard Tronche. And the national press is shining its light on the Glen Rose area's Rough Creek Lodge, where comforting rooms and chef Gerard Thompson's stellar New American menu add up to a perfect mini-vacation. Other 'must-program' numbers for your cell phone are the ultra-modern Downtown Mediterranean Fizzi and Lonesome Dove, Reata alumnus Tim Love's newcomer in the Stockyards, which serves upscale ranch-style cuisine.

Similar to the growth in north Dallas, the explosion of multi-acre manses in Tarrant County has created an opportunity to feed its well-heeled inhabitants. First the chains obliged, and now more upscale establishments are moving in.

Rounding out the overall positive picture is an average cost per meal of $23.71 in Dallas and $21.93 in Fort Worth, further impetus to treat yourself to a night out.

Dallas, TX
Fort Worth, TX
February 27, 2001

Suzanne Hough
Kay Winzenried

Dining Tips

Over our 20-plus years of surveying restaurant-goers, we've heard from hundreds of thousands of people about their dining-out experiences. Most of their reports are positive – proof of the ever-growing skill and dedication of the nation's chefs and restaurateurs. But inevitably, we also hear about problems.

Obviously, there are certain basics that everyone has the right to expect when dining out: 1. Courteous, hospitable, informative service; 2. Clean, sanitary facilities; 3. Fresh, healthful food; 4. Timely honoring of reservations; and 5. Smoke-free seating.

Sadly, if these conditions aren't met, many diners simply swallow their disappointment, assuming there's nothing they can do. However, the truth is that diners have far more power than they may realize. Every restaurateur worth his or her salt wants to satisfy customers, since happy clients equal a successful business. Rather than the adversaries they sometimes seem to be, diners and restaurateurs are natural allies – both want the same outcome, and each can help the other achieve it. Toward that end, here are a few simple but sometimes forgotten tips that every restaurant-goer should bear in mind:

1. Speak up: If dissatisfied by any aspect of your experience – from the handling of your reservation to the food, service or physical environment – tell the manager. Most problems are easy to resolve at the time they occur – but not if management doesn't know about them until afterward. The opposite is also true: if you're pleased, speak up.

2. Spell out your needs ahead of time: If you have specific dietary requests, wish to bring your own wine, want a smoke-free (or smoking) environment, or have any other special needs, you can avoid disappointment by calling ahead to make sure the restaurant can satisfy you.

3. Do your part: A restaurant's ability to honor reservations, for example, is largely dependent on diners honoring reservations and showing up on time. Make it a point to cancel reservations you're unable to use and be sure to notify the restaurant if you'll be late. The restaurant, in turn, should do its best to seat parties promptly, and, if there are delays, should keep diners informed (a free drink doesn't hurt either).

4. Vote with your dollars: Most people tip 15 to 19%, and often 20% or more at high-end restaurants. Obviously, you have the right not to tip at all if unhappy with the service; but in that case, many simply leave 10% to get the message across. If you like the restaurant, it's worth accompanying the low tip with a word to the management. Of course, the ultimate way to vote with your dollars is not to come back.

5. Put it in writing: Like it or not, all restaurants make mistakes. The best ones distinguish themselves by how well they acknowledge and handle mistakes. If you've expressed your complaints to the restaurant management but haven't gotten a satisfactory response, write to your local restaurant critic, with a copy to the restaurant, detailing the problem. That really gets the restaurateur's attention. Naturally, we also hope you'll express your feelings, pro and con, by voting on zagat.com.

Key to Ratings/Symbols

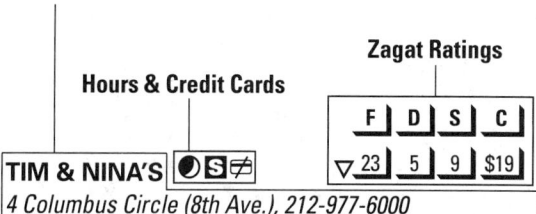

Review with surveyors' comments in quotes

Restaurants with the highest overall ratings, greatest popularity and importance are printed in CAPITAL LETTERS.

Before each review a symbol indicates whether responses were uniform ■ or mixed ◪.

Hours: ☾ serving after 11 PM
  🅂 open on Sunday

Credit Cards: ⊄ no credit cards accepted

Ratings: Food, Decor and Service are rated on a scale of **0** to **30**. The Cost (C) column reflects our surveyors' estimate of the price of a meal including one drink.

F	Food	D	Decor	S	Service	C	Cost
23		5		9		$19	

- **0–9** poor to fair
- **10–15** fair to good
- **16–19** good to very good
- **20–25** very good to excellent
- **26–30** extraordinary to perfection
- ∇ low response/less reliable

A place listed without ratings is either an important **newcomer** or a popular **write-in**. For such places, the estimated cost is indicated by the following symbols.

- **I** $15 and below
- **M** $16 to $30
- **E** $31 to $50
- **VE** $51 or more

www.zagat.com

Most Popular

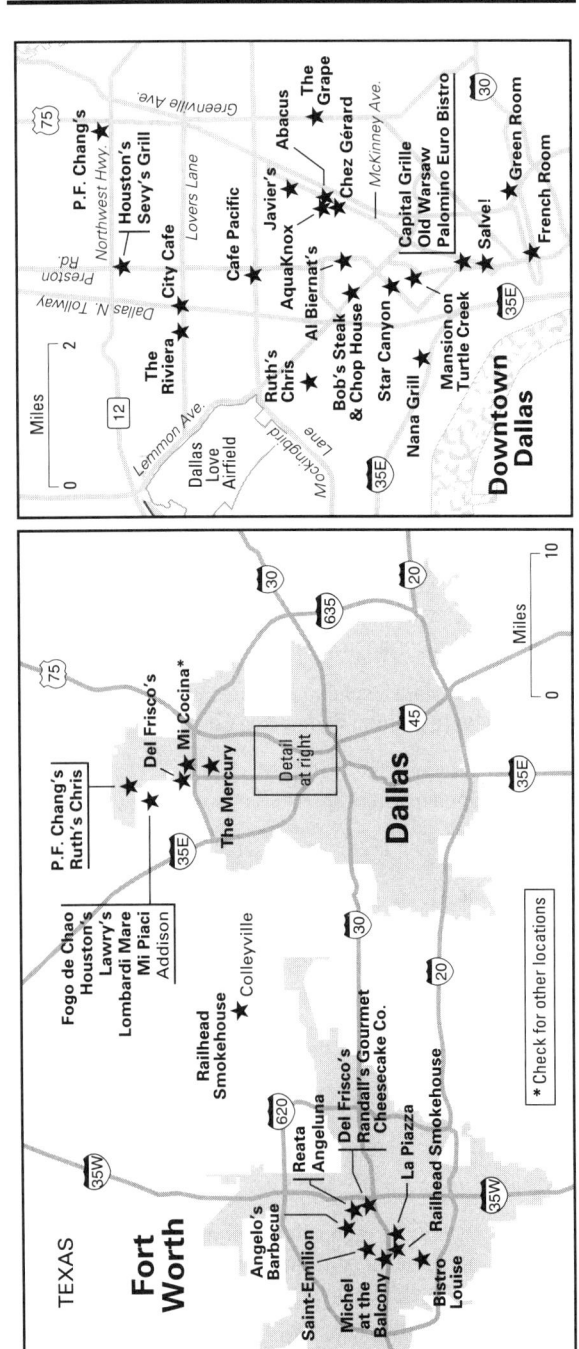

Most Popular

Each of our reviewers has been asked to name his or her five favorite restaurants. The 40 spots most frequently named, in order of their popularity, are:

Dallas

1. Mansion on Turtle Creek
2. Cafe Pacific
3. French Room
4. Riviera
5. Abacus
6. Star Canyon
7. Bob's Steak & Chop
8. Javier's
9. Del Frisco's
10. City Cafe
11. Mi Piaci*
12. Mi Cocina
13. Nana Grill
14. P.F. Chang's
15. Green Room
16. Houston's
17. Ruth's Chris
18. Salve!
19. Chez Gérard
20. Fogo de Chao
21. Capital Grille
22. Palomino
23. Grape
24. Al Biernat's
25. AquaKnox
26. Sevy's Grill*
27. Lawry's
28. Lombardi Mare
29. Mercury
30. Old Warsaw*

Fort Worth/Mid-Cities

1. Bistro Louise
2. Del Frisco's*
3. Reata
4. Saint-Emilion
5. La Piazza
6. Angeluna
7. Michel at the Balcony*
8. Randall's Cheesecake
9. Railhead Smokehse.
10. Angelo's Barbecue

It's obvious that many of the restaurants on the above list are among the most expensive, but Dallas/Fort Worth diners also love a bargain. Were popularity calibrated to price, we suspect that a number of other restaurants would join the above ranks. Thus, we have listed 80 Best Buys on page 17.

---

* Tied with the restaurant listed directly above it.

Top Ratings*

Top 40 Food Ranking

- **28** French Room
  Saint-Emilion/FW
  Riviera
- **27** Laurels
  Mansion on Turtle Creek
  Cafe Pacific
  Del Frisco's/FW
  Bob's Steak & Chop
  La Piazza/FW
- **26** Hôtel St. Germain
  Cacharel/FW
  Pyramid Grill
  Nana Grill
  Green Room
  Pappas Bros. Steakhse.
  Del Frisco's
  Old Warsaw
  Star Canyon
  Randall's Cheesecake/FW
  Mi Piaci

  Abacus
- **25** Bistro Louise/FW
  Modo Mio
  Tei Tei Robata Bar
  City Cafe
  Chamberlain's
  Capital Grille
  Lawry's
  York St.
  Morton's of Chicago
  Fogo de Chao
  Ruth's Chris
  Kincaid's/FW
  Grape
  Railhead Smokehse./FW
  Mercury
  Suze
  Sammy's Barbecue
  Tramontana
  Palm

Top Spots by Cuisine

American (New)
- **27** Laurels
- **26** Pyramid Grill
  Nana Grill
  Green Room
  Abacus

American (Traditional)
- **22** Highland Park Pharmacy
  Buffet at the Kimbell/FW
  Zodiac
- **21** Mac's/FW
  Lucile's Stateside/FW

Asian
- **24** Citizen
- **23** P.F. Chang's
  Liberty
- **21** Tong's House
- **20** Szechuan/FW

Barbecue
- **25** Railhead Smokehse./FW
  Sammy's Barbecue
- **24** Clark's Outpost
- **23** Angelo's Barbecue/FW
- **21** Sonny Bryan's/FW

Cajun/Creole
- **22** Margaux's
  Pappadeaux/FW
- **20** Charleston's/FW
  Nate's
- **16** Razzoo's/FW

Coffee Shop/Diner
- **22** Paris Coffee Shop/FW
  Mama's Daughters'/FW
- **21** Mecca
- **20** Barbec's
- **18** Cafe Brazil

* Excluding restaurants with low voting.
FW= Restaurant in Fort Worth/Mid-Cities or also has locations there.

Top Food

Continental
- **26** Old Warsaw
- **23** Hofstetter's
  Jennivine
  Franki's Li'l Europe
- **22** Chaparral Club

Deli/Sandwich Shop
- **23** Carshon's Deli/FW
- **21** Yogi's Bagel/FW
  Gilbert's
- **20** Street's
- **18** Bagelstein's

Eclectic/International
- **26** Randall's Cheesecake/FW
- **25** Grape
  Suze
- **23** Angeluna/FW
- **20** Grape Escape/FW

French
- **28** French Room
  Saint-Emilion/FW
  Riviera
- **26** Hôtel St. Germain
  Cacharel/FW

Hamburger
- **25** Kincaid's/FW
- **20** Chips Hamburgers
  Snuffer's
- **19** Angry Dog
- **18** Ball's Hamburgers

Italian
- **27** La Piazza/FW
- **26** Mi Piaci
- **25** Modo Mio
- **24** Lombardi Mare
  Salve!

Japanese
- **25** Tei Tei Robata Bar
- **23** Mr. Sushi
  Yamaguchi
- **22** Blue Fish
  Sushi on McKinney

Mediterranean
- **25** Bistro Louise/FW
- **24** Ziziki's
  Mediterraneo
  Palomino
- **23** Il Sole

Mexican
- **24** Javier's
  La Valentina
- **22** La Hacienda/FW
  La Calle Doce
  Monica's

Middle Eastern
- **25** Cafe Izmir
- **22** Ali Baba
  Hedary's Lebanese Oven
- **21** Hedary's Lebanese/FW

Pizza
- **22** Arcodoro & Pomodoro
- **20** Sal's Pizza
  Campisi's/FW
- **19** Sipango
- **18** California Pizza Kitchen

Seafood
- **27** Cafe Pacific
- **24** Nick & Sam's
- **23** AquaKnox
  Al Biernat's
  Newport's Seafood

Southwestern
- **27** Mansion on Turtle Creek
- **26** Star Canyon
- **24** Reata/FW
- **23** Michaels/FW
- **20** Blue Mesa Grill/FW

Steakhouse
- **27** Del Frisco's/FW
  Bob's Steak & Chop
- **26** Pappas Bros. Steakhse.
- **25** Chamberlain's
  Capital Grille

Tex-Mex
- **23** Mia's
- **22** La Hacienda/FW
- **21** Matt's Rancho Martinez
  Pappasito's
  Mi Cocina/FW

Thai
- **23** Chow Thai
- **21** Royal Thai
- **20** Thai Soon
- **19** Thai Taste
- **17** Cathy's Wok

www.zagat.com

Top Food by Special Feature

Breakfast*
- **23** Carshon's Deli/FW
- **22** Paris Coffee Shop/FW
- **21** Breadwinners
     Gilbert's
     Mecca

Brunch
- **27** Mansion on Turtle Creek
- **26** Nana Grill
- **24** Lombardi Mare
- **23** Rooster
- **20** Abuelo's/FW

Business Dining
- **27** Del Frisco's/FW
- **25** Morton's of Chicago
- **23** Al Biernat's
- **22** Gershwin's
     Dakota's

Hotel Dining
- **28** French Room
     Hotel Adolphus
- **27** Mansion on Turtle Creek
     Mansion on Turtle Creek
- **26** Hôtel St. Germain
     Hôtel St. Germain
     Pyramid Grill
     Fairmont Hotel
     Nana Grill
     Wyndham Anatole

Newcomers/Unrated
- Jeroboam
- Lola
- Lonesome Dove/FW
- Mignon
- Sapristi!/FW

People-Watching
- **25** Voltaire
- **24** Nick & Sam's
     Palomino
- **23** Angeluna/FW
- **19** We Oui

---

* Other than hotels.

Top 40 Decor Ranking

29 French Room
28 Hôtel St. Germain
    Mansion on Turtle Creek
27 Abacus
    Laurels
    Reata/FW
    Voltaire
    Nana Grill
26 Star Canyon
    La Piazza/FW
    Del Frisco's/FW
    Pyramid Grill
    Capital Grille
25 Saint-Emilion/FW
    Cafe Pacific
    Lady Primrose's
    AquaKnox
    Pappas Bros. Steakhse.
    Beau Nash
    Cacharel/FW
    Riviera
    Palomino
    Citizen
24 Mi Piaci
    Chaparral Club
    Lombardi Mare
    Bistro Louise/FW
    Rainforest Cafe/FW
    Old Warsaw
    Randall's Cheesecake/FW
    Dakota's
    Salve!
    Nick & Sam's
    Del Frisco's
23 Sullivan's
    Cafe Capri
    Al Biernat's
    Lavendou
    Abuelo's Mexican/FW
    Angeluna/FW

Outdoor

Angeluna/FW
Dakota's
Grape
Il Sole
Joe T. Garcia's/FW
Lauderdale's on the Lake/FW
Matt's Rancho Martinez
Oasis/FW
Primo's
Rooster
Salve!
Star Canyon

Romantic

Cacharel/FW
Chez Gérard
Dakota's
French Room
Grape
Hôtel St. Germain
Mansion on Turtle Creek
Randall's Cheesecake/FW
Saint-Emilion/FW
York St.

Room

Abacus
Angeluna/FW
AquaKnox
Cool River Cafe/FW
Dakota's
Lombardi Mare
Palm
Palomino
Salve!
Star Canyon
Tenaya/FW
Voltaire

View

Angeluna/FW
Antares
Chaparral Club
Joe T. Garcia's/FW
Laurels
Mustang Cafe/FW
Nana Grill
Reata/FW

Top 40 Service Ranking

- **28** French Room
- **27** Mansion on Turtle Creek
- **26** Riviera
  Laurels
  Hôtel St. Germain
  Del Frisco's/FW
  Saint-Emilion/FW
  Cafe Pacific
- **25** Nana Grill
  Reata/FW
  Cacharel/FW
  Capital Grille
  Bob's Steak & Chop
- **24** Pyramid Grill
  Pappas Bros. Steakhse.
  York St.
  La Piazza/FW
  Fogo de Chao
  Star Canyon
  Lawry's

  Morton's of Chicago
  Ruth's Chris
  Del Frisco's
  Ferrari's Italian Villa
- **23** Old Warsaw
  Voltaire
  Chamberlain's
  Randall's Cheesecake/FW
  Palm
  Abacus
  Al Biernat's
  Sullivan's
  Nick & Sam's
  Green Room
  Addison Cafe
  Kobe Steaks
  Mi Piaci
  Ruggeri's Ristorante
  City Cafe
  Newport's Seafood

Best Buys

40 Top Bangs for the Buck

This list reflects the best dining values in our *Survey*. It is produced by dividing the cost of a meal into the combined ratings for food, decor and service.

1. Highland Park Pharmacy
2. Bagel Chain
3. Wild About Harry's
4. Kincaid's/FW
5. Paris Coffee Shop/FW
6. Empire Baking Co.
7. Mecca
8. Bubba's
9. Norma's Cafe
10. Yogi's Bagel/FW
11. Chipotle/FW
12. Street's
13. Chips Hamburgers
14. Mama's Daughters'/FW
15. Railhead/FW
16. Buffet at the Kimbell/FW
17. Sammy's Barbecue
18. Carshon's Deli/FW
19. Barbec's
20. Original Pancake House
21. Ball's Hamburgers
22. Cowboy Chicken
23. Bagelstein's
24. Texadelphia
25. Fresh Choice/FW
26. Angelo's Barbecue/FW
27. Baker's Ribs
28. Celebrity Cafe
29. Corner Bakery/FW
30. Mai's Vietnamese
31. Angry Dog
32. Jason's Deli/FW
33. EatZi's
34. Purdy's
35. Peggy Sue BBQ
36. Purple Cow/FW
37. Ez's
38. Taco Cabana
39. Cindi's Deli
40. Fuddruckers/FW

Additional Good Values
(A bit more expensive, but worth every penny)

Abuelo's Mexican/FW
Al's Pizzeria
Avila's
Aw Shucks
Babe's Chicken Dinner/FW
Benito's/FW
Black-eyed Pea
Blue Goose Cantina
Blue Mesa Grill/FW
Breadwinners Cafe
Cafe Brazil
Cafe Express
Campisi's/FW
Cathy's Wok
Covino's
Hedary's Lebanese/FW
Hot Damn, Tamales!/FW
Il Grano
Joe T. Garcia's/FW
Jubilee Cafe/FW

Kalachandji's
Kel's
Leonardo's
Lover's Egg Roll/FW
Luna de Noche
Mainstream Fish House
Mai's Vietnamese
Matt's Rancho Martinez
Mi Cocina/FW
Nuevo Leon
Poor Richard's Cafe
Primo's
Red Hot & Blue/FW
Rockfish Seafood Grill/FW
Sal's Pizza
Sonny Bryan's/FW
Snuffer's
Szechuan/FW
Tin Star
Tupinamba

www.zagat.com

Alphabetical Directory of Restaurants

Dallas

	F	D	S	C
ABACUS	26	27	23	$58

4511 McKinney Ave. (Knox St.), 214-559-3111

■ "If I could afford it, I'd eat here every night" gush acolytes of chef-owner Kent Rathbun's Uptown New American where dazzling tasting menus, "novel appetizers" like "delicious lobster shooters" and an "interesting wine list" are complemented by a "visually stunning", geometrically themed interior with "lovely orchids" on every table; the bottom line: a smart choice for "special-occasion dining."

Abuelo's Mexican Food Embassy S	20	23	18	$20

3420 N. Central Expwy. (bet. Parker Rd. & Spring Creek Pkwy.), Plano, 972-423-9290
See review in Fort Worth Directory.

Addison Cafe S	22	20	23	$38

5290 Belt Line Rd. (Montfort Dr.), Addison, 972-991-8824

■ A 16-year-old peacock still struts around a cage in one of the dining rooms of this Addison Classic French stop where the waiters "remember you by name" and the "refreshingly quiet" atmosphere allows you to "hear yourself think"; expect "consistently good" cuisine that's highlighted by "wonderful desserts" like crème brûlée.

Adelmo's	23	17	22	$35

4537 Cole Ave. (Knox St.), 214-559-0325

■ "Personal attention from the staff", complimentary pickled vegetables and salad and "excellent" blackboard specials like the famous thick, juicy veal chop explain the popularity of this "rustic", "romantic" Uptown Mediterranean, a "charming" place to "settle in for the evening."

A.J. Gonzales' Mexican Oven	▽ 17	12	15	$24

703 McKinney Ave. (Record St.), 214-754-8070

■ It's "pretty much what you'd expect from a cheapie West End Tex-Mex"/Mexican eatery note voters weighing in on this unprepossessing entry; nonetheless, loyalists vouch for the brisket enchiladas ("oh yeah") and vegetarian options like chile rellenos.

Akbar S	▽ 21	16	17	$18

Ruisseau Village, 301 W. Parker Rd. (Central Expwy.), Plano, 972-235-0260

■ Decorated with Mogul-era paintings, this "warm, hospitable" Plano BYO is one of "the best Indians in the Metroplex"; in addition to an "excellent lunch buffet", there's also standout chicken tikka, lamb curry and rice pudding.

Dallas | F | D | S | C |

Al-Amir ⑤ | ▽ | 19 | 14 | 16 | $22 |
7402 Greenville Ave. (Pineland Dr.), 214-739-2647
◪ Middle Eastern victuals and late-night fun come together at this Greenville ethnic where after chowing down on solid grilled meats like the shish kebab, patrons can party with a DJ and belly dancer until 2 AM (Thursday–Saturday); if "nightclub atmosphere" isn't your thing (don't expect to have a quiet conversation), there's always takeout.

AL BIERNAT'S ⑤ | 23 | 23 | 23 | $49 |
4217 Oak Lawn Ave. (Herschel Ave.), 214-219-2201
◪ "Personal attention" from "consummate host-owner" Al Biernat wins over many to this Oak Lawn seafooder/steakhouse where it's best to dress up and "ask for a booth" to take in the boisterous, "see-and be-seen" scene; "huge portions", "delicious salads" and great beef go a long way as well, though a few tough-to-please types note that the "excellent" service is even "better when they know you."

Alfredo Trattoria | 22 | 16 | 21 | $27 |
5404 Lemmon Ave. (Dorothy Ave.), 214-526-3331
■ "Very tasty" Italian cooking garners converts to this family-run Downtown spot where you shouldn't be surprised if the staff "makes you feel welcome" and rightly encourages you to order the homemade mozzarella, potent garlic soup, chicken piccata and osso buco.

Ali Baba Cafe | 22 | 8 | 14 | $16 |
1905 Greenville Ave. (Oram St.), 214-823-8235
■ "When your body craves Middle Eastern food, this is the place to go" advise regulars of this Greenville bohemian hot spot, known for its hummus and garlicky golden chicken; heady odors further whet the appetite, though the "no-frills" interior argues for takeout from the adjacent market.

Al's Pizzeria ⑤ | ▽ | 23 | 11 | 17 | $12 |
3701 W. Northwest Hwy. (Webb Chapel Rd.), 214-350-2714
■ Sure there are "great calzones" and marvelous meatball sandwiches at this Suburban Northwest pie palace, but it's the super thin-crust pizzas that draw folks from miles around; an interior filled with checked vinyl cloths and TVs blaring sports seems just right, as does the informal self-service setup (order from the "nice people" at the counter, grab some napkins and silverware and stake out a table).

Amici Signature Italian | ▽ | 24 | 15 | 22 | $34 |
1022 S. Broadway St. (south of Belt Line Rd.), Carrollton, 972-245-3191
■ Up a creaky flight of stairs to the second floor of a historic Downtown Carrolltown building lies this cozy trattoria, which is "worth finding" for both its Italian basics and "creative", Med-focused dinner specials; "caring service" and a BYO policy that "allows you to pair your best wines with their wonderful food" negate the dated decor.

Dallas | F | D | S | C |

Amore Italian | 19 | 15 | 20 | $20 |
Snider Plaza, 6931 Snider Plaza (Westminster Ave.), 214-739-0502
■ "Seniors, SMU faculty and students after that monthly check" arrives head to this Snider Plaza Italian for "very welcoming service", "generous portions" of "reliable" "traditional fare", a "cozy", "candlelit" setting and the spectacle of "staring at a Mona Lisa on every wall"; P.S. as a "neighborhood favorite" it can be "hard to get into", so reservations are recommended.

Anderson's BBQ House | ▽ 21 | 9 | 17 | $10 |
5410 Harry Hines Blvd. (Butler St.), 214-630-0735
■ Don't be surprised if the "guy in front of you buying that beef sandwich plate is a cardiologist from one of the nearby hospitals" note ironic-minded regulars commenting on this "very affordable" country-western–themed Suburban Northwest BBQ joint; it "does a booming lunch business", so "go early" to get your share of baked potatoes, pork ribs and peach cobbler.

Angelo's Italian Grill S | ▽ 19 | 15 | 17 | $18 |
6341 La Vista Dr. (Gaston Ave.), 214-823-5566
■ Puppy-eyed couples on dates love the "candlelight, soft music" and booths at this popular Lakewood Italian, but it's also relaxed enough for families on the lookout "for pizzas" and cheap, all-you-can-eat weekday lunch buffets.

Angry Dog ●S | 19 | 14 | 16 | $13 |
2726 Commerce St. (Crowdus St.), 214-741-4406
■ No pooch would be peeved to eat the "to-die-for hot dogs" or "terrific burgers" served at this Deep Ellum restaurant and pub where "beer and beer food reign" and "loud" members of Gen X are out in force; while service isn't flawless, the "swift" staff works hard to handle the crowds.

Antares S | 16 | 22 | 19 | $41 |
Hyatt Regency Dallas, 300 Reunion Blvd. (Commerce St. & I-35E), 214-712-7145
◪ Rotating high, high atop the Downtown Hyatt Regency, this New American offers a "great" 360-degree view of Dallas; while ratings suggest the seasonal menu is good but "not excellent", this is still an obvious spot to take out-of-towners, especially for Sunday brunch, an early evening drink or when the acrobatic window washers are scheduled.

AQUAKNOX S | 24 | 25 | 22 | $51 |
3214 Knox St. (Cole Ave.), 214-219-2782
◪ "Fine, fresh fish" and a "cool, contemporary" look, including a wall of water and a minimalist Asian credenza centerpiece, are the hallmarks of this "trendy" Knox/Henderson aquatic haven, which is a "great place to go at someone else's expense"; those paying their own way knock it as "overpriced" and "overrated."

Dallas | F | D | S | C |

Arc-en-Ciel S | 20 | 10 | 15 | $19 |
3555 W. Walnut St. (Jupiter Rd.), Garland, 972-272-2188
■ "You almost forget you're in Dallas" at this enormous Garland Asian where dim sum carts at lunch bring a "wide variety" of appetizer-size morsels (steamed dumplings, spring rolls and the like); lots of Chinese and Vietnamese offerings further justify why it's "worth a trip", but since many of the servers speak limited English, it helps to point.

Arcodoro & Pomodoro ● S | 22 | – | 19 | $30 |
2708 Routh St. (McKinney Ave.), 214-871-1924
■ These two longtime Uptown Italian favorites have joined together and moved a few blocks east to a new space that's been renovated to resemble an Italian villa; they now share a kitchen and the same Sardinian menu, with the exception of the popular wood-oven pizzas, which are served only in Arcodoro, the more casual bar/cafe area.

August Moon S | 17 | 16 | 16 | $18 |
Pepper Sq., 15030 Preston Rd. (Belt Line Rd.), 972-385-7227
2300 N. Central Expwy. (Park Blvd.), Plano, 972-881-0071
◪ One august group of surveyors finds this North Dallas and Plano Chinese duo a "reliably good" choice for "house specialties such as five-flavor shrimp"; critics, however, say "the moon is waning" but concede that it's still "impressive to see the waitresses peel off the snow pea strings."

Avanti Euro Bistro S | ▽ 22 | 21 | 20 | $29 |
5001 Addison Circle (bet. Addison Rd. & Quorum Dr.), Addison, 972-386-7800
■ Leopard-print banquettes add decorative zip to this "attractive", global-influenced French-Moroccan in Addison where meals often begin with bountiful meze platters and end with "delicious desserts" (try the chocolate profiterole) and "wonderful" nightly jazz.

Avanti Restaurant at Fountain Place | ▽ 22 | 20 | 21 | $27 |
Fountain Pl., 1445 Ross Ave. (Field St.), 214-965-0055
■ Martha Stewart would salivate upon seeing this Downtown Italian's enormous courtyard containing a waterfall, fountains and "amply spaced tables"; keep it in mind as an ideal place for a quiet, "romantic" dinner ("wonderful spinach lasagna") or large private party; N.B. dancing and live entertainment are no longer offered.

Avanti Ristorante S | 22 | 18 | 20 | $29 |
2723 McKinney Ave. (Worthington St.), 214-871-4955
■ This small, cozy Uptown Italian doesn't get much press ("a sleeper"), but it's been attracting steady crowds for the past 12 years; its secret: an "excellent" menu of favorites like the veal chop, as well as plenty of "late-night fun" Thursday–Saturday when the kitchen stays open until the wee hours and offers a 'moonlight breakfast.'

Dallas | F | D | S | C |

Avila's Mexican Restaurant ▽ | 25 | 14 | 19 | $13 |
4714 Maple Ave. (Kings Rd.), 214-520-2700

■ "Don't let the exterior scare you off" because "some of the best Mexican food around" can be found at this modestly decorated Downtown "institution" where marvelous moles, enchiladas, tamales and creamy homemade flans lead the hit parade.

Aw Shucks S | 18 | 10 | 14 | $15 |
3601 Greenville Ave. (Longview St.), 214-821-9449

■ "Definitely a jeans and T-shirt place", this "hectic" Greenville seafooder works "when you need a fix" of Louisiana Bay oysters and some "messy-but-worth-it" Dungeness crab legs – or simply want a bowl of gumbo and a cold beer; pampered types may be surprised to learn that "service consists of a walk-up counter."

Baby Doe's Matchless Mine S | 14 | 19 | 15 | $28 |
3305 Harry Hines Blvd. (I-35, Oak Lawn Ave. exit), 214-871-7310

◪ "Interesting mine-shaft decor" and a panoramic view of Dallas are the draws of this theme Oak Lawn steakhouse, which gets some votes for its Sunday brunch but otherwise doesn't endear itself to critics who find it "kind of hokey" and for "tourists only."

Bagel Chain S | 21 | 10 | 17 | $7 |
5555 W. Lovers Ln. (Inwood Rd.), 214-350-2245

■ Bagel fans find they "couldn't make it a week" without a "cheap, fast lunch" of "great chicken salad" at this Lovers Lane NYC–style deli; a sparse interior means "get it to go or sit outside."

Bagelstein's S | 18 | 11 | 15 | $11 |
8104 E. Spring Valley Rd. (Coit Rd.), 972-234-3787

◪ Open for almost 25 years "but still one of the better delis in town", this North Dallas eatery serves "dependable" breakfasts, overstuffed sandwiches and chicken soup with truly huge matzo balls; aesthetes think the "cheesy" decor should be spiffed up.

Baker's Ribs | 20 | 12 | 14 | $12 |
2724 Commerce St. (bet. Crowdus & Henry Sts.), 214-748-5433
4844 Greenville Ave. (bet. Lovers Ln. & University Blvd.), 214-373-0082 S
488 I-30 W. (Belt Line Rd.), Garland, 972-226-7447 S

■ I'm "ready to lasso the cows myself!" declare rabid fans of this family-owned 'cue minichain whose "juicy", "smoky" ribs, "tender chopped-beef sandwiches" and "succulent chicken" are complemented by sassy sides like the black-bean-and-corn salad.

Dallas

| F | D | S | C |

Ball's Hamburgers S — 18 | 13 | 15 | $11
Village of Preston Hollow, 4343 W. Northwest Hwy. (Midway Rd.), 214-352-2525
Snider Plaza, 3404 Rankin St. (Hillcrest Ave.), 214-373-1717
■ Filled with "soccer moms and tots", these North Dallas and Park Cities patty parlors may not look fancy and may seem "a little noisy", but they make "low-priced" "fun, fattening" stops for "very good", "hearty" hamburgers, onion rings and "yummy shakes"; N.B. the basket of three mini-burgers is perfect for the kids.

Bangkok City S — ▽ 24 | 11 | 17 | $15
4301 Bryan St. (Peak St.), 214-824-6200
4503 Greenville Ave. (Yale Blvd.), 214-691-8233
■ Ignore the decor and concentrate on the "authentic Thai" cuisine at these Downtown and Greenville Siamese twins where the service is "personal" and the fare is "consistently excellent"; a number of voters favor the Bryan Street branch for its relatively more "festive" atmosphere.

Barbec's S⌀ — 20 | 11 | 16 | $11
8949 Garland Rd. (Emerald Isle Dr.), 214-321-5597
■ "Go for the beer biscuits, beer biscuits, beer biscuits" is the exhortation from commentators on this "crowded" East Dallas breakfast landmark whose "diner food" "restores your cholesterol level" (assuming it's too low) and "trailer-park decor" argues for a renovation.

Basha Mediterranean — 20 | 15 | 17 | $26
2217 Greenville Ave. (Richmond Ave.), 214-824-7794
■ "Sit in the tent room" to get a "ringside" seat for the belly dancers (Friday and Saturday) at this Lower Greenville Mediterranean, which appeals to Gen Xers looking to unwind over traditional breads and dips as well as a "don't-miss" pistachio-crusted chicken.

Bavarian Grill — 18 | 17 | 18 | $20
Ruisseau Village, 221 W. Parker Rd. (Central Expwy.), Plano, 972-881-0705
■ "Authentic German" cuisine ("good sausages"), 60 types of suds, a *biergarten*, decor "straight from Munich" and "enough live polka music to tap your feet to" make this Plano Deutsch choice a "fun" pick "for cold-weather" dining.

Beau Nash S — 22 | 25 | 22 | $41
Hotel Crescent Court, 400 Crescent Ct. (Cedar Springs Rd.), 214-871-3240
■ The "place to be seen in Uptown Dallas", this boisterous American "oldie but goodie" oozes "city sophistication" thanks to "lots of beautiful people", correct "unobtrusive" service and a softly lit interior with polished wood and bountiful floral displays; try to visit for lunch on the "pretty" enclosed conservatory, after-work cocktails at the bar ("one of the best martinis") or Sunday brunch.

Dallas

	F	D	S	C

Benihana Grill ⓢ   21 | 20 | 21 | $27
3848 Oak Lawn Ave. (Blackburn St.), 214-559-3450
■ Kids "love the knife tricks" performed by the "animated", "entertaining" teppanyaki chefs who cook in front of diners at this Oak Lawn Japanese, "a good, smaller offshoot of the original" branch; if dining alone, grab a seat at one of the large communal tables and start chatting.

Benihana of Tokyo ⓢ   22 | 21 | 22 | $29
7775 Banner Dr. (Coit Rd.), 972-387-4404
■ Prepare for "an adventure, not just a meal" at this old-time North Dallas Japanese chain venue where the chefs nimbly slice and dice steaks, seafood and chicken; while not for everyone, it's "fun for groups" and birthday parties.

Big Fish, Little Fish ⓢ   21 | 16 | 19 | $24
2810 N. Henderson Ave. (Richard Ave.), 214-821-4552
■ A menu that allow patrons to "mix and match dozens of fish with dozens of sauces" is the concept behind this "rustic" Knox/Henderson seafooder, "one of the better kept secrets in town", with a "well-chosen wine list" and warm servers; P.S. "for a real treat, reserve the 'in-the-boat' table."

Bistral ⓢ   18 | 18 | 18 | $33
2900 McKinney Ave. (N. Lamar St.), 214-220-1202
■ More than 450 labels comprise the "lovely" wine list at this intimate Uptown New American whose menu ranges from solid burgers to "imaginative takes on bistro fare" like orange-and-pepper-marinated chicken; a "hip crowd", "fun booths" and a worthwhile Sunday brunch are pluses too.

Bistro A   21 | 18 | 19 | $37
Snider Plaza, 6815 Snider Plaza (Lovers Ln.), 214-373-9911
◪ Surveyors are of mixed minds on chef-owner Avner Samuel's soothing-looking Mediterranean near SMU: boosters focus on "light", "tasty" edibles like the "refreshing meze appetizer plate" and "gorgeous fish"; detractors would like less "attitude" and more food ("miniscule portions").

Black-eyed Pea ⓢ   15 | 13 | 14 | $13
3857 Cedar Springs Rd. (Reagan St.), 214-521-4580
7778 Forest Ln. (N. Central Expwy.), 214-361-7221
5601 Greenville Ave. (Lovers Ln.), 214-361-5979
5600 W. Lovers Ln. (Inwood Rd.), 214-352-3781
2212 W. Northwest Hwy. (Stemmons Frwy.), 214-654-0112
4460 Belt Line Rd. (Midway Rd.), Addison, 972-701-0166
2625 Old Denton Rd. (Trinity Mills Rd.), Carrollton, 972-245-9744
3825 Pavillion Ct. (I-635), Mesquite, 972-686-1787
1905 Preston Rd. (Plano Pkwy.), Plano, 972-248-6096
605 W. 15th St. (Alma Rd.), Plano, 972-423-5565
◪ "Aimed at families and senior citizens", there's "something for everyone" on this chain's midpriced menu of American "comfort" eats; while gourmands call the fare "mediocre", "if you can't find anything else, it does the trick."

Dallas

| | F | D | S | C |

Blue Fish 🅢   22 | 19 | 19 | $28
18149 N. Dallas Pkwy. (Frankford Rd.), 972-250-3474
3519 Greenville Ave. (McCommas Blvd.), 214-824-3474

■ "Fun" and trendy, these North Dallas and Greenville Japanese magnets attract raw fish fiends as well as those hankering for Pacific Rim–influenced dishes, a huge selection of sake, delicious green-tea frozen custard and eye-catching decor.

Blue Goose Cantina 🅢   18 | 15 | 15 | $17
2905 Greenville Ave. (Goodwin Ave.), 214-823-6786
14920 Midway Rd. (Beltway Rd.), Addison, 972-726-8771
4757 W. Park Blvd. (Preston Rd.), Plano, 972-596-8882

■ Homemade tortilla chips, "epic portions" of Tex-Mex edibles and "funky" decor (lots of neon bar signs) appease the "hordes of twenty- and thirtysomethings" that patronize this decent trio; surveyors add that the Greenville branch is a nice spot to "sit on the patio and watch everybody drive by."

Blue Mesa Grill 🅢   20 | 20 | 18 | $21
Lincoln Park Shopping Ctr., 7700 W. Northwest Hwy. (Central Expwy.), 214-378-8686
Village on the Pkwy., 5100 Belt Line Rd. (Dallas Pkwy.), Addison, 972-934-0165

■ "Don't miss happy hour" (free appetizers!) insist fans of these "crowded", cacophonous Southwesterns, much-loved for their "dangerous blue margaritas", "excellent guacamole", "belt-popping brunch" buffet and "snazzy" Santa Fe–style decor; while service is a nonissue, it is possible to get a "waiter who's descriptive, pithy and witty, like a Zagat comment."

BOB'S STEAK & CHOP HOUSE   27 | 22 | 25 | $47
4300 Lemmon Ave. (Wycliff Ave.), 214-528-9446

■ "As close as you can get to a private club without paying dues" is how close-knit regulars describe this "dark" Lemmon Avenue steakhouse, which serves some of "the best prime beef in Dallas" as well as critically acclaimed lamb chops and enormous glazed carrots that are "out of this world"; N.B. while sensitive types may not like walking through the cigar smoke–filled bar, the dining rooms are well-ventilated.

Breadwinners Cafe & Bakery 🅢   21 | 18 | 18 | $18
3301 McKinney Ave. (Hall St.), 214-754-4940

■ Warning: "you can gain 10 pounds by just looking" at the "wonderful breads", pastries and desserts in the display case of this North of Downtown American cafe/bakery, which has an "especially nice courtyard" to linger over some of the "best breakfasts" and brunches in town.

Dallas | F | D | S | C |

Bronx, The ⓢ | 18 | 15 | 17 | $22 |
3835 Cedar Springs Rd. (Oak Lawn Ave.), 214-521-5821
■ For almost 25 years this wood-paneled Oak Lawn New American has been a "hidden treasure" for "above-average" cuisine and "friendly service"; migas at the "great Sunday brunch", the wilted spinach salad and grilled rosemary salmon are popular ways to approach it.

Bubba's ⓢ⊘ | 21 | 12 | 15 | $10 |
Snider Plaza, 6617 Hillcrest Rd. (Lovers Ln.), 214-373-6527
■ "This is the place for fried chicken and delicious dinner rolls" declare members of the SMU set, who get "all the fat intake that a student needs" at this Snider Plaza diner; P.S. early-birds love the "great cheap breakfasts."

Cafe Athenée | 20 | 18 | 20 | $27 |
5365 Spring Valley Rd. (Montfort Dr.), 972-239-8060
■ "One of North Dallas' best-kept secrets", this "romantic little jewel" is a "delightful, family-run" Romanian-focused Eastern European entry; its "unusual" offerings (at least for these parts) include a white caviar mousse appetizer, an eggplant-and-ham salad and housemade sausages.

Cafe Brazil ⓢ | 18 | 12 | 14 | $14 |
2815 Elm St. (Crowdus St.), 214-747-2730 ◐
2221 Abrams Rd. (Belmont Ave.), 214-826-9522
6420 N. Central Expwy. (bet. Dyer St. & University Blvd.), 214-691-7791 ◐
3847 Cedar Springs Rd. (Oak Lawn Ave.), 214-461-8762
2071 N. Central Expwy. (Campbell Rd.), Richardson, 972-783-9011
◪ Gen Xers head to these "hip" coffee shops "for late-night snacks" and "hangover-cure" breakfasts of massive omelets, "scrumptious French toast" and "bottomless" cups of jumpin' java; service can be "spotty" at times, but that's almost a prerequisite for "colorful" "hangouts" anyway.

Cafe Capri | 23 | 23 | 22 | $37 |
15107 Addison Rd. (Belt Line Rd.), Addison, 972-960-8686
■ Tucked away in Addison, this longtime Continental destination has "romantic atmosphere" (there's a harpist nightly), "excellent" service and plenty of classic renditions such as Dover sole, Châteaubriand and dessert soufflés; regulars add that coming here has become "a nice tradition."

Cafe Express ⓢ | 19 | 16 | 15 | $14 |
5600 W. Lovers Ln. (Greenway Blvd.), 214-352-2211
3230 McKinney Ave. (bet. Bowen & Hall Sts.), 214-999-9444
4101 Belt Line Rd. (west of Midway Rd.), Addison, 972-991-9444
■ Possibly "the future of fast food", this whimsical-looking American chain requires patrons to order at the counter then gives them the option of stopping by an upscale condiment bar (with oils, vinegars, mustards, etc.) before enjoying huge salads and zesty soups; while usually good for a "quick", "light" meal, the lines can get "out of control at lunch."

Dallas

| | F | D | S | C |

Cafe Expresso | 23 | 17 | 23 | $25
Preston Ctr., 6135 Luther Ln. (Preston Rd., off W. Northwest Hwy.), 214-361-6984

■ "As comfortable as our own dining room but with no dishes" to contend with is the consensus on this "high-quality" Italian, a "Preston Center haunt" near the Northwest Highway, where "cheerful" owner Dieter Paul is "always on hand" to "make sure things are done right"; reliable options include any veal dish and the grilled shrimp.

Cafe Highland Park S | 22 | 20 | 21 | $31
Highland Park Village, 69 Highland Park Village (Mockingbird Ln. & Preston Rd.), 214-521-7300

■ This Highland Park Mediterranean has an elegant dining room with windows overlooking a "peaceful" garden, along with a few second-story tables that couples find "romantic"; unobtrusive, formal service, "towering crab cakes" and dishes with well-made sauces further argue for a visit.

Cafe Istanbul S | 21 | 17 | 19 | $23
Inwood Village, 5450 W. Lovers Ln. (Inwood Rd.), 214-902-0919

■ "Small" and "unassuming", this Lovers Lane source for "authentic" Turkish cuisine is best enjoyed with a group; regulars suggest starting with some "warm pita bread" and hummus, ending with "yummy baklava" and trying to visit when the gyrating belly dancers perform.

Cafe Izmir S | 25 | 21 | 22 | $26
3711 Greenville Ave. (south of Mockingbird Ln.), 214-826-7788

■ Could ordering be any simpler than at this impressive Greenville Middle Eastern where your waiter says "'this is really easy: there's no menu, just tell me whether you want food with meat or without'"?; most meals are prix fixe, but some à la carte options also please picky types, as do "plenty of wines by the glass."

Cafe Madrid ◐ | 21 | 16 | 17 | $24
4501 Travis St. (Armstrong Ave.), 214-528-1731

■ Sangria "that will knock you off your feet" is one good reason why this Knox/Henderson Iberian reminds surveyors of "times spent in Barcelona"; there are also "excellent tapas" ("try the baked tomatoes with manchego"), "fine paella" and an all-Spanish wine list.

CAFE PACIFIC | 27 | 25 | 26 | $42
Highland Park Village, 24 Highland Park Village (Mockingbird Ln. & Preston Rd.), 214-526-1170

■ "Blue bloods and high-maintenance women" agree that this Highland Park seafood "institution" is "always at the top of its game" thanks to marvelous "maitre d' and local legend Jean-Pierre" Albertinetti, a "professional staff with personality and polish", an old-world setting that feels "like a private club", an "impressive wine list" and "the freshest fish in land-locked Dallas" (try the "heavenly sole").

Dallas | F | D | S | C |

Cafe Panda S | 19 | 16 | 18 | $17 |
7979 Inwood Rd. (Lovers Ln.), 214-902-9500
■ "Very good" Chinese food "graciously served" by tuxedo-clad waiters is the story behind this pink-walled Inwood ethnic where it's smart to let them know when you want it spicy; while the "upscale" interior argues for a sit-down meal, takeout is available as well.

California Pizza Kitchen S | 18 | 15 | 16 | $16 |
5505 Belt Line Rd. (bet. Montford Dr. & Preston Rd.), 972-490-8550
8411 Preston Rd. (south of W. Northwest Hwy.), 214-750-7067
Stonebriar Ctr., 2601 Preston Rd. (Hwy. 121), Frisco, 972-712-0884
◪ A "good standby" to "take the kids" for salads, pastas and a variety of "creative, upscale" pizzas (order the Thai chicken or Philly cheese steak versions), this pie link receives mixed reviews for its decor: foes find the stark rooms "too chainlike", while defenders appreciate that they're "clean" and "brightly lit."

Campisi's | 20 | 12 | 16 | $16 |
1522 Main St. (Akard St.), 214-752-0141
5610 E. Mockingbird Ln. (Greenville Ave.), 214-827-0355 S
5360 Lovers Ln. (Inwood Rd.), 214-350-2595 S
3115 W. Parker Rd. (Independence Dr.), Plano, 972-612-1177 S
7632 Campbell Rd. (Coit Rd.), Richardson, 972-931-2267 S
■ "Top-notch", thin-crust pies that perennially vie for "the best in Dallas" and an impressive chicken Marsala recipe endear voters to these pizza and pasta "legends"; the dimly lit original branch on Mockingbird is still "the only way to go" because of its tableside mini-jukeboxes, often tuned to Sinatra.

Cantina Laredo S | 19 | 19 | 18 | $17 |
Preston Royal, 250 Preston Rd. (Royal Ln.), 214-265-1610
4546 Belt Line Rd. (Midway Rd.), Addison, 972-458-0962
■ *Architectural Digest* readers say the Preston-Royal branch of this "classy", family-friendly Mexican twosome is "the one to go to" because its decor "exceeds expectations"; aesthetics aside, "don't miss the baby-goat" meatloaf and "excellent tortilla soup" at either branch.

Canyon Cafe S | 20 | 21 | 19 | $22 |
17808 Dallas Pkwy. (Briargrove Ln.), 972-267-0506
■ "Unusual" Southwestern choices make this "hip" North Dallas spot a clear choice "for out-of-towners" as well as locals; whether it's best to sit inside on a raised booth "to get away from the noise" or on the enclosed patio is still unclear, but either way the service will be snappy; N.B. free quesadillas are served at happy hour Thursday–Friday.

Dallas | F | D | S | C |

CAPITAL GRILLE S   25 | 26 | 25 | $46
Crescent Shops & Galleries, 500 Crescent Ct. (bet. Cedar Springs Rd. & McKinney Ave.), 214-303-0500
■ "You know the drill" at this "quiet" Uptown outpost of a steakhouse chain: expect the "best liver and onions" (just ask Neiman's Stanley Marcus), "great" cuts of beef like the prime-aged sirloin, a comprehensive wine list, an unobtrusive, "well-taught" staff and "classy", "clubby" digs with stuffed-animal heads, booths and a piano lounge; in sum, a true masculine "power trip" and slice of "high-roller heaven."

Carrabba's Italian Grill S   19 | 18 | 20 | $22
17548 Dallas Pkwy. (Trinity Mills Rd.), 972-732-7752
■ An offshoot of the national chain, this North Dallas Italian allows patrons to call in their order, drive up to one of the reserved parking spaces near the carry-out doorway and briefly wait as the staff rushes to deliver the goods; those who choose to dine in may find it a "new favorite" with ample portions of "very tasty" dishes prepared in an open kitchen.

Casa Rosa S   17 | 17 | 15 | $16
Inwood Village, 165 Inwood Village (Inwood Rd. & Lovers Ln.), 214-350-5227
◪ Drawing the Inwood Village set for the last 20 years, this mammoth Mexican staple serves the basics like frosty margaritas and "good handmade guacamole", as well as some updated twists ("go for the enchiladas with goat cheese"); the "Spanish-style setting" has its adherents too, but critics call the place "unremarkable."

Cathy's Wok S   17 | 11 | 14 | $14
4250 Frankford Rd. (N. Dallas Tollway), 972-818-7667
3948 Legacy Dr. (Coit Rd.), Plano, 972-491-7267
◪ "You feel healthy when you leave" this popular North Dallas and Plano Thai-Chinese duo where dieters can opt for nonfat and low-fat choices and learn precisely the number of fat grams and calories they'll be consuming (i.e. the "excellent sesame chicken" has 495 cals); still, despite the feel-good theme, critics find the cuisine a little too "greasy."

Celebration S   21 | 16 | 19 | $18
4503 W. Lovers Ln. (bet. Inwood Rd. & Lemmon Ave.), 214-358-0612
■ "Huge portions" of "reasonably priced", "consistently" "solid" American "comfort dishes" (including the "best pot roast anywhere") as well as a staff that's "easy with kids" explain why this Lovers Lane eatery has been a "local favorite" with families for almost 30 years; N.B. there's now a market next door for takeout.

Dallas F | D | S | C

Celebrity Cafe & Bakery   20 | 14 | 14 | $12
2418 Fairmount St. (McKinney Ave.), 214-922-9866 S
Highland Park Village, 65 Highland Park Village
(Mockingbird Ln. & Preston Rd.), 214-528-6612 S
Preston Royal, 10720 Preston Rd. (Royal Ln.), 214-373-0783
Village on the Pkwy., 5100 Belt Line Rd. (Dallas Pkwy.),
Addison, 972-866-0011
4709 W. Parker Rd. (Preston Rd.), Plano, 972-599-0835
■ Famous for its chocolate-topper cake and the "best-looking and best-tasting sugar cookies in town", these sweet-tooth havens are also popular "for girls'-day-out" "light" lunches of satisfying soups, salads and sandwiches.

CHAMBERLAIN'S S   25 | 22 | 23 | $46
5330 Belt Line Rd. (east of N. Dallas Tollway), Addison,
972-934-2467
■ "Always a class act", "charming" owner Richard Chamberlain's smartly located Addison steakhouse wins over patrons with a "killer corn side dish", some of the "best crab cakes" and superior cuts of beef; a very "warm", "professional" staff, mahogany-wood paneling and original lithographs from the '20s further explain why this is "where all the big-name people eat" (Chuck Norris, Hulk Hogan), as well as tourists.

Champps Americana S   17 | 17 | 16 | $18
4951 Belt Line Rd. (Quorum Dr.), Addison, 972-991-3335
■ Remember, guys, "platinum cards attract women", so if you want to meet some of the "wonderful eye candy" that frequents this "loud" Addison sports bar on Friday and Saturday night, break out the shiny plastic – and "wear your Rolex" while you're at it; on weekdays, parents feed the kids burgers and overstuffed sandwiches as they watch games on the more than two dozen big-screen TVs.

Chaparral Club, The   22 | 24 | 22 | $48
Adam's Mark Hotel, 400 N. Olive St. (Pearl St.),
214-922-8000
■ Located on the 38th floor of a Downtown hotel, this Continental has a "super view of Dallas" and lots of "old-fashioned glamour", courtesy of an "elegant" setting with live music; the courtly, tuxedo-clad staff adds to the pleasantness, as does the "consistently good food", especially the innovative appetizers; N.B. a lovely, wood-paneled private room hits the mark for small parties.

Charolais S   – | – | – | E
5950A Royal Ln. (Preston Rd.), 214-692-0900
This elegant new steakhouse has stampeded into North Dallas with a decidedly Gallic gait; its name derives from a breed of French cattle prized for its tenderness and flavor; signature dishes include steak Stanley (filet mignon), Dover sole and a tasty variety of dessert soufflés.

Dallas F | D | S | C

Cheesecake Factory S   21 | 20 | 18 | $20
Lincoln Park Shopping Ctr., 7700 W. Northwest Hwy. (Central Expwy.), 214-373-4844
Stonebriar Ctr., 2601 Preston Rd. (Hwy. 121), Frisco, 972-731-7799
■ "Gigantic servings" of "quality" American cuisine and "a menu with as many choices as cheesecake has calories" ("anyone can find a favorite dish here") are the appeal of these contemporary-looking North Park and (new) Frisco chain outlets; just remember to "get there early" or late to avoid the "long waits" and "save room for dessert."

CHEZ GERARD   25 | 20 | 23 | $38
4444 McKinney Ave. (Armstrong Ave.), 214-522-6865
■ "Notable regulars" say "don't miss the soufflés, steak frites" and "best frogs' legs" when dining at this "consistently high-quality" Uptown French veteran, which is staffed by a family of "unpretentious", Gallic-tongued charmers and has a petite, floral-patterned dining room as well as a tented warm-weather terrace.

Chili's Grill & Bar S   16 | 15 | 16 | $14
Casa Linda Plaza, 246 Casa Linda Plaza (Garland Rd.), 214-321-9485
7567 Greenville Ave. (Meadow Rd.), 214-361-4371
3230 Knox St. (Travis St.), 214-520-1555
7035 Marvin D. Love Frwy. (Hwy. 67), 214-330-4829
Preston Valley, 12815 Preston Rd. (LBJ Frwy.), 972-991-3855
9239 Skillman St. (LBJ Frwy.), 214-553-0444
2222 W. Northwest Hwy. (I-35E), 214-358-5274
4500 Belt Line Rd. (Midway Rd.), Addison, 972-233-0380
■ An omnipresent Tex-Mex chain that began a quarter-century ago with one unpretentious eatery on Greenville Avenue, this veteran remains "a better choice than fast food" for most voters, who call it a "decent" "standby" for salads and burgers that "kids love"; critics counter that they only go because it's "cheap and easy, not for the eats."

Chipotle Mexican Grill S   16 | 13 | 15 | $10
2705 McKinney Ave. (Boll St.), 214-871-3100
11930 Preston Rd. (Forest Ln.), 972-789-1900
Preston Ctr., 8301 Westchester Dr. (Northwest Hwy.), 214-619-7755
371 Belt Line Rd. (Marsh Ln.), Addison, 972-243-9009
3401 Preston Rd. (Hwy. 121, opp. Stonebriar Ctr.), Frisco, 972-668-1540
Collin Creek Mall, 1009 N. Central Expwy. (15th St.), Plano, 972-423-5115
■ "Very large burritos" (weighing in at 20 ounces) stuffed with "everything you can imagine" are the specialty of this rapidly expanding Tex-Mex chain, known for its "huge" portions, "reasonable prices", "very fast" service and "hip" (if "sterile") metal-and-blond-wood settings; the only quibble: "thumbs down" on "charging for chips and salsa."

www.zagat.com

Dallas F D S C

Chips Old Fashioned Hamburgers S
20 | 13 | 15 | $10

4501 Cole Ave. (Knox St.), 214-526-1092
4530 W. Lovers Ln. (N. Dallas Tollway), 214-691-2447
■ This duo of "really old-fashioned" "mainstays" in Knox/Henderson and Lovers Lane is always jam-packed with "kids" and other fans of the "best banana shakes in the world", "to-die-for onion fries" and "hall-of-fame burgers" ("cooked the way you want 'em"); given such glorious "grease fixes", who cares if the interior's a bit "dingy"?

Chow Thai Addison S
23 | 20 | 20 | $20

Prestonwood Pl., 5290 Belt Line Rd. (east of N. Dallas Tollway), Addison, 972-960-2999
■ For "Thai food with a California twist", aficionados can't get enough of the "awesome" "gourmet" cuisine turned out by this Addison Siamese, which rises above a "not-optimal strip mall location" with its stylish, "beautifully decorated interior"; factor in "excellent" service and some diehards are inspired to visit "60 times a year."

Chow Thai Pacific Rim S
– | – | – | M

3309 Dallas Pkwy. (Parker Rd.), Plano, 972-608-1883
Already a standout among Plano Asians, this smartly decorated newcomer, a cousin to Chow Thai Addison, offers a user-friendly menu with lots of mix-and-match options; savor the soups and appetizers, but save room for such entrees as the smoked pork chop and pad Thai.

Chubby's S
▽ 16 | 12 | 16 | $11

11333 E. Northwest Hwy. (Buffalo St.), 214-348-6065
910 W. Parker Rd. (bet. Alma Dr. & Thunderbird Ln.), Plano, 972-881-1348
3307 W. Pleasant Run Rd. (I-35E), Lancaster, 972-228-4101
■ "We love it" profess patrons of this "down-home" outfit specializing in American and Tex-Mex comfort food (chicken-fried steak, enchiladas and the like); really just "your average diner", this booth-filled favorite is especially beloved for its breakfasts, which are available all day long.

Chuck E. Cheese's S
10 | 14 | 10 | $13

13125 Montfort Dr. (LBJ Frwy.), 972-458-7649
7110 S. Westmoreland Rd. (Camp Wisdom Rd.), 972-298-8850
1340 W. Centerville Rd. (I-635, Centerville Rd. exit), Garland, 972-681-0832
1604 Preston Rd. (Plano Pkwy.), Plano, 972-599-0512
1235 E. Belt Line Rd. (bet. Glenville Dr. & Plano Rd.), Richardson, 972-234-8778
☒ It's a "guaranteed winner" with the ankle-biters (they "love and demand it"), but there's no question that food and service take a backseat to the "fun and games" (rides and other mouse-themed entertainment) at this pizza chain; weary parents confide they'll "be glad when they don't have to go anymore."

Dallas | F | D | S | C |

Chuy's S | 19 | 19 | 17 | $16 |
4544 McKinney Ave. (Knox St.), 214-559-2489
■ A Tex-Mex "icon" of kitsch, this Uptown "feel-good family spot" attracts swarms of "college" kids with its swirled margaritas, "addictive banditos" (tortillas fried with cheese and green chiles) and other "great-value" classics; the devoted enthuse "any place with a Graceland lounge" – an over-the-top "ode to Elvis" – "is ok in our book."

Cindi's Delicatessen S | 17 | 10 | 15 | $12 |
7522 Campbell Rd. (Coit Rd.), 972-248-0608
11111 N. Central Expwy. (Royal Ln.), 214-739-0918
■ "Ruling the morning hours", this no-frills North Dallas "NY deli" duo is "great for breakfasts" (try the "awesome pecan pancakes"), but it also hits the spot later in the day with "huge sandwiches", "better-than-homemade" latkes and "excellent blintzes."

Cisco Grill | 18 | 16 | 19 | $16 |
Snider Plaza, 6630 Snider Plaza (Lovers Ln.), 214-363-9506
■ "Funky" Santa Fe decor with Native American–style artwork lends a festive air to this "steady" Snider Plaza "standby" for "real Southwestern dishes", including some of the "best" salsa around and "great tortilla soup"; it draws a "big SMU crowd at lunch", no surprise given the quick service and "reasonable prices."

Citizen S | 24 | 25 | 21 | $39 |
Two Turtle Creek, 3858 Oak Lawn Ave. (Lemmon Ave.), 214-522-7253
■ "Chic and delicious" declare denizens of this "loud" Oak Lawn "creative Pan-Asian" that's a darling of the "go-to-be-seen" crowd, thanks to its "dramatic", "contemporary" interior boasting an "LA look and feel"; every bit as stylish as the decor is the "inventive, tasty" cuisine borrowed from every corner of Asia and "presented with flair."

CITY CAFE S | 25 | 20 | 23 | $33 |
5757 W. Lovers Ln. (N. Dallas Tollway), 214-351-2233
■ "Consistently one of the finest in the city", this Lovers Lane New American offers the "comfortable" "feel of a neighborhood" eatery but with "first-class food and service"; its seasonal menu of "uniquely prepared" and "creatively presented" dishes "changes often enough to pique your curiosity", and the crowning touch is an "exquisite" wine list that oenophiles rank among "the best in Dallas."

City Cafe to Go S | 24 | 12 | 17 | $19 |
5757 W. Lovers Ln. (N. Dallas Tollway), 214-351-3366
■ It should be no surprise that this offshoot of the City Cafe on Lovers Lane is usually "crowded", given that it has just five tables; surveyors suggest bypassing the "cramped" dining area and ordering the "excellent" salads, signature shrimp-and-crawfish cakes and tempting desserts to go.

www.zagat.com

Dallas | F | D | S | C |

Ciudad ⑤ | 21 | 22 | 21 | $30 |
Turtle Creek One, 3888 Oak Lawn Ave. (bet. Blackburn & Irving Sts.), 214-219-3141
■ "Wow" – it's "almost ahead of its time" marvel admirers of the "creative, authentic" Mexican cuisine at this "upscale" Oak Lawn newcomer, which features flavors from the Yucatán and Mexico City (try the red mole-braised veal short ribs); it also wins friends with "warm service" and "trendy", "fun" atmosphere, though it's often "very loud" "unless you sit outside" on the "great patio."

Clair de Lune ⑤ | 22 | 20 | 21 | $32 |
Preston Royal, 5934 Royal Ln. (bet. Dallas Tollway & Preston Rd.), 214-987-2028
◪ Tucked away in a sleepy North Dallas strip mall, this "simple yet elegant" "neighborhood place" is a "lovely" choice for traditional French dishes presented with "classic" formal service; it's a fine "girls' lunch place" and makes a "classy" choice for special occasions, though the less enthusiastic complain the kitchen is "not consistent."

Clark's Outpost ⑤ | 24 | 13 | 18 | $17 |
101 Hwy. 377 (Gene Autry Dr.), Tioga, 940-437-2414
■ "Still worth the trip" 50 miles outside of Dallas to rural Tioga, this quarter-century-old smokehouse produces what "food mavens" deem some of the "best BBQ in North Texas"; Dallas' top chefs can sometimes be spotted among the crowds packing its many rooms, chowing down on chicken and ribs bathed in a famously "sensational" sauce.

Compari's | 22 | 21 | 21 | $19 |
621 W. Plano Pkwy. (Custer Rd.), Plano, 972-423-1234 ⑤
4020 Preston Rd. (bet. Parker Rd. & Spring Creek Pkwy.), Plano, 972-612-1234
■ Family-pleasers, plain and simple, this Italian pair in Plano dishes out copious portions of red sauce classics (veal Florentine, pastas, and the like) accompanied by bottomless bowls of salad; add wallet-friendly prices, speedy service, and casual, comfortable decor and it's no surprise they "get crowded", especially on weekends.

Copeland's of New Orleans ⑤ | 18 | 17 | 16 | $21 |
5353 Belt Line Rd. (Prestonwood Blvd., next to Prestonwood Mall), Addison, 972-661-1883
◪ Surveyors are of two minds when it comes to this Addison branch of the Cajun chain: while boosters appreciate its festive Big Easy atmosphere ("everything's here but the Mardi Gras"), which always draws a "good crowd" for potent drinks and "authentic" caloric classics in jumbo portions, critics retort "New Orleans it ain't!"

Dallas | F | D | S | C |

Corner Bakery | 18 | 16 | 15 | $12 |
301 N. Market St. (Pacific Ave.), 214-651-8650
Galleria Mall, 13350 N. Dallas Pkwy. (LBJ Frwy.), 972-934-7001 S
NorthPark Ctr. Mall, 205 NorthPark Ctr. (Northwest Hwy.), 214-361-1316 S
4019 Villanova St. (Northwest Hwy.), 214-368-7101 S
11700 Preston Rd. (Forest Ln.), 214-891-1690 S
2401 Preston Rd. (Park Blvd.), Plano, 972-398-1955 S

◣ A self-proclaimed 'European-style' bakery, this bustling chain with locations mostly in shopping centers provides "innovative sandwiches", "unusual salads" and a wide assortment of baked goods that may just be "the best mall food ever"; the less enchanted, however, call it little more than an "average" coffee shop.

Covino's S | 21 | 12 | 19 | $15 |
3265 Independence Pkwy. (Parker St.), Plano, 972-519-0345

◣ Hidden amidst a labyrinth of strip malls in Plano, this bare-bones Southern Italian BYO is a "great family place"; owned by a transplanted NYC couple – he oversees the thin-crust pizza and she bakes the cheesecakes – who "always make you feel welcome", the only rub is the no-reservations policy, which means there's often a "long wait" for a table.

Cowboy Chicken S | 20 | 8 | 15 | $10 |
17437 Preston Rd. (Summerside Dr.), 972-732-6281

■ While the setup and decor look like any old fast-food joint, the "great" rotisserie chicken roasted over a hickory flame at this North Dallas "longtime family favorite" is anything but ordinary; given the modest digs, however, many opt to get the juicy "fresh" birds and all of the go-withs to go; the only question: "do real cowboys eat chicken?"

Cozymel's Coastal Mexican Grill S | 18 | 18 | 16 | $19 |
5021 W. Park Blvd. (Preston Rd.), Plano, 972-964-2809
See review in Fort Worth Directory.

Crescent City Cafe | ▽ 19 | 13 | 14 | $16 |
2615 Commerce St. (bet. Good-Latimer Expwy. & Henry St.), 214-745-1900

■ Long considered a Deep Ellum fixture, this laid-back Cajun/Creole hangout is a swell place to start the day with a cafe au lait and a few beignets, or, later on, to kick back with a hefty muffaletta (many consider it the "best" in town) or one of the daily specials that are "always very, very good"; either way, the place "makes you feel like family."

www.zagat.com

Dallas F | D | S | C

Daddy Jack's Lobster & Chowder House S
22 | 16 | 19 | $27

1916 Greenville Ave. (bet. Belmont & Ross Aves.), 214-826-4910

■ "Be ready to lick your fingers" at this "busy" rough-hewn seafood house in Lower Greenville where the weekly lobster specials are "a must" and the bisque sets the standard "to measure all others by"; while longtimers lament that owner Jack Chaplin ("the greatest man") has "moved away" to Connecticut, the vibe remains "friendly"; N.B. the Preston-Royal branch has closed.

Daddy Jack's Wood Grill S
23 | 17 | 20 | $28

2723 Elm St. (Crowdus St.), 214-653-3949

◪ "You get exactly what you came for" at this Deep Ellum no-frills fish house spin off of Daddy Jack's Lobster & Chowder House; it's a welcoming, "neat place" with "always-good grilled seafood", so no one complains too much if the dining area is a bit "cramped" and gets "very loud" when crowded.

Dakota's S
22 | 24 | 21 | $35

600 N. Akard St. (San Jacinto St.), 214-740-4001

■ Known as a Downtown "classic" for "business dinners" and "before-theater" meals, this "very cool" subterranean American, reached only via glass-walled elevator, is Dallas' "best underground restaurant" (of course, there's not much competition); though it gets raves mostly for its "neat location" featuring a "beautiful patio" replete with cascading waterfall, the cuisine and service are "great" too.

Dave & Buster's S
14 | 18 | 15 | $18

10727 Composite Dr. (east of I-35), 214-353-0620
8021 Walnut Hill Ln. (N. Central Expwy.), 214-361-5553

◪ "Go for the games, not the [American] food" suggests the majority of surveyors weighing in on this pair of hangar-size, "noisy" North Dallas entertainment palaces; it's "always a party", but the longer of tooth caution that this "casual" "playpen" is the most "fun" for "kids" – "definitely not for the grown-up crowd."

Deep Ellum Cafe S
20 | 17 | 17 | $23

2706 Elm St. (bet. Crowdus St. & Good-Latimer Expwy.), 214-741-9012

◪ "A fine spot on a Saturday night", this eclectic American in oh-so-happening Deep Ellum draws a young, "hip crowd" into its quirky, casual interior for fusion favorites like Cajun chicken egg rolls; it remains popular for weekend brunches as well, though sticklers suggest the place "needs updating."

Dallas | F | D | S | C |

DEL FRISCO'S DOUBLE EAGLE STEAKHOUSE | 26 | 24 | 24 | $53 |
5251 Spring Valley Rd. (N. Dallas Pkwy.), 972-490-9000
◪ Possibly "the best steaks in the West" come off the grill at this "prime" North Dallas steakhouse that's simply "tops in all categories", from its "perfectly cooked" beef and 850-bottle wine list to its clubby, high-"energy" environs and "superior" service; there's a price for being this "near to heaven", however: hefty tabs make it "strictly for the expense-account crowd", and its popularity means there's often a "long wait for a table", even "with a reservation."

Desperados Mexican S | 18 | 17 | 17 | $16 |
4818 Greenville Ave. (University Blvd.), 214-363-1850
3443 Campbell Rd. (Jupiter Rd.), Garland, 972-530-8886
■ The "freshest guacamole" leads the list of winners at these longtime Greenville/Garland crowd pleasers, which also satisfy Mexican taste buds with their sultry seviche, deep-fried tacos and "seriously good margaritas."

Dickey's Barbecue | 17 | 12 | 14 | $12 |
4610 N. Central Expwy. (Knox St.-Henderson Ave. exit), 214-370-4550 S
14999 Preston Rd. (Belt Line Rd.), 972-661-2006 S
2445 W. Northwest Hwy. (Harry Hines Blvd.), 214-350-3095 S
9230 Skillman St. (LBJ Frwy.), 214-349-9335 S
726 N. Harwood St. (Federal St.), 214-740-1661
2919 Forest Ln. (Josey Ln.), 972-247-1534 S
3700 Gus Thomasson Rd. (Oates Dr.), Mesquite, 972-686-6822 S
1211 14th St. (Ave. M), Plano, 972-423-9960 S
1150 N. Plano Rd. (Arapaho Rd.), Richardson, 972-907-8494 S
5000 Rowlett Rd. (bet. Lake Shore Dr. & Main St.), Rowlett, 972-475-6838 S
◪ Opinions are all over the map when it comes to this Dallas "institution", but then Texans have rarely been in agreement on the subject of BBQ; fans shout yee-haw over the chain's "yummy" brisket, solid sausages and "good sides", served cafeteria-style, but vocal dissenters snipe "dry and uninspired" ("I'll travel to Kansas City before I eat this again").

Dick's Last Resort ●S | 14 | 16 | 16 | $18 |
1701 N. Market St. (Record St.), 214-747-0001
◪ "Be prepared for fun" when visiting this West End BBQ theme joint, that is, if you enjoy "eating with your hands" and "being treated badly" by a "purposely irreverent", "hysterically rude" staff; customers looking to "act like kids" again call the experience a "blast", but the more thin-skinned advise "avoid this place."

Dallas | F | D | S | C |

Dodie's Seafood Cafe S ▽ 22 | 13 | 17 | $15
2129 Greenville Ave. (Bell St.), 214-821-8890
■ "A lot closer than New Orleans", this "laid-back", family-run Cajun in Lower Greenville makes Big Easy types "feel right at home" with its "authentic" crawfish boils, po' boys and blackened catfish served with "great hospitality"; while the "throwback-to-the-'50s" decor has a certain charm, sitting out on the patio may be the best bet.

Dovie's S 18 | 20 | 18 | $25
14671 Midway Rd. (bet. Belt Line & Spring Valley Rds.), Addison, 972-233-9846
◪ Quartered in a '30s stone farmhouse with seven dining rooms, this quaint Addison American offers "great", romantic "atmosphere" and prompt service ("they want your biz and show it!"); however some surveyors have a hard time warming up to the cooking, which tends toward the "nondescript", even if it is of "reasonable quality for the price."

Dream Cafe S 20 | 14 | 15 | $18
2800 Routh St. (bet. Cedar Springs Rd. & McKinney Ave.), 214-954-0486
■ "Run by earth mothers", this American Uptowner offers "very healthy food" that actually "tastes good" (imagine that); especially popular is the "great outdoor dining area" and grassy, "huge lawn" that's "nice for kids to play on" and perfect for "bringing the dogs."

Dunston's Steakhouse S 17 | 13 | 17 | $19
3565 Forest Ln. (bet. Marsh Ln. & Webb Chapel Rd.), 972-241-9204
8526 Harry Hines Blvd. (Brookfield Ave.), 214-637-3513
5423 W. Lovers Ln. (Inwood Rd.), 214-352-8320
11817 Lake June Rd. (bet. Hickory Tree & Peachtree Rds.), Balch Springs, 972-285-2879
■ Regulars (and there are "lots") of this cowboy-themed steak chain know that while at every location the "cheap" grub's "very good", it's still the Lovers Lane branch, with its "fine", "old-fashioned salad bar" and "back room" with "slice-of-the-'70s" decor that's the place to be (it's "where Ross Perot eats").

East Wind S 22 | 19 | 19 | $22
2711 Elm St. (Crowdus St.), 214-745-5554
■ Surveyors seeking to escape from it all find refuge in this tranquil Downtown Vietnamese, a "great place for a quiet two-hour lunch" amid "simple", "attractive" environs; its "terrific" Americanized fare (beef carpaccio, charcoal-grilled catfish) is "wonderfully light" and "flavorful", and the service is both "helpful" and unobtrusive.

Dallas

EatZi's S 23 | 18
3403 Oak Lawn Ave. (Lemmon Ave.), 214-526-1515
■ "Listen to opera while browsing" this "feast for the senses" on Oak Lawn, where the overflowing spread of Eclectic "gourmet take-out" choices, from hot entrees, soups and salads to cheeses and "nice wines", means "folks on the go" can enjoy meals of "excellent taste and quality"; given the crowds it attracts, regulars wish there were more tables on the premises.

El Chico S 15 | 14 | 15 | $15
9005 Bruton Rd. (bet. McKim Dr. & Prairie Creek Rd.), 214-381-5870
2031 Abrams Rd. (bet. Oram St. & Prospect Ave.), 214-821-5785
13937 N. Central Expwy. (Spring Valley Rd.), 972-238-0011
1902 Eastgate Dr. (Northwest Hwy.), Garland, 972-270-7580
1700 N. Central Expwy. (bet. 16th & 18th Sts.), Plano, 972-578-0070
■ "Basic Tex-Mex" with "attentive service" (the staff "moves you in and out quickly") is the lowdown on this longtime chain; it's a "favorite" for its "great-value margaritas" and "chile rellenos big enough to feed two", even if the food's really "nothing special" and it gets "very noisy."

El Fenix 18 | 15 | 18 | $14
Casa Linda Plaza, 255 Casa Linda Plaza (Garland Rd.), 214-327-6173 S
120 E. Colorado Blvd. (Beckley Ave.), 214-941-4050 S
5622 Lemmon Ave. (Inwood Rd.), 214-521-5166
1601 McKinney Ave. (bet. Akard & Field Sts.), 214-747-1121
Webb Forest Shopping Ctr., 3128 Forest Ln. (Webb Chapel Rd.), 972-241-3248 S
6811 W. Northwest Hwy. (Hillcrest Rd.), 214-363-5279 S
9090 Skillman St. (LBJ Frwy.), 214-349-3815 S
5280 Belt Line Rd. (Montfort Dr.), Addison, 972-387-2533 S
3904 Town Crossing Blvd. (east of I-30), Mesquite, 972-279-8900 S
810 N. Central Expwy. (Plano Pkwy.), Plano, 972-578-1020 S
■ Among the "oldest Tex-Mex" eateries in town, this ubiquitous chain is a "reliable" purveyor of "affordable" border-fare "quick fixes" served by a "swift, always pleasant" staff; its famous, cut-price Wednesday enchilada special is "still the best", so "get there early" because sometimes the "line wraps around the building."

El Norte Grill S ∇ 21 | 16 | 20 | $14
2205 W. Parker Rd. (Custer Rd.), Plano, 972-596-6783
■ Located in a former fast-food stop and now sporting a funky '70s look, this respectable Plano Mexican impresses with memorable margaritas, "chicken dishes that tend to be the best" choices and a snappy hot sauce.

	F	D	S	C
	23	13	16	$10

...kford Rd.), 972-769-1600
...ood Rd.), 214-350-0007
...ycliff Ave.), 214-526-3223
... Rd.), 972-851-5711

■ Cherry walnut, pumpernickel rye and sourdough lead an all-star lineup of "fantastic breads" ("the best in Dallas") at these "quality" bakeries, which also do a big business in cookies, pastries and sandwiches like the "great chicken salad"; P.S. the "sparse surroundings" have limited seating, so don't hesitate to do takeout.

Enigma S ▽ 16 | 23 | 20 | $62
3005 Routh St. (Cedar Springs Rd.), 214-999-0666
◪ The "most bizarre restaurant experience of my life" declare baffled surveyors commenting on this mysterious, two-story Uptown Eclectic "wackily decorated" with ornate furniture, nude statues and other "over-the-top" Liberace-like touches; different place settings and menus for each diner add to the "interesting" approach, though there's nothing enigmatic about the "ridiculous" prices.

Ez's S 17 | 13 | 14 | $12
6833 W. Northwest Hwy. (Hillcrest Rd.), 214-750-6677
■ "Bring back memories" of those *Happy Days* with a visit to this brightly colored, neon-filled North Dallas diner, which serves "EZ food" like "good burgers and onion rings" and "the best shakes"; "great for kids" at all times, it's especially appealing Monday–Thursday after 5PM, when one child (under 12) eats free for every parent who orders an entree.

Ferrari's Italian Villa 24 | 21 | 24 | $29
14831 Midway Rd. (bet. Belt Line & Spring Valley Rds.), Addison, 972-980-9898
■ Kudos abound for this Addison Italian where the conscientious owner "always seems to be there", the staff "makes you feel right at home" and the feeling is "homey" whether you sit near the centerpiece wood-burning oven or in the semi-private room; luscious lasagna, "super" veal (the specialty) and the seriously fresh antipasti bar all make smart choices.

Firehouse S ▽ 22 | 17 | 19 | $26
1928 Greenville Ave. (north of Ross Ave.), 214-826-2468
■ "Bang-Bang Chicken that's a bulls-eye" leads the International Mix of fiery, "spicy" dishes at this Lower Greenville entry where it's cool to begin the evening with a "fabulous martini" (try the "decadent chocolate" version) at the bar; only macho heat-seekers claim "the food is never as hot as they say it will be."

42   www.zagat.com

Dallas

| F | D | S | C |

First Chinese Barbeque S | ▽ 21 | 10 | 13 | $17
111 S. Greenville Ave. (bet. Main & Polk Sts.), Richardson, 972-680-8216

◪ Two chopsticks up for the "authentic" Chinese BBQ and noodle dishes at this unpretentious Richardson favorite, which admittedly could use a makeover (the "decor is still early Communist"); the staff's friendly, though language barriers can make it "hard to communicate" at times.

Fish | 21 | 18 | 18 | $41
Paramount Hotel, 302 S. Houston St. (Jackson St.), 214-747-3474

◪ "Good for a pre–Reunion Arena meal or business lunch" because of its convenient Downtown location and crisp, smart "NYC feel", this dimly lit seafooder may have momentarily stumbled after losing its award-winning chef but is now back on track ("getting better") with *poisson* pleasers like the sesame-crusted ahi.

Fishbowl S | 20 | 22 | 19 | $33
3214 Knox St. (Cole Ave.), 214-521-2695

■ Order a Trader Vic–style cocktail, a few pupu platters and "relax" at this "cool, contemporary" Knox/Henderson Pan-Asian, which occupies the former lounge area of Star Canyon; as it's a "fun", "see-and-be-seen spot", don't be surprised if your hostess is "absolutely stunning."

Flying Saucer Draught Emporium ●S | 14 | 18 | 16 | $15
1520 Greenville Ave. (south of Ross Ave.), 214-824-7468
14999 Montfort Dr. (Belt Line Rd.), Addison, 972-991-7093

◪ Hundreds of souvenir plates line the walls and ceilings of these funky German emporiums in Greenville and Addison known for their "world-class selection" of more than 200 varieties of draft and bottled suds; the "best wurst" and "to-die-for" beer-cheese soup also get some notices, but clearly it's "more about the beer than the food."

FOGO DE CHAO S | 25 | 21 | 24 | $41
4300 Belt Line Rd. (Midway Rd.), Addison, 972-503-7300

■ "Nirvana for carnivores", this Addison churrascaria presents "food with a show", as "fantastic" gaucho-clad waiters serve unlimited quantities of "excellent" skewered meat and poultry until you turn your coaster from green to red; an "outstanding" salad bar adds to the "gluttony", so "skip breakfast and lunch" before Chao-ing down here.

Fox & Hound English Pub & Grill ●S | – | – | – | I
18918 Midway Rd. (Frankford Rd.), 972-732-0804

Tally ho to this chain link offering billiards, darts and sports on the telly for clubbable sorts, as well as a substantial selection of beers; traditional American and English pub food helps players keep their strength up for games (including the singles scene at the bar).

www.zagat.com

Dallas   F | D | S | C

Francesca   – | – | – | M
18101 Preston Rd. (Frankford Rd.), 972-447-9000
Attentive service that lets you set your own pace is the draw of this cream-colored North Dallas Italian, a subtle charmer where the trout and beef tenderloin tips are winners.

Franki's Li'l Europe S   23 | 17 | 21 | $21
Casa Linda Plaza, 362 Casa Linda Plaza (Buckner Blvd.), 214-320-0426
■ What other eatery can you go to "where the owner greets you in a red shirt and suspenders" ask fans of Franki Kovacic, the lovable proprietor of this small East Dallas Eastern European specialist, which puts out some "very good", "hard-to-find" dishes, such as paprika chicken.

FRENCH ROOM, THE   28 | 29 | 28 | $69
Hotel Adolphus, 1321 Commerce St. (Akard St.), 214-742-8200
■ Uncontestedly elected No. 1 for Food, Decor and Service in the Dallas *Survey*, this Downtown New French–American "throwback to more elegant times" is "magnificently decorated" with a cherub-painted ceiling, soft candlelights and beautiful flowers; factor in "impeccable service" from a staff that makes you "feel like a king and queen" and "fabulous", exquisitely plated dishes and you have the city's "perfect" spot "for special-occasion dining"; N.B. gourmet diners on a budget should consider the prix fixe menus.

Fresco Grill & Pasta S   ▽ 20 | 14 | 17 | $17
4015 Lemmon Ave. (Throckmorton St.), 214-520-2232
◪ "Good pasta" dishes make for "modestly priced" dinners at this Lemmon Avenue Italian, whose "strip-mall location" and somewhat "clichéd decor" (replete with hanging grapevines) "may keep away" some potential customers; all agree, however, it's a good bet for "pizza delivery."

Fresh Choice S   16 | 13 | 13 | $10
4080 Belt Line Rd. (bet. Marsh Ln. & Midway Rd.), Addison, 972-385-7353
601 W. 15th St. (bet. Alma Dr. & N. Central Expwy.), Plano, 972-881-9792
◪ An AYCE buffet format that includes soups, salads, pastas, pizzas and desserts means "enough choices for everyone" at these "fairly priced" chain outlets; advocates endorse them for "satisfying" lunches or lazy weeknight meals, but thrill seekers may find them "boring after two visits."

Fuddruckers S   17 | 14 | 14 | $12
4520 Frankford Rd. (Dallas Pkwy.), 972-818-3833
Old Town Shopping Ctr., 5500 Greenville Ave. (Lovers Ln.), 214-360-9390
2205 N. Central Expwy. (Park Blvd.), Plano, 972-881-1890
■ Foodies get to affix their own fixins to the "surprisingly good" burgers purveyed at these patty parlors; game rooms at some branches add to their "family-friendly" feel.

Dallas

F | D | S | C

Gennie's Bishop Grill ⊘   ▽ 25 | 11 | 18 | $11
321 N. Bishop Ave. (8th St.), 214-946-1752
■ "Don't change" a thing implore fans of this 30-year-old, lunch-only Oak Cliff regional American where customers gladly stand in a cafeteria-style line for "to-die-for" "Texas home cooking", headlined by homemade breads, vibrant veggies, chicken-fried steak and peanut butter pie.

Gershwin's   22 | 21 | 20 | $30
8442 Walnut Hill Ln. (Greenville Ave.), 214-373-7171
■ Now under new ownership but still popular with the business-lunch crowd, this North Dallas New American veteran has fans waxing rhapsodic over its "elegant" food, including "great mushroom soup" and "the ultimate" chocolate-sack dessert; "sharp" decor (dark wood paneling) and nightly piano music are other reasons why this "nice tradition" should continue to thrive.

Gilbert's N.Y. Delicatessen-Restaurant S   21 | 12 | 14 | $14
Preston Forest Village Shopping Ctr., 11661 Preston Rd. (Forest Ln.), 214-373-3333
◪ "Arguably the best deli in town" opine pastrami pundits weighing in on this Preston/Forest Jewish-style favorite whose "terrific breakfasts" ("to-die-for omelets") are matched by corned beef to crow about and challah to holler over; if the pickles are served with some occasional "attitude", don't allow that to half-sour the experience.

Gloria's S   21 | 15 | 17 | $19
4140 Lemmon Ave. (Douglas Ave.), 214-521-7576
600 W. Davis St. (bet. Bishop Ave. & Tyler St.), 214-948-3672
3715 Greenville Ave. (bet. Martel & Matalee Aves.), 214-874-0088
5100 Belt Line Rd. (Dallas Tollway), Addison, 972-387-8442
■ There's no shame if you're one of the many weak-willed worshippers who "can't pass up" the outrageous black bean dip served at these "bustling" Salvadoran-Mexicans, whose original Oak Cliff location "maintains its funky charm" and popularity with "hip" customers; P.S. the "different flavored margaritas" and seafood are other can't-miss options.

Good Eats S   17 | 14 | 15 | $15
6950 Greenville Ave. (Park Ln.), 214-691-3287
4727 Frankford Rd. (N. Dallas Tollway), 972-447-0624
Turtle Creek, 3888 Oak Lawn Ave. (Blackburn St.), 214-522-3287
14905 Midway Rd. (Belt Line Rd.), Addison, 972-392-3287
Town East Mall, 2034 Town East Blvd. (LBJ Frwy.), Mesquite, 972-270-6255
1101 N. Central Expwy. (15th St. exit), Plano, 972-516-3287
◪ Good eats? – "says who?" scoff critics of this chain of homestyle American meals, which gets criticized for merely "adequate" food and "slow" service at some locations; defenders say the menu has "something for everyone" including a respectable chicken-fried steak.

Dallas | F | D | S | C |

Gopal 🆂 | – | – | – | I |
758 S. Central Expwy. (Spring Valley Rd.), 972-437-0155
With all of the high-tech industries around the Richardson area, you'll see lots of short-sleeved plaid shirts and, yes, even pocket protectors among the clientele at this newcomer; but these geeks know their food, because this is vegetarian Indian that doesn't dumb itself down for Americans; be sure to make friends with the staff, who will steer you to specialties not listed on the menu.

Grady's American Grill 🆂 | 17 | 18 | 18 | $19 |
8024 Walnut Hill Ln. (Central Expwy.), 214-265-9193
4525 Belt Line Rd. (bet. Beltway Dr. & Midway St.), Addison, 972-991-0008
3811 Pavillion Ct. (opp. Town East Mall), Mesquite, 972-686-1919
5013 W. Park Blvd. (Preston Rd.), Plano, 972-612-8099
■ "Large portions", "reasonable prices" and "friendly" ("hi, I'm Mike") employees that are "good with kids" make for "nice family outings" to these American chain links; popular choices include the grilled chicken with pasta, pork tenderloin and meat loaf.

GRAPE, THE 🆂 | 25 | 20 | 22 | $30 |
2808 Greenville Ave. (Vickery Blvd.), 214-828-1981
■ Going on 30 years old, this "very romantic" New American–Eclectic bistro on Lower Greenville has been "a perennial winner" from day one thanks to a renowned mushroom soup (the "best I ever ate"), an award-winning wine list and "attentive" service; close tables mean "unavoidable eavesdropping", which is just fine if you have a dull "first-date dinner" companion.

GREEN ROOM, THE 🆂 | 26 | 19 | 23 | $40 |
2715 Elm St. (Crowdus St.), 214-748-7666
■ Put away those jackets and ties, because this "noisy" Deep Ellum New American is a "brash", "refreshingly casual" spot where twentysomethings lap up chef Marc Cassel's "magnificent", "innovative" cuisine, revel in the "dark", "delightfully funky" atmosphere and bond with the appropriately "trendy" staff; P.S. regulars add that this "tablecloth Bohemian" experience should always include the "superb mussels", the 'Feed Me' prix fixe and wine sold at "cherry-picking prices."

Hard Rock Cafe 🆂 | 14 | 22 | 14 | $19 |
2601 McKinney Ave. (Routh St.), 214-855-0007
◪ "A fun place for music lovers" and tourists, this McKinney Avenue branch of the rock 'n' roll–themed chain features live bands and tons of memorabilia, including Lenny Kravitz's guitar and Madonna's blouse; critics find it too "loud", with all-American grub that's "overpriced for the quality."

Dallas F | D | S | C

Hedary's Lebanese Oven & Grill S | 22 | 15 | 17 | $19
Spring Creek Shopping Ctr., 7915 Belt Line Rd. (Coit Rd.), 972-233-1080

■ Adventurous diners love to belly up to this North Dallas Lebanese (a little sister to the FW original) for "large portions" of "light", "high-quality food" (try a combination plate or "great lunch buffet"); adding to the authentic feel is an owner who makes his own yogurt and raises his own lamb, as well as live entertainment on Thursdays.

Henk's European Deli ▽ | 20 | 14 | 19 | $13
5811 Blackwell St. (N. Central Expwy.), 214-987-9090

■ This East Dallas German restaurant/bakery/deli is marking 10 years of serving "great" suds, sausages and "superb cakes"; admirers say "don't miss the beer-cheese soup" and "better omelets than you're likely to find anywhere else" and toss in a *danke* for live music Fridays and Saturdays.

Herrera's Mexican Restaurant 19 | 11 | 16 | $15
5427 Denton Dr. (Inwood Rd.), 214-630-2599 S
2853 W. Illinois Ave. (bet. Hampton & Westmoreland Rds.), 214-330-6426 S
4001 Maple Ave. (Reagan St.), 214-528-9644 S
9404 Ovella Ave. (Loop 12/Northwest Hwy.), 214-956-0150
3790 Belt Line Rd. (bet. Marsh Ln. & Midway Rd.), Addison, 972-488-2202 S
1905 N. Josey Ln. (bet. Belt Line & Keller Springs Rds.), Carrollton, 972-242-4912 S

◪ "The kind of place you can go to over and over again without breaking the bank", this old-time Dallas chain serves *grande* Mexican portions, albeit in modest – some say "uncomfortable" – digs; tip: since choosing from the large menu can be daunting, consider ordering a combo plate.

Highland Park Pharmacy 22 | 21 | 22 | $9
3229 Knox St. (Frances St.), 214-521-2126

■ Locals happily take their medicine at this "step back in time" Knox/Henderson American institution – the Dallas *Survey's* No. 1 Bang for the Buck – that's been around since 1912; diners have good chemistry with the waitresses who work the "old-fashioned soda counter" serving "terrific shakes" and the "best grilled cheese in town."

Hoffbrau Steaks & Brewery S 17 | 15 | 16 | $20
3205 Knox St. (Cole St.), 214-559-2680
311 N. Market St. (Ross Ave.), 214-742-4663
4180 Belt Line Rd. (Midway Rd.), Addison, 972-392-1161
1530 N. Peachtree St. (Gross Rd.), Mesquite, 972-289-1889
3310 N. Central Expwy. (Parker Rd.), Plano, 972-423-4475

◪ Surveyors of this moderately priced steakhouse/microbrewery chain steer in opposite directions: some hop for "fresh beer" and "more food for the money than anywhere else", while others advise customers to "break out the A.1." for the "bland" beef.

www.zagat.com

Dallas | F | D | S | C |

Hofstetter's Spargel Cafe S | 23 | 22 | 21 | $28 |
4326 Lovers Ln. (bet. Dallas Tollway & Douglas Ave.), 214-368-3002
■ In addition to pleasing desserts and "excellent authentic German food" like "*sehr gut*" Wiener schnitzel and a tasty 'butcher's platter' (smoked pork chop, pork loin and bratwurst with sauerkraut), this Lovers Lane staple also attracts a "loyal following" for its solid, "no-attitude" service and "airy", art-filled setting.

Homemade Delights Tearoom & Bakery ⊭ | – | – | – | I |
Cobwebs Antique Mall, 1400 Ave. J (bet. 14th & 15th Sts.), Plano, 972-424-5982
When you're browsing Cobwebs Antiques Mall, catch this cheerful Plano tearoom; menu choices are inexpensive and plentiful and come nicely garnished with surprises – a sampling of fruit here, a mini-muffin there.

HOTEL ST. GERMAIN | 26 | 28 | 26 | VE |
2516 Maple Ave. (bet. Cedar Springs Rd. & McKinney Ave.), 214-871-2516
■ "Escape from reality" to this "quaintly European" Uptown French-Continental whose mutely lit, widely spaced tables are staffed by attentive white-gloved waiters; "the ultimate place for an intimate celebration", it exclusively offers a multicourse tasting menu ("a bargain at $85"), so à la carte cats should consider rendezvousing at the new Champagne Bar, which also serves appetizers; N.B. Sharon Hage (ex Salve!) is now behind the stove.

HOUSTON'S S | 23 | 20 | 20 | $22 |
Preston Ctr., 8300 Preston Rd. (Northwest Hwy.), 214-691-8991
5318 Belt Line Rd. (Preston Rd.), Addison, 972-960-1752
■ Despite the fact that there's "always a wait" ("no matter what time of day"), "everyone seems to be happy" at this high-quality American chain where it's fun to pass the time at the bar taking in "great people-watching" before sitting down for the "outstanding spinach artichoke dip" and "wonderful salads"; "superior service" and "romantic", "comfortable" surroundings are other reasons why it may be the "best of its genre."

Humperdink's ◐S | 18 | 17 | 16 | $20 |
18438 N. Dallas Tollway (bet. Frankford Rd. & Plano Pkwy.), 972-248-7970
6050 Greenville Ave. (north of Southwestern Blvd.), 214-368-6597
2208 W. Northwest Hwy. (Loop 12), 214-358-4159
3820 Belt Line Rd. (bet. Business Ave. & Commercial Dr.), Addison, 972-484-3051
1601 N. Central Expwy. (Collins Blvd.), Richardson, 972-690-4867
See review in Fort Worth Directory.

Dallas | F | D | S | C |

Huntington's S | ▽ 18 | 18 | 19 | $41 |
Westin Galleria Dallas, 13340 Dallas Pkwy. (LBJ Frwy.), 972-851-2882
■ Located off the lobby of a Galleria hotel, this Continental is known to savvy surveyors as one of the better places to take a break from shopping; while it's a quiet spot for everything from soup and salad to a three-course meal, seek your sales elsewhere, because prices tend to be "expensive."

Il Grano S | 18 | 16 | 15 | $14 |
5960 W. Parker Rd. (N. Dallas Tollway), Plano, 972-473-4747
◪ "Once you decipher the ordering system" at this Plano Southern Italian cafeteria (requests for starters, entrees and beverages are placed at separate stations), it can be a decent choice for a "good", "quick, tasty" meal; granted, the food is "nothing to write home about", but there are some "buried treasures" like the focaccia and the marinated portobello mushrooms.

Il Sole Restaurant & Bar S | 23 | 23 | 21 | $38 |
Travis Walk, 4514 Travis St. (Fitzhugh Ave.), 214-559-3888
■ This "romantic" Mediterranean yearling in Knox/Henderson has an "excellent staff", a second-story patio perfect for people-watching and an overall subdued, soothing atmosphere; it draws a "classy, not flashy" group of regulars who love the award-winning "great wine list" (especially the offerings "by the glass or even half glass") and menu filled with "delicious" options like the "to-die-for" calamari and maple crème brûlée.

Il Sorrento S | 20 | 22 | 20 | $31 |
8616 Turtle Creek Blvd. (Northwest Hwy.), 214-352-8759
■ "Celebrating 50 years under the same owner", this Turtle Creek Italian is a favorite of the Park Cities set, who wouldn't change a thing, not the "solid" food, solicitous service, "excellent roving accordion player" or "throwback" decor replete with "over-the-top fountains and statues."

India Palace S | 23 | 19 | 20 | $22 |
12817 Preston Rd. (LBJ Frwy.), 972-392-0190
■ Considered "royalty" within its category, this North Dallas Indian has quietly ruled for over 15 years thanks to a "serene" setting that's "better than most" and "spicy, consistent" victuals, including "saag panir that's perfect"; newcomers shouldn't be surprised if they start to visit "every week or two" for the "bargain" brunch and lunch buffets.

Into My Garden | – | – | – | I |
1017 E. 15th St. (bet. Ave. K & I-75), Plano, 972-509-0292
Don't skimp on time when you lunch at this quaint tearoom/antique store yearling in historic Downtown Plano, where it's no secret that the combo plate (a sampling of soup, salad, quiche and fruit) and desserts are the specialties; N.B. call two days ahead if you want the full afternoon tea service.

Dallas   F | D | S | C

Jasmine S   22 | 20 | 19 | $20
4002 Belt Line Rd. (Surveyor Blvd.), Addison, 972-991-6867
■ Known for its "above-average" Chinese food, this "reliable" Addison ethnic serves innovative dishes like shrimp in a fried potato 'bowl'; "good service" and live piano music on weekends add to its staying power.

Jason's Deli   17 | 12 | 14 | $11
5400 E. Mockingbird Ln. (bet. Central Expwy. & Greenville Ave.), 214-821-7021 S
7412 Greenville Ave. (Walnut Hill Ln.), 214-739-1800
104 Preston Royal Shopping Ctr. (Royal Ln.), 214-373-9173 S
18111 N. Dallas Pkwy. (Frankford Rd.), 972-818-3354 S
4021 Belt Line Rd. (bet. Marsh Ln. & Midway Rd.), Addison, 972-239-0074 S
906 W. McDermott Dr. (Waters Rd.), Allen, 972-727-3440 S
1681 N. Central Expwy. (University Dr.), McKinney, 972-542-9393 S
1725 N. Town East Blvd. (Emporium Circle), Mesquite, 972-681-7878 S
4801 Parker Rd. (Preston Rd.), Plano, 972-519-0022 S
◪ Fans feel these well-known chain links offer "fast, fresh" sandwiches and "good salad bars", but critics counter that they're "not really delis" and have "uninspired" eats; still, the low-key settings and "reasonable" prices make these ubiquitous eateries "great places to bring the kids."

JAVIER'S S   24 | 22 | 23 | $31
4912 Cole Ave. (Harvard Ave.), 214-521-4211
■ The faithful have "been going once a month for 20 years" to this Knox/Henderson "icon", which "raises the bar on Mexican food" ("excellent fish and chicken dishes"); the festive and "fun" interior is "dark and cozy like a womb" and the service is cordial and "fast", but a warning: the popular cigar room is definitely "not for asthmatics."

Jaxx Cafe   23 | 20 | 21 | $27
14925 Midway Rd. (Commander Dr.), Addison, 972-458-7888
■ With attractive dark wood and beveled glass decor and "attentive" service, this American in Addison is "the best interview restaurant in the Tech sector" and "great for a business lunch"; favorites "always prepared to perfection" include the classic club sandwich made with house-roasted turkey and the white-chocolate bread pudding.

Jennivine S   23 | 21 | 21 | $30
3605 McKinney Ave. (Lemmon Ave.), 214-528-6010
■ Loyalists hope the sun never sets on this beloved Uptown institution that's been serving Continental-English fare for nearly 25 years; despite being situated near massive construction projects, its "romantic" private-home environs feel like a refuge, and the staff gives the royal treatment to Anglophiles, who return for "great" cheese plates, pâtés and puddings; N.B. try to make a reservation for afternoon tea.

Dallas F | D | S | C

Jeroboam ⑤ – | – | – | E
Kirby Bldg., 1501 Main St. (Akard St.), 214-748-7226
Already being hailed as a Downtown destination, this newly minted, sleek brasserie uncorks casual French cuisine, including such favorites like pâté, cassoulet and selections from the cheese cart; regulars also know that the curried cauliflower soup is the way to start a meal.

Jimmy Lu's ⑤ – | – | – | M
17727 Dallas Pkwy. (Trinity Mills Rd.), 972-852-8888
Specializing in Pan-Asian food downed with wicked mai tais but offering fairly straightforward steak and seafood dishes as well, this immense North Dallas newcomer likes to publicize its huge patio, but seeing that it overlooks a parking lot, you might be better off eating inside.

Joe's Crab Shack ⑤ 15 | 17 | 15 | $19
10250 Technology Blvd. E. (Northwest Hwy.), 214-654-0909
3855 Belt Line Rd. (bet. Marsh Ln. & Midway Rd.), Addison, 972-247-1010
◪ Lured by the "great crabs" and "good family fun", some voters have a merry time at these laid-back seafooders where the tables are covered in paper and shells are tossed into a bucket; still, crabby detractors say "bring earplugs and leave your taste buds at home."

Johnny Orleans Pasta Kitchen ⑤ 17 | 15 | 15 | $17
11661 Preston Rd. (Forest Ln.), 214-363-3133
2704 Worthington St. (McKinney Ave.), 214-871-0808
1310 W. Campbell Rd. (Coit Rd.), Richardson, 972-808-0777
◪ Regulars go for the bomba bread and "giant portions" of "unusual pastas" at this "good" Italian-Cajun chain, which has an extensive menu; foes find it no Mardi Gras, citing "mediocre service" and "standard" flavors.

Kalachandji's ⑤ ▽ 22 | 23 | 19 | $12
Dallas Hare Krishna Temple, 5430 Gurley Ave. (bet. Fairview & Graham Aves.), 214-821-1048
■ This East Dallas Vegetarian "oasis" offers "a relaxing environment", solicitous service and "excellent food" that's been enlightening regulars for almost 20 years; devotees especially delight in the easy-on-the-wallet lunch and dinner buffets; P.S. since it's located in a Hare Krishna temple, be prepared to "put up with the religious overtones."

Kathleen's Art Cafe ⑤ 19 | 14 | 16 | $20
4424 Lovers Ln. (bet. N. Dallas Tollway & Preston Rd.), 214-691-2355
◪ Connoisseurs crave the "good brunch" at this "funky" Lovers Lane Southwestern cafe/bakery, as well as the "changing art exhibits" and "huge delicious cakes"; while critics may pan occasional staff "attitude" and atmosphere that's "too rustic", they still vie for the Sunday night half-price meal deals.

Dallas | F | D | S | C |

Kel's 🆂 ▽ | 17 | 9 | 18 | $11 |
5337 Forest Ln. (N. Dallas Tollway), 972-458-7221
■ It may "look like a truck stop", but good buddies have been wheeling over to this Forest Lane stalwart since 1963; the reason: "old-fashioned" Texas "home cooking", such as chicken-fried steak and comforting banana pudding.

Kirby's Steakhouse 🆂 | 22 | 22 | 21 | $36 |
3525 Greenville Ave. (McCommas Blvd.), 214-821-2122
Preston Parker Crossing, 3408 Preston Rd. (Parker Rd.), Plano, 972-867-2122
◪ "These guys know a good steak" declare partisans of this high-scoring trio (there's an FW branch as well), which is "not too casual, nor too dressy" and thus appropriate for a certain type of "business dinner"; dissenters "miss the original" branch, finding the sibs "inconsistent", but take solace in the "great salad with house garlic dressing."

Kobe Steaks 🆂 | 25 | 22 | 23 | $30 |
5000 Belt Line Rd. (Quorum Dr.), Addison, 972-934-8150
■ An Addison Japanese steakhouse where the chefs cook at your table, this restaurant-row veteran offers "wonderful food"; despite "long waits", it's a "great business-dinner spot" with a "fun" "bar area for just meeting friends."

Kostas Cafe 🆂 | 21 | 15 | 19 | $21 |
4914 Greenville Ave. (University Blvd.), 214-987-3225
4621 W. Park Blvd. (Ohio Dr.), Plano, 972-596-8424
■ You won't have to excavate to find the treasures of this Greenville and Plano Greek duo, which offers a "very comfortable" taverna experience suitable for family dining or a special evening with a date; regulars go *opa* for the "friendly" service, affordable prices and "traditional" food like dolmas and not-so-spartan combination plates.

Kuby's Sausage House 🆂 | 21 | 13 | 17 | $15 |
Snider Plaza, 6601 Snider Plaza (Daniel Ave.), 214-363-2231
■ An "institution with the highest-quality German fare", this Snider Plaza veteran is a combination specialty food store/restaurant where the heady cooking aromas immediately activate taste buds; "great for a sandwich" and a beer, as well as "authentic" dishes that "bring back memories of Munich" (or maybe it's the accordion music), its butcher department is also "the only place to buy meat."

La Calle Doce 🆂 | 22 | 17 | 19 | $19 |
415 W. 12th St. (bet. Adams & Bishop Aves.), 214-941-4304
1925 Skillman St. (Live Oak St.), 214-824-9900
■ This family-run Oak Cliff veteran, tucked into a charming Victorian, specializes in "outstanding" "seafood with Mexican flair" – particularly the "superb grilled catfish" and octopus; it may be one of "the best-kept secrets in town", and its new "romantic" sister restaurant in East Dallas should also please folks, as long as they "go early."

Dallas   F | D | S | C

La Creme   ▽ 18 | 12 | 14 | $12
4448 Lovers Ln. (N. Dallas Tollway), 214-369-4188
■ Perking away on Lovers Lane since the '80s, this coffeehouse makes a sweet stop for a quick taste of roasted chicken salad or a cup of java and a gooey bakery treat; it's also a comfortable respite to relax and read the paper.

La Dolce Vita S   ▽ 22 | 21 | 19 | $21
1924 Abrams Pkwy. (Gaston Ave.), 214-821-2608
■ Hardly Fellini-esque, this "friendly place" in Lakewood offers Southern Italian dishes, sweet service and romantic atmosphere; creative types delight in "wonderful design-your-own pastas", and theater buffs drop in for dessert after the play; tip for wallet-watchers: it's a "great value" too.

Lady Primrose's Thatched   20 | 25 | 20 | $21
Cottage Pantry
Hotel Crescent Court, 500 Crescent Ct. (bet. Maple & McKinney Aves.), 214-871-8334
◪ Co-owned by Dallas doyenne Caroline Rose Hunt, this antique-shop-cum-tearoom in Uptown's Crescent Court with "*Alice in Wonderland* atmosphere" is an "ideal location for girls' time" lunch and high tea; some of its Laura Ashley–clad "mother and daughter" guests find the fare "tasty", while others feel the "ambiance is better than the food"; N.B. reservations and bonnets are recommended.

La Hacienda Ranch S   22 | 23 | 19 | $22
3300 I-35 (Frankford Rd.), Carrollton, 972-323-5242
4110 Preston Rd. (north of Hwy. 121), Frisco, 972-335-2232
■ A "Tex-Mex-themed steakhouse" with "wonderful lodge decor" is the concept behind these spacious Metroplex eateries, which reel in both locals and tourists with the "most tender beef fajitas" and "good" enchiladas.

La Madeleine French   19 | 18 | 15 | $15
Bakery & Cafe
3906 Lemmon Ave. (Oak Lawn Ave.), 214-521-0182 S
3072 Mockingbird Ln. (N. Central Expwy.), 214-696-0800 S
NorthPark Ctr. Mall, 628 NorthPark Ctr. (Northwest Hwy.), 214-696-2398 S
Preston Ctr., 8319 Preston Rd. (south of Northwest Hwy.), 214-346-9733 S
2121 San Jacinto St. (Pearl St.), 214-220-3911
4343 W. Northwest Hwy. (Midway Rd.), 214-357-5621 S
11930 Preston Rd. (Forest Ln.), 972-233-6446 S
5290 Belt Line Rd. (east of Dallas Pkwy.), Addison, 972-239-9051 S
5000 W. Park Blvd. (Preston Rd.), Plano, 972-407-1878 S
1320 W. Campbell Rd. (Coit Rd.), Richardson, 972-671-4887 S
◪ Cheered for the "best basil tomato soup" as well as "*très bon*" Caesar salad, croissants and desserts, this French bakery/cafe chain exemplifies "consistently good quality"; critics counter that it's "overpriced."

Dallas   F | D | S | C

La Mirabelle   22 | 20 | 22 | $44
17610 Midway Rd. (Trinity Mills Rd.), 972-733-0202
■ Run by a husband/wife team who share cooking and hosting duties, this cozy North Dallas French venue is a smart choice for "truly gourmet" "classic" renditions like lobster bisque and Dover sole as well as bistro favorites that come with "wonderful *pommes frites*"; diners also appreciate the "appealing decor" and "warm", "personal touches", such as tableside "visits" from the chef.

L'Ancestral   24 | 20 | 21 | $38
Travis Walk, 4514 Travis St. (Knox St.), 214-528-1081
■ This "charming" Knox/Henderson bistro has been dishing out country Gallic hits – escargots, pepper steak and floating island – for some 20 years; though some carp that the "menu never changes", "loyal regulars" praise its "old-fashioned" setting and authenticity ("even our waiter was French").

Landmark Restaurant S   22 | 22 | 22 | $42
Melrose Hotel, 3015 Oak Lawn Ave. (Cedar Springs Rd.), 214-522-1453
■ Some claim they "never had a bad meal" at this Melrose New American, which features marble floors, crown moldings and "very romantic" muted lighting that explains why "my husband proposed here"; consider ordering the signature smoked salmon–wrapped salmon, or if your budget allows it, the prix fixe menu with matching wines.

Landry's Seafood S   15 | 15 | 15 | $21
306 N. Market St. (Elm St.), 214-698-1010
4440 Belt Line Rd. (Midway Rd.), Addison, 972-960-6878
◪ These Downtown and Addison branches of a national seafood chain are "good for cheapie meals" of mostly fried shore eats; harsh critics, however, protest that the edibles are reminiscent of "mom's Friday fish sticks" and that the overall experience is "forgettable."

La Trattoria Lombardi S   24 | 19 | 21 | $32
2916 N. Hall St. (McKinney Ave.), 214-954-0803
■ The owner and his "team make everyone feel welcome" at this Uptown "touch of Italy" with "consistently good" food and a "warm, homey atmosphere"; if available, try the signature seafood cioppino, otherwise, go with the chef's recommendation; P.S. lunch is a "great value."

LAURELS   27 | 27 | 26 | $62
Westin Park Central Hotel, 12720 Merit Dr. (Coit Rd.), 972-851-2021
■ It's food score may be in question since the departure of award-winning chef Danielle Custer, but this North Dallas global-influenced New American still epitomizes "elegant, elevated dining" thanks to "unobtrusive" service and an intimate beige-and-gold room with a "terrific", 20th-floor panoramic view; N.B. tasting menus are no longer available.

Dallas   F | D | S | C

La Valentina de Mexico ⓢ   23 | 23 | 21 | $31
14866 Montfort Dr. (south of Belt Line Rd.), 972-726-0202
■ Lose your heart to this capacious North Dallas eatery where the "Mexico City–style" cuisine's "way above" standard fare – "no enchiladas here" – especially the "to-die-for steak"; its "wonderful" service and strolling mariachi band "set a nice tone for the evening", and the bar is a fun place to meet for a drink; oenophiles should come on Wednesdays when bottles are 50 percent off.

Lavendou   24 | 23 | 21 | $34
Preston Lloyd Ctr., 19009 Preston Rd. (bet. Frankford Rd. & Plano Pkwy.), 972-248-1911
◪ Chez Gérard's North Dallas sibling, this "Country French surprise" is decked out in Provençal colors of cornflower blue and sunny yellow and has "excellent cuisine" (try the lavender crème brûlée); service plays to mixed reviews ("impeccable" vs. "snooty"), but this is still a "good place to take out-of-towners" because it "proves we're not hicks."

LAWRY'S THE PRIME RIB ⓢ   25 | 23 | 24 | $38
14655 Dallas Pkwy. (bet. Belt Line & Spring Valley Rds.), 972-503-6688
■ "The definitive prime rib" carved tableside, "great creamed spinach" and a famous 'spinning bowl salad' are the highlights of this upscale North Dallas chain link; granted, trendy types might think the decor "could use updating" and find the staff uniforms "hokey", but this is still a "favorite for celebrations" and an "excellent lunch value."

Lefty's Lobster & Chowder House ⓢ   22 | 15 | 19 | $24
4021 Belt Line Rd. (Runyon Rd.), Addison, 972-774-9518
◪ "Hiding out" in an Addison strip mall, this seafooder may have nautical decor and snappy service, but its big hook is lobsters, which bibbed-up patrons gently wrestle with when they're not chowing on sides like corn on the cob; landlubbers find it "way too noisy" and "crowded" ("felt like a sardine") but appreciate the chicken and beef options.

Leonardo's   ▽ 26 | 14 | 23 | $18
9741 Preston Rd. (Main St.), Frisco, 972-335-1244
■ It's worth the drive to Frisco for the "fabulous" Italian fare at this "hidden treasure", a wood-paneled, family-owned BYO with super garlic rolls, a "wonderful veal Guisseppe" and "the best linguini with clam sauce" ("trust me").

Le Paris Bistrot ⓢ   21 | 21 | 20 | $34
2533 McKinney Ave. (Routh St.), 214-720-0225
■ Set in a former antique shop with lots of romantic nooks and murals, this Uptown French bistro has an "exceedingly accommodating staff", a "superb wine list" and "quality" fare like braised lamb shanks and roasted chicken with herbs de Provence; N.B. free valet parking at lunch and dinner.

Dallas | F | D | S | C |

Les Saisons ⑤ | 22 | 22 | 20 | $37 |
Centrum Bldg., 3102 Oak Lawn Ave. (Cedar Springs Rd.), 214-528-1102
■ Seemingly "of another era", this Oak Lawn veteran makes a "dependable" French connection to classics like "to-die-for brie soup", Dover sole and rack of lamb; skilled tableside preparations and rich dishes mean you can expect a leisurely meal, more time to take in the Monet-style murals.

Liberty ⑤ | 23 | 18 | 19 | $26 |
5631 Alta Ave. (Greenville Ave.), 214-887-8795
◪ Soba, so good, say slurpers who give the nod to the "heavenly" noodle dishes served at this Lower Greenville Pan-Asian, which features a "strong wine list" and a slate bar perfect for dining alone; dissenters say it's "overrated" but concede that a visit makes a "good change of pace."

Lola, The Restaurant | – | – | – | E |
2917 Fairmont St. (Cedar Springs Rd.), 214-855-0700
Following the lead of its predecessor, Barclays, this Uptown New American serves innovative fixed-price meals in two, three or four courses; suave servers and a house-turned-restaurant setting mean the evening can get very romantic.

Lombardi Mare ⑤ | 24 | 24 | 22 | $38 |
Village on the Pkwy., 5100 Belt Line Rd. (Montfort Dr.), Addison, 972-503-1233
■ "As hot as a hot Texas summer" sums up the "trendy" scene at this sleek Addison Italian-seafooder, which dazzles with bowls of live goldfish dangling above the bar and candlelit communal tables; risotto to relish and "impeccably fresh" offerings like cioppino and pick-your-own lobsters are other reasons to swim upstream for a table; N.B. Tom Fleming (ex The Riviera) is now behind the stove.

Los Vaqueros ⑤ | 17 | 14 | 18 | $16 |
Snider Plaza, 6615 Snider Plaza (Lovers Ln.), 214-361-9885
■ "Family-owned and -operated", this "old-fashioned" Snider Plaza Tex-Mex "haunt" is a casual stop where the kids are treated well and the "good, basic" renditions (tacos, fajitas, etc.) are zipped up with the "best hot sauce"; P.S. "try the 'Willis Tate'" an off-the-menu chicken enchilada platter.

Lover's Egg Roll ⑤ | 16 | 9 | 13 | $11 |
5360 Lovers Ln. (Inwood Rd.), 214-358-1318
13901 Midway Rd. (Spring Valley Pkwy.), 972-991-1668
3501 McKinney Ave. (Cole St.), 214-443-1888
1501 Preston Rd. (Plano Pkwy.), Plano, 972-735-8646
5960 W. Parker Rd. (Dallas Tollway), Plano, 972-378-9292
◪ Clearly, some love this egg roll and others do not, since this Chinese chain gets a real sweet-and-sour response: boosters say it's a "decent" "last-minute pickup" choice for "generous portions" of steamed dumplings and fried rice; resourceful critics claim "there are much better" options.

Dallas   F | D | S | C

Lucky's Cafe S 18 | 13 | 16 | $14
3531 Oak Lawn Ave. (north of Lemmon Ave.), 214-522-3500
■ Oak Lawn "comfort food" connoisseurs feel lucky to live near this humble-looking, "old-fashioned" American cafe whose breakfasts are "a must" (try the biscuits and omelets) and whose spinach salad is breathlessly called "the best anywhere"; hit-the-spot homemade desserts like apple pie and cobbler round out the "down-home" experience.

Luna de Noche Tex-Mex Grill ▽ 20 | 14 | 20 | $18
7927 Forest Ln. (Coit Rd.), 972-233-1880 S
Spring Park Ctr., 7602 Jupiter Rd. (Campbell Rd.), Garland, 972-414-3616
■ The new Forest/Central location of this family-run Tex-Mex twosome may silence those who find the Garland branch "too hard to find"; either way, both have "very good" victuals, homemade sangria and cosseting, "above-average" service, so "get there early."

Mac's Bar & Grill S 21 | 19 | 19 | $26
2301 N. Central Expwy. (Enterprise Dr.), Plano, 972-881-2804
See review in Fort Worth Directory.

Maggiano's Little Italy S 21 | 22 | 20 | $25
NorthPark Ctr. Mall, 205 NorthPark Ctr. (Northwest Hwy.), 214-360-0707
■ "Huge portions" are the hallmark of this mammoth NorthPark Center chain link, a "family-style" Italian where large tables of friends and relatives share solid salads ("try the chopped" one) and platters of respectable red sauce renditions (manicotti, meatballs, etc.) N.B. half portions are now offered, so you no longer have to invite everyone you know to clean the plate.

Magic Time Machine S 15 | 22 | 18 | $27
5003 Belt Line Rd. (N. Dallas Tollway), Addison, 972-980-1903
◪ Its American "food is definitely not the main attraction", but kids (and a few parents) still love this Addison storybook-themed eatery for its "delightful", "campy" costumed staff, whose hijinks make this "not the place for uptight people."

Maguire's Regional Cuisine S 22 | 22 | 22 | $33
17552 Dallas Pkwy. (Trinity Mills Rd.), 972-818-0068
■ Uniformly high marks and glowing comments reflect voter enthusiasm for this smartly "trendy" but "reasonably priced" New American along the North Dallas Tollroad corridor; it's become "a new favorite" with voters for its "great Bloody Mary's at brunch", "especially good salads", "excellent meat loaf", "exceptional" pistachio-crusted halibut and "wonderful dessert menu", led by the chocolate lava cake.

Dallas   F | D | S | C

Mainstream Fish House S 23 | 16 | 20 | $22
11661 Preston Rd. (Forest Ln.), 214-739-3474
■ "We never met a fish we didn't like here" reflects mainstream views of this "moderately priced" Forest "neighborhood" seafooder where it helps to "get there early" for the "large variety" of offerings, including "super clam chowder" and fish tacos; though "short on decor", it nonetheless makes for "a great quick meal during the week."

Mai's Vietnamese 21 | 11 | 19 | $13
4812 Bryan St. (Fitzhugh Ave.), 214-826-9887
■ While its Downtown environs "leave a lot to be desired" and its plain, no-frills interior is nothing to brag about, this Vietnamese BYO has thrived for almost 20 years thanks to soups that "are a meal in themselves", "fresh", "flavorful" dishes and service that gets you "in and out in a flash."

Mama's Daughters' Diner 22 | 11 | 20 | $12
2610 Royal Ln. (Harry Hines Blvd.), 972-241-8646
Wynnewood Village Shopping Ctr., 718 Wynnewood Village (Illinois Ave.), 214-948-6200
2015 N. Galloway Ave. (I-80), Mesquite, 972-289-6262
■ These Southern diners work for "pig-out breakfasts" and plate lunches of chicken-fried steak and "the best desserts"; adding to the Mayberry RFD experience are fawning waitresses who get to know you pretty quickly.

Mango Thai Cuisine S – | – | – | M
4701 W. Park Blvd. (Preston Rd.), Plano, 972-599-0289
The artistic decor, cooled by sherbet hues, ensures a creative experience even before you try the food at this Plano colony of a prominent local Siamese empire; you'll find both tame choices for novices and richly layered flavors for those who want to Thai one on.

MANSION ON TURTLE CREEK S 27 | 28 | 27 | $64
2821 Turtle Creek Blvd. (Gillespie St.), 214-559-2100
■ Once again the Most Popular restaurant in the Dallas *Survey* and the "gold standard" in its category, this Downtown Southwestern features acclaimed chef Dean Fearing's "consistently innovative" combinations, which are likely to leave you "speechless"; moreover, the "outstanding" staff provides a "never-ending flow of attention" and the "beautiful rooms" convey an "exclusive feel" that's "like dining in someone's house"; in sum, a "first-class night out", even if the "amazing wine list" is "overpriced."

Margaux's 22 | 17 | 20 | $34
2404 Cedar Springs Rd. (Maple Ave.), 214-740-1985
■ "Delightful owner" Kay Agnew and her "gracious" staff ensure a "pleasant" meal at this small Uptown Cajun-Creole outlet, open for weekday lunches, dinner on Thursdays and private functions; the "constantly changing menu" usually includes crawfish étouffée and shrimp scampi.

Dallas   F | D | S | C

Marie Gabrielle   ▽ 19 | 24 | 19 | $20
Centex Bldg., 2728 N. Harwood St. (Payne St.), 214-871-2097

■ Sprawled out along the base of Uptown's Centex building, this stylish International boasts a floor-to-ceiling view of the elaborate gardens and fountains outside; really two eateries, its cafeteria serves salads, sandwiches and stick-to-your-ribs hot dishes, while its upscale, full-service dining room offers more sophisticated fare; N.B. it's open for breakfast and lunch only, but can be rented out for parties.

Mario & Alberto   20 | 17 | 19 | $19
Preston Valley Shopping Ctr., 12817 Preston Rd. (LBJ Frwy.), 972-980-7296

◪ If you believe regulars, the "Kahlua pie alone is worth the trip" to this "fairly quiet", pink-colored Northwest Dallas family stop where the "extensive menu" means "good choices between Mex and Tex-Mex" items.

Mario's Chiquita   21 | 20 | 20 | $18
221 W. Parker Rd. (N. Central Expwy.), Plano, 972-423-2977

◪ Offering both Mexican and Tex-Mex cuisine, this popular Plano cantina draws plenty of folks who appreciate its "cheerful" pink decor, "friendly service" and generous portions; a few sensitive types think the "high noise level" is a drawback.

Martinez Cafe S   – | – | – | I
2001 Coit Rd. (Park Blvd.), Plano, 972-964-7898

While this beige Plano venue isn't very fancy, it sure feels like home to the faithful who flock here for enormous, cheap Tex-Mex standards like beef fajitas, pork carnitas and chile rellenos.

Martini Ranch ☽   ▽ 15 | 18 | 18 | $23
2816 Fairmount St. (Cedar Springs Rd.), 214-220-2116

◪ With 15 types of some of the "best martinis in town" to choose from, this NYC–style Uptown American presents a challenge to ambitious drinkers; some might argue that trying "two is too few and having three is too many to remember dinner", but that may not be the worst thing, since the edibles are called "average" and "uninteresting."

Marty's Wine Bar & Cafe TuGogh   22 | 15 | 18 | $26
3316 Oak Lawn Ave. (bet. Cedar Springs Rd. & Lemmon Ave.), 214-526-7796

■ This "real find" in Oak Lawn wears many hats: it's a fine wine store with "hard-to-find" bottles, a *vin* bar with "superb choices by the glass", a full-scale gourmet market, a take-out shop for "when you invite food snobs to dinner", a self-service lunch cafe and an evening restaurant with "low-key" live music and "excellent New American" cuisine.

Dallas F | D | S | C

Mattito's Cafe Mexicano S   19 | 17 | 18 | $18
3011 Routh St. (Cedar Springs Rd.), 214-526-8181
■ "If you like tequila, this is the place to drink it" – "every variety that's legal to sell in Texas" – note voters drawn to this Tex-Mex veteran, which moved Uptown to more colorful environs but still prepares "great margaritas" and a Sunday brunch buffet with at least 60 choices.

Matt's No Place   24 | 18 | 21 | $28
Lakewood Theater Plaza, 6326 La Vista Dr. (Gaston Ave.), 214-823-9077
■ Lakewood residents say there's "no place like this No Place", a "very cool neighborhood" spot with "a mural of local dignitaries" ("a little racy but very funny") and a Texas-themed menu of "steaks, wild game and such"; N.B. reservations are recommended on weekends.

Matt's Rancho Martinez   21 | 13 | 18 | $18
Lakewood Theater Plaza, 6332 La Vista Dr. (Gaston Ave.), 214-823-5517
Matt's at Macy's
Galleria Mall, 13350 Dallas Pkwy. (LBJ Frwy.), 972-851-5123
■ A "longtime favorite" in Lakewood (and now also at the Macy's Food Court), this huge Tex-Mex cantina has many attractive seating options, such as a downstairs room, upstairs balcony and spacious patio; either way, owner Matt Martinez (wearing his omnipresent cowboy hat) and his family provide *muy bueno* service, "yummy" chile rellenos and a 'Bob Armstrong dip' that's "a must."

May Dragon S   19 | 17 | 19 | $21
Inwood Quorum Shopping Ctr., 4848 Belt Line Rd. (Inwood Rd.), Addison, 972-392-9998
■ "You won't be hungry an hour after leaving" this Addison Chinese institution, which is known for "the best smoked duck in town" and a "warm, helpful" staff that unobtrusively moves in and out of its small, screened rooms.

Mecca   21 | 11 | 21 | $11
10422 Harry Hines Blvd. (Lombardy Ln.), 214-352-0051
■ Open for more than 60 years, this "best little roadhouse cafe" in Northwest Dallas might have limited, time-warp decor, but its "truck-stop waitresses sure can sling" the "down-home" victuals like chicken-fried steak and pecan pie, especially during the "awesome breakfasts", which attract everyone from long haulers to bankers.

Medieval Times S   10 | 22 | 15 | $35
2021 N. Stemmons Frwy. (Market Ctr. Blvd.), 214-761-1801
◪ Who needs utensil etiquette when you can "eat with your hands" (just "make sure they're clean") at this Medieval-themed American eatery where parents "take the kids once" for the show and souvenirs ("bring the checkbook"); foes who fault flavors from the Dark Ages say "forget the food."

Dallas   F | D | S | C

Mediterraneo S   24 | 23 | 21 | $41
18111 Preston Rd. (Frankford Rd.), 972-447-0066
■ Its "beautiful" decor remains intact, but this sunny North Dallas Mediterranean has otherwise "undergone a transformation" over the past year courtesy of new management; while the menu has been shortened somewhat, there's still plenty of "aromatic dishes with enough panache to please", especially the "well-prepared seafood."

Melting Pot, The S   ▽ 19 | 18 | 19 | $29
4900 Belt Line Rd. (bet. Inwood Rd. & Quorum Dr.), Addison, 972-960-7027
◪ "Plan to stay a while" when dining at this popular Addison fondue specialist, which is "fun for groups" and also "romantic" couples as long as they avoid the occasional "splattering of grease"; those who don't melt for the savory and sweet specialty "order the coq au vin."

Mercado Juarez S   17 | 15 | 16 | $17
1901 W. Northwest Hwy. (Spangler Rd.), 972-556-0796
◪ This "old-fashioned" Tex-Mex chain is respected for its "good flour tortillas", fajitas, cabrito (goat) and fried ice cream balls; the less impressed say the edibles are just "ok."

Mercury, The S   25 | 22 | 22 | $42
11909 Preston Rd. (Forest Ln.), 972-960-7774
■ For "fine food in an improbable strip mall location" head to this North Dallas New American where "innovative" dishes "dazzle the senses" and a "trendy" clientele looks glamorous in the understated, modern setting; the only quibble: it's "one of the loudest restaurants" around.

Mia's Tex-Mex   23 | 14 | 19 | $18
4322 Lemmon Ave. (Wycliff Ave.), 214-526-1020
◪ "Who doesn't love Mia's?" is a common refrain on this Oak Lawn Tex-Mex haven where "the elite and the not-so-elite" chow down on "don't-miss" brisket tacos and chile rellenos; despite "hundreds of pictures of locals on the walls", regulars call it "sort of a dive", but if the occasional Dallas Cowboy or two can feel comfortable, so can you.

MI COCINA S   21 | 19 | 19 | $20
Galleria Mall, 13350 Dallas Pkwy. (LBJ Frwy.), 972-239-6426
7201 Skillman St. (Kingsley Rd.), 214-503-6426
11661 Preston Rd. (Forest Ln.), 214-265-7704
Highland Park Village, 77 Highland Park Village (Mockingbird Ln. & Preston Rd.), 214-521-6426
18352 Dallas Pkwy. (Frankford Rd.), 972-250-6426
1370 W. Campbell Rd. (Coit Rd.), Richardson, 972-671-6426
■ "We're addicted" confess regulars of this "popular" chain that cooks up some of the "best Tex-Mex", washed down with the "world's deadliest" margaritas; the "hip" Highland Park branch gets the "highest marks for people-watching", especially at happy hour, when young "eye candy" abounds.

Dallas | F | D | S | C |

Mignon 🆂 | – | – | – | E |
4005 Preston Rd. (bet. Parker Rd. & Spring Creek Pkwy.), Plano, 972-943-3372
High-wattage types enjoy the energy at this stylish French newcomer in Plano, featuring a large dining patio where *les chiens* are welcome; the menu offers what you'd expect, like steak frites, as well as other must-tries like braised pork shank and pan-seared sea bass.

Mimi's Cafe 🆂 | – | – | – | I |
810 W. McDermott Dr. (bet. I-75 & Watters Rd.), Allen, 214-547-1440
See review in Fort Worth Directory.

MI PIACI RISTORANTE 🆂 | 26 | 24 | 23 | $38 |
14854 Montfort Rd. (Belt Line Rd.), Addison, 972-934-8424
■ "Luscious ingredients, creative combinations and lovely presentations" add up to "absolutely spectacular" cuisine at this "upscale" Addison Northern Italian known for its "marvelous risotto" and osso buco; its "sophisticated", "sleek" and "open" room "overlooking the water" (a manmade duck pond) and "exemplary" service also win kudos; P.S. a small dining room in the wine cellar can be rented out for private parties.

MODO MIO CUCINA RUSTICA ITALIANA | 25 | 21 | 22 | $35 |
Frankford Crossing, 18352 Dallas Pkwy. (Frankford Rd.), 972-671-6636
■ Rino Brigliadori (chef-owner) and his son Rino Jr. (manager) "make a welcoming team" at this "great neighborhood" Northern Italian trattoria in North Dallas where the "fantastic", "authentic" dishes (including sea bass that's the "best ever") are always served "with a smile"; given this "warm an atmosphere", no one minds much if it can get a bit "crowded" and "noisy."

MoMo's Italian Specialties 🆂 | 20 | 16 | 17 | $22 |
9191 Forest Ln. (Greenville Ave.), 972-234-6800
Preston Ctr. Plaza, 8300 Preston Ctr. Plaza (Northwest Hwy.), 214-987-2082
■ "Brick walls give warmth" to these "reliable", "reasonably priced" Forest Lane and Preston Center Italians, which are "fun for dinner with friends" as well as "good family restaurants"; popular choices include the meat ravioli and T-bone steak stuffed with prosciutto and gruyere.

MoMo's Pasta 🆂 | 19 | 16 | 17 | $21 |
2704 Elm St. (bet. Crowdus St. & Good-Latimer Expwy.), 214-748-4222

(continued)

Dallas F | D | S | C

(continued)
MoMo's Pasta
3312 Knox St. (Travis St.), 214-521-3009
Prestonwood Pl., 5290 Belt Line Rd. (Montfort Dr.),
Addison, 972-386-7373

■ "Authentic Italian that thumbs its nose at imposters" is how defenders describe the edibles at this trio serving "tasty and creative" fare that has folks still "coming in at 10 PM on a Sunday night"; nono-sayers find it "overpriced", with occasional service problems.

Monica's Aca y Alla S   22 | 19 | 20 | $21
2914 Main St. (bet. Malcolm X Blvd. & Walton St.),
214-748-7140

■ "Salsa dance with the fun crowd" at this "quintessential" Deep Ellum Mexican where the "well-crafted" fare, washed down with "great margaritas", "is the best this side of the Rio Grande" ("try the sumptuous flank steak"); amigos also acclaim the jovial staff and "delightful" eponymous owner Monica Greene, but caution: "be prepared for a wait on the weekends."

MORTON'S OF CHICAGO S   25 | 23 | 24 | $52
501 Elm St. (Houston St.), 214-741-2277
14831 Midway Rd. (bet. Belt Line Rd. & Spring Valley Rd.),
Addison, 972-233-5858

■ "Go with a client – you'll get the contract" declare savvy surveyors weighing in on these acclaimed Elm and Addison haute steakhouses where the beef ranges from "excellent" to "the best", the seafood catches are "superb" and the molten chocolate cake is "to die for"; cigars sold on premises and an extensive martini menu are further grease for the business-deal wheels, though those without an expense account find it "overpriced."

Mr. G's Deli   ∇ 21 | 11 | 15 | $11
1453 Coit Rd. (15th St.), Plano, 972-867-2821

■ With a "huge sandwich selection" of more than 80 choices and deli-gates who call its offerings "the best in the area" ("especially the Reubens, there's even a meatless variety"), it should be no surprise that this Plano sandwich shop/wine store has served more than 2 million of 'em since opening in '88; but alas, that pace will be difficult to keep up, since the Campbell Road branch has closed.

Mr. Sushi S   23 | 17 | 19 | $28
4860 Belt Line Rd. (Addison Rd.), Addison, 972-385-0168

■ In addition to "the best sushi in town for the price", this Addison Japanese venue has "relaxed atmosphere" that exerts "no pressure on beginners"; however, management also offers "special variations for the less timid."

Dallas   F | D | S | C

Nakamoto Japanese Cuisine S ▽   24 | 21 | 22 | $29
3309 N. Central Expwy. (Parker Rd.), Plano, 972-881-0328
■ "Excellent" "fresh sushi" and "great hospitality" combine most winningly at this Plano Japanese, which caters to all, from novices to roll aficionados who venture off-menu; the tatami room is perfect for private parties (just make sure your socks don't have holes – it's strictly no-shoes).

NANA GRILL S   26 | 27 | 25 | $54
Wyndham Anatole Hotel, 2201 N. Stemmons Frwy. (Market Ctr. Blvd.), 214-761-7470
■ "What a view" exclaim enthusiasts admiring the vista from this Downtown New American favorite; its "luxurious room" is "where you go to impress someone", and the "excellent food and service" complement the "wonderful atmosphere" (enhanced by live jazz Wednesday–Saturday); admirers also recommend it for the "best brunch in Texas", a buffet accompanied by "buckets of champagne."

Natalie's S   19 | 15 | 17 | $17
5944 Royal Ln. (Preston Rd.), 214-739-0362
■ This "quiet, little neighborhood" American cafe in Preston-Royal has been a "nice spot for a ladies' lunch" for years; the bakery items are especially popular, with sweet tooths constantly asking for "more cinnamon rolls!"; regulars, however, rue "that prices have gone up."

Nate's Seafood & Steakhouse S   20 | 15 | 17 | $24
14951 Midway Rd. (Belt Line Rd.), Addison, 972-701-9622
■ The food's big and the prices easy on the wallet at this popular Cajun institution in Addison, where you'll "bark like a dog for the hush puppies"; the service is "swift and friendly", and despite the funky, even "white-trash", decor, you may find that you're "dining next to a celebrity."

Newport's Seafood S   23 | 22 | 23 | $32
The Brewery Bldg., 703 McKinney Ave. (I-35), 214-954-0220
■ Located in a historic former brewery, this Downtown old-timer's casual rustic interior provides "a great meeting place" to dine on "impeccably fresh" seafood (including some "unusual combinations") that's "competitive with the best restaurants in town", and often "less expensive" too; a "classy staff" rounds out the "dependable" experience.

Nicholini's Seafood Grill S   24 | 22 | 22 | $33
Preston Trails, 17370 Preston Rd. (Frankford Rd.), 972-735-9868
■ Tucked away in a North Dallas strip mall, this Italian-accented seafooder turns out to be a "pleasant surprise" thanks to "crisp service", a "relaxing atmosphere" (abetted by a saltwater aquarium) and "wonderful", "pleasing-to-the-eye" dishes like crab-stuffed salmon.

Dallas

F | D | S | C

Nick & Sam's S   24 | 24 | 23 | $50
3008 Maple Ave. (Oak Lawn Ave.), 214-871-7444
◪ This "see-and-be-seen" Uptown steakhouse attracts admirers with amenities such as a rolling caviar cart, grand piano in the kitchen and "smart, sophisticated decor"; beef takes center stage, but the lamb and fish offerings are also "excellent"; some warn that it's "incredibly loud" and "priced for a roaring economy."

Nicola's S   ▽ 21 | 17 | 20 | $21
Galleria Mall, 13350 Dallas Pkwy. (LBJ Frwy.), 972-788-1177
■ Sandwich in the time for some of the "excellent panini" offered at this sleek North Dallas Italian, with equally sleek service; although it overlooks the Galleria's ice-skating rink, advocates say its menu is the city's closest thing "to favorites in Venice, Padua and Verona", especially the pizza with a killer crust and homemade sorbetto.

Norma's Cafe S   20 | 14 | 18 | $11
1123 W. Davis St. (Willomet Ave.), 214-946-4711
3647 W. Northwest Hwy. (Webb Chapel Rd.), 214-357-7771
3300 Belt Line Rd. (bet. Marsh Ln. & Webb Chapel Rd.), Farmers Branch, 972-243-8646
■ For "good" regional "home cooking" walk (or drive) a country mile to these casual "original greasy spoons" where "you won't be disappointed with the blue plate specials" (order the chicken-fried steak) and filling breakfasts.

Nuevo Leon S   21 | 16 | 18 | $19
3211 Oak Lawn Ave. (Cedar Springs Rd.), 214-522-3331
2013 Greenville Ave. (Ross Ave.), 214-887-8148
12895 Josey Ln. (bet. Belt Line Rd. & Valwood Pkwy.), Farmers Branch, 972-488-1984
■ "At last, Mexican rather than Tex-Mex" declare amigos of this trio of simply decorated spots where families who appreciate a "reliable" "good value" habitually dine "once a week" on the likes of "fresh salsas" and "great fajitas."

Old Chicago ☻S   ▽ 20 | 18 | 16 | $15
4060 Belt Line Rd. (bet. Marsh Ln. & Midway Rd.), Addison, 972-490-3900
◪ With its "down-home" atmosphere, this Addison American is an easy place for parents to take the kids for burgers, pizzas and a nice selection of root beers, while they sip a beer and grab some pasta; critics are less than kind about the edibles and staff ("lax service"), but they're outvoted.

Old San Francisco Steakhouse S   19 | 19 | 18 | $30
10965 Composite Dr. (Walnut Hill Ln.), 214-357-0484
◪ The "terrific atmosphere" at this North Dallas veteran steakhouse includes a woman on a red velvet swing, honky-tonk piano players and other Gold Rush–era touches; forty-niners also mine the free blocks of Swiss cheese and the "excellent" steaks, though spoilers call the food "overrated."

www.zagat.com

Dallas | F | D | S | C |

OLD WARSAW ⓈⒶ | 26 | 24 | 23 | $56 |
2610 Maple Ave. (McKinney Ave.), 214-528-0032
◪ An "elegant and romantic hideaway", this Uptown French-Continental has been exuding "old-world charm" for more than 50 years and recently received a much-needed remodeling (don't miss the shark tank); the "superb food" is formally served, and the menu offers "the best chocolate soufflé ever made"; nonetheless, wallet-watchers warn "take your heaviest credit card."

Olive Garden Ⓢ | 15 | 14 | 16 | $18 |
9079 Vantage Point Dr. (Greenville Ave.), 972-234-3292
4240 Belt Line Rd. (Midway Rd.), Addison, 972-239-9096
3816 Towne Crossing Blvd. (I-635), Mesquite, 972-270-1582
◪ Some assert "you can't beat the all-you-can-eat soup and salad" and "gigantic portions" offered by this national Italian chain, adding that a visit makes for "one of the best values around"; foes find it a version of "suburban hell" with "inconsistent" service and just "ok" victuals.

On the Border Ⓢ | 17 | 16 | 16 | $17 |
3130 Knox St. (bet. Cole & McKinney Aves.), 214-528-5900
1801 N. Lamar St. (Corbin St.), 214-855-0296
4400 Belt Line Rd. (Midway Rd.), Addison, 972-788-4400
1350 Northwest Hwy. (Saturn Rd.), Garland, 972-686-7867
1505 N. Central Expwy. (15th St.), Plano, 972-881-2257
◪ Surveyors are divided over this Tex-Mex chain: one camp calls it "good family dining" with "decent" fare like veggie quesadillas and "rice and beans that actually have flavor"; those on the opposite side acknowledge the "top-shelf margaritas" but find the food "standard issue", the service "slow" and the atmosphere "noisy."

Original Pancake House Ⓢ | 21 | 13 | 17 | $12 |
2900 Lemmon Ave. W. (bet. McKinney & Oak Grove Aves.), 214-528-7215
4343 W. Northwest Hwy. (Midway Rd.), 214-351-2012
5100 Belt Line Rd. (N. Dallas Tollway), Addison, 972-385-6468
2301 N. Central Expwy. (bet. Park Blvd. & Parker St.), Plano, 972-423-2889
▪ "Be prepared for a line" at these perennially popular breakfast nooks where you'll flip for "pancakes like grandma used to make" (the "apple [version] is a must") and "huge omelets"; those who've grown accustomed to the waits see these places as "great weekend hangouts" with plenty of people-watching.

Osaka Sushi Ⓢ | – | – | – | M |
5012 W. Park Blvd. (Preston Rd.), 972-931-8898
Don't be surprised if you're drawn to the nicely priced lunch and dinner buffets at this North Dallas Japanese noshery where the staff replenishes the offerings way before they're empty; the sushi selection is diverse, but you'll also eat well if you order from the regular menu.

Dallas | F | D | S | C |

Outback Steakhouse S | 20 | 17 | 19 | $24 |
2225 Connector Dr. (Northwest Hwy.), 214-956-8999
9049 Vantage Point Dr. (Greenville Ave.), 972-783-0397
15180 Addison Rd. (Belt Line Rd.), Addison, 972-392-0972
3903 Towne Crossing Blvd. (Towne East Blvd.), Mesquite, 972-686-0555
1509 N. Central Expwy. (15th St.), Plano, 972-516-4100

■ "Great steaks at fair prices" hit the barbie at this beef chain, which some city slickers are "almost ashamed to say they like"; less pretentious patrons pick "the best bloomin' onions", savor the "super prime rib" and relish the rustic atmosphere.

Palm Restaurant S | 25 | 21 | 23 | $47 |
701 Ross Ave. (Market St.), 214-698-0470

◪ Those who go "to be seen" say "you're nobody unless you lunch" at this clubby, "upscale" West End steakhouse, which has one of "the best porterhouses in Dallas" and "great lobsters"; caricatures of famous locals ("fun wall reading") and snappy service add to the lively, expense-account experience; still, a few impossible-to-please types quibble that "it helps to be a regular."

PALOMINO EURO BISTRO S | 24 | 25 | 23 | $37 |
Hotel Crescent Court, 500 Crescent Ct. (bet. Cedar Springs Rd. & Pearl St.), 214-999-1222

■ "Sleek", "upscale" digs, "wonderful service" and "consistently creative", "well-prepared" Mediterranean food (start with the "great crab dip") mean few neighsayers for this "trendy" Uptown chain link; P.S. its bar is quite the "people-watching" scene, so don't be surprised if you see men jockeying to meet "women with big hair."

Pappadeaux Seafood Kitchen S | 22 | 19 | 19 | $26 |
10428 Lombardy Ln. (I-35 & Northwest Hwy.), 214-358-1912
3520 Oak Lawn Ave. (Lemmon Ave.), 214-521-4700
18349 Dallas Pkwy. (Frankford Rd.), Plano, 972-447-9616
725 Central Expwy. (Spring Valley Rd.), Richardson, 972-235-1181

■ Serving "huge portions" of the only "decent Louisiana-style seafood in the Metroplex", this "always packed", "well-priced" chain is a slice of "crawfish heaven" ("the best étouffée"), with "addictive fried shrimp" and beatific bread pudding too; the *bon temps* atmosphere can get "too loud", but overall, "who can argue with success?"

PAPPAS BROS. STEAKHOUSE | 26 | 25 | 24 | $47 |
10477 Lombardy Ln. (I-35 & Northwest Hwy.), 214-366-2000

■ "Outstanding every time" declare devotees of this Northwest Dallas jewel in the crown of the Pappas family restaurant empire, which is "Texas to the core", with "Lone Star state–size drinks, big steaks and great Southwestern decor"; a "huge wine selection" ("from $25 to $70,000") and practically "flawless service" add to its superb rep – just get "someone else to pay for you."

Dallas | F | D | S | C |

Pappasito's Cantina ⑤   21 | 20 | 19 | $21
10433 Lombardy Ln. (I-35E & Northwest Hwy.), 214-350-1970
723 S. Central Expwy. (Forest Park Blvd. & I-30), Richardson, 972-480-8595
■ This Northwest Dallas and Richardson duo offers "big" Tex-Mex portions of winning enchiladas and "the hands-down best fajitas in town"; "long waits" and "noisy" environs are drawbacks, but hey, that's "a Pappas trademark."

Parigi ⑤   23 | 20 | 19 | $35
3311 Oak Lawn Ave. (Hall St.), 214-521-0295
■ "A wonderfully intimate spot" that's modeled after a Parisian open-air cafe, this "long-standing" Oak Lawn "gem" continues to shine with "interesting" Eclectic offerings; while the menu changes often, the beef tenderloin and chocolate glob (a half-baked brownie) are staples.

Patrizio ⑤   22 | 21 | 20 | $25
Highland Park Village, 25 Highland Park Village (Mockingbird Ln. & Preston Rd.), 214-522-7878
Preston Park Village, 343 Preston Park Village (Park Ln.), Plano, 972-964-2200
■ These "chic", "lively" Highland Park and Plano Italian sibs are prized for their "lush patios" that evoke a "hidden cove in Venice"; of course, "you can't go and not order a Bellini", but there's also "affordable", "impressive food" including "terrific salads" and a signature artichoke ravioli.

Paul's Porterhouse ⑤   ▽ 21 | 18 | 20 | $37
10960 Composite Dr. (Walnut Hill Ln.), 214-357-0279
■ Carnivores flock to this Northwest Dallas veteran for its "out-on-the-range", early-1900s Western decor and extensive menu, which includes quail soup, prime fillet and game dishes; so go "impress your out-of-town guests" and, with the relatively low prices, you'll "come out ahead."

Peggy Sue BBQ ⑤   21 | 14 | 18 | $14
Snider Plaza, 6600 Snider Plaza (bet. Daniel Ave. & Hillcrest Rd.), 214-987-9188
■ "Dallas' rich and famous" as well as lots of ordinary folk like to lasso up the "brisket beyond belief" and "incredibly sweet ribs" served at this Snider Plaza BBQ senior citizen, which features "eclectic Western decor" and has a "chummy, homey" feel.

P.F. CHANG'S CHINA BISTRO ⑤   23 | 23 | 19 | $24
NorthPark Ctr. Mall, 225 NorthPark Ctr. (Northwest Hwy.), 214-265-8669
18323 N. Dallas Pkwy. (Frankford Rd.), 972-818-3336
◪ Many voters "can't live without the lettuce wraps" and crispy honey shrimp from these "chic" North Dallas area "Nouvelle Chinese" stops; "reasonable prices" and "dark", muraled interiors that give an artistic feel are other pluses, but the no-reservations policy causes "long" waits.

Dallas

Picardy's Shrimp Shop ⑤
Snider Plaza, 6800 Snider Plaza (Milto...
◪ This "basic neighborhood seafood..." Plaza garners mixed reviews: old salt... "the best fish 'n' chips", solid gumbo and "good shrimp" sandwiches", while landlubbers lament that the edibles are "average" and "nothing special."

Pietro's ⑤ ▽ 15 | 12 | 16 | $23
5722 Richmond Ave. (Greenville Ave.), 214-824-6960
■ Heroically described as "the last of the really great mom-and-pop places in Dallas", this "down-home" old-timer in the lower Greenville area pleases *paesani* with "hearty" Italian dishes (try the lasagna and veal); proud regulars boastfully add that "if you want to pay for fancy decor and kiss-up service, go elsewhere."

Planet Hollywood ⑤ 12 | 18 | 13 | $20
603 Munger Ave. (Market St.), 214-749-7827
◪ Undeniably a "tourist spot," this Uptown Hollywood-themed chain link showcases "cool" movie memorabilia (such as John Travolta's suit from *Saturday Night Fever*), which helps, since the American "food isn't that great."

Plano Cafe ⑤ 19 | 14 | 18 | $25
1915 N. Central Expwy. (Park Blvd.), Plano, 972-516-0865
■ Under new ownership for the past two years, this "small, intimate" Plano New American remains a "good" choice for "nicely presented" cuisine, especially the baked salmon and signature crème brûlée.

Poor Richard's Cafe ⑤∅ ▽ 21 | 13 | 20 | $10
Park Mall, 2442 Ave. K (Park Blvd.), Plano, 972-423-1524
◪ While it's "atmosphere is not the same" since it was completely remodeled and expanded, this "local politician's hangout" in Plano continues to be a "favorite for breakfasts" (try the BBQ chicken omelet) slapped snappily on the table by an efficient staff.

PoPoLos Cafe ⑤ 20 | 20 | 19 | $30
707 Preston Royal Shopping Ctr. (Royal Ln.), 214-692-5497
◪ Now "back in action" after closing temporarily, this popular North Dallas Mediterranean is a bankable choice for wood-fired pizzas, savvy salads and solid fish entrees; if some feel it's "not as good as it used to be", they're still "glad it reopened."

Primo's ◐⑤ 19 | 15 | 18 | $17
3309 McKinney Ave. (Hall St.), 214-220-0510
■ Since "eating at Primo's is like hanging out with your buddies at home", it should be no surprise that even big-name chefs like to congregate out on the patio of this legendary Tex-Mex venue; objectively, the decor may be pedestrian, but the eats are quite "good" and prices are on the "value" side.

www.zagat.com

	F	D	S	C
	17	12	14	$11

...'s S

..., Belt Line Rd. (Inwood Rd.), Addison, 972-960-2494
...03 E. Campbell Rd. (Plano Rd.), Richardson, 972-480-0288

☑ Purdy "good" burgers, chicken and hot dogs served on homemade rolls have allowed these Addison/Richardson patty parlors to thrive for more than 15 years; just order at the counter, top your food at the condiment bar and grab a table alongside the many businesspeople and families chowing down to oldies.

Purple Cow S   16 | 16 | 16 | $13

110 Preston Royal Shopping Ctr. (Royal Ln.), 214-373-0037
Lakeside Mkt., 5809 Preston Rd. (Spring Creek Pkwy.), Plano, 972-473-6100

☑ Elevated electric trains and '50-style diner decor fuel the "fun" atmosphere at these "loud" soda shops/burger joints, de facto "soccer-mom retreats", where "screaming kids" moo with delight over the "wonderful" purple milk shakes (adults like the spiked versions).

PYRAMID GRILL S   26 | 26 | 24 | $54

(fka Pyramid Room)
Fairmont Hotel, 1717 N. Akard St. (Ross Ave.), 214-720-5249

■ Formerly called the Pyramid Room, this elegant Uptown New American is still "one of our favorites" "to celebrate an anniversary and my husband's promotion", thanks to well-spaced tables, "terrific" courtly service, "excellent" grilled fare and many touches from its previous incarnation, such as sorbets in lighted ice sculptures.

Queen of Sheba S   ▽ 19 | 15 | 17 | $19

3527 McKinney Ave. (Lemmon Ave.), 214-521-0491

■ Almost 20 years old, this iconoclastic Uptown Ethiopian-Italian hybrid has a "quiet, relaxing setting" and a "very helpful staff that explains how to order, what to order and how to consume what comes to the table"; try not to *injera* yourself trying everything on the prix fixe 'Queen's Dinner'.

Randy's Steakhouse S   ▽ 18 | 18 | 20 | $35

7026 Main St. (5th St.), Frisco, 972-335-3066

■ Set in a converted, historic Victorian house in Frisco, this "quaint" beef zone is run by chef-owner Randy Burks, who "comes around" to check up on patrons as they work their way through hand-cut steaks that are "notably better than some of the overrated places in Plano and Addison."

Razzoo's Cajun Cafe S   16 | 18 | 17 | $18

13949 N. Central Expwy. (Spring Valley Rd.), 972-235-3700
3712 Towne Crossing Blvd. (Towne East Blvd.), Mesquite, 972-686-9100
See review in Fort Worth Directory.

Dallas F | D | S | C

Red Hot & Blue 🆂   19 | 15 | 17 | $16
9810 N. Central Expwy. (Walnut Hill Ln.), 214-368-7427
5017 W. Plano Pkwy. (Preston Rd.), Plano, 972-248-3866
■ "A taste of Dixie in Dallas", these BBQ joints are one of the few places in town that sell pulled pork and dry-rubbed ribs ("the way Elvis liked them"); "the best potato salad I've ever tasted" adds to their Southern charm.

Remington's Seafood Grill 🆂   22 | 17 | 20 | $24
4580 Belt Line Rd. (Midway Rd.), Addison, 972-386-0122
■ "Consistency" thy name is Remington's, report surveyors weighing in on this Addison standby for seafood, which has been serving "delicious", "reasonably priced" dishes for more than 20 years; while merry-makers might want to "liven up" the tranquil atmosphere, everyone, from dates to families, feels special.

RIVIERA, THE   28 | 25 | 26 | $60
7709 Inwood Rd. (Lovers Ln.), 214-351-0094
■ Chef Michael Marshall (ex Hôtel St. Germain) is now behind the stoves of this "cosmopolitan" North Dallas French-Mediterranean stalwart, which is where celebration-minded diners go "when they want to be pampered" by a "graceful, welcoming" European-style staff serving "superb" cuisine ("to-die-for Dover sole", rack of lamb that rules); decor that's "like walking into a room in Provence" adds to its "fancy shmancy" allure.

Rock Bottom Brewery 🆂   17 | 18 | 16 | $19
4050 Belt Line Rd. (bet. Marsh Ln. & Midway Rd.), Addison, 972-404-7456
☑ Six kinds of "good" brews are produced on site at this gigantic Addison suds house, a chain outfit whose "huge portions" of American victuals are "average" ("ok for salads and burgers").

Rockfish Seafood Grill 🆂   19 | 16 | 18 | $19
5331 E. Mockingbird Ln. (I-75), 214-823-8444
4701 W. Park Blvd. (Preston Rd.), Plano, 972-599-2190
7639 Campbell Rd. (Coit Rd.), Richardson, 972-267-8979
■ "Reasonably priced", "well-prepared", New Orleans–influenced seafood ("excellent" fried shrimp), "very casual" settings and assuredly "friendly" service are the hallmarks of this chain where it's fun to scoop up a handful of peanuts on the way in and later dump the shells on the floor.

Rodolfo's Italian & Seafood Restaurant 🆂   17 | 14 | 17 | $23
5956 Royal Ln. (Preston Rd.), 214-368-5039
☑ Diners know for certain that the "light choices" at this unpretentious Preston-Royal Italian are really low in fat and calories because management lists the nutritional content of every dish; still, that's not enough for bored critics who feel the edibles are "satisfying, but not exciting."

Dallas

| | F | D | S | C |

Romano's Macaroni Grill S | 20 | 20 | 20 | $21
388 N. Hwy. 67 (FM 1382), Cedar Hill, 469-272-0272
5858 W. Northwest Hwy. (Douglas Rd.), 214-265-0770
4535 Belt Line Rd. (Midway Rd.), Addison, 972-386-3831
5005 W. Park Blvd. (Preston Rd.), Plano, 972-964-6676
■ "Loud" and "happy", these Italian chainlets are "good casual spots to take the family", since kids can be kids and scribble on the paper-topped tables and adults feel like adults as they consume wine on the "wonderful honor system"; free herbed foccacia, "value" prices and "tasty" food (especially for a chain) round out their appeal.

Rooster S | 23 | 21 | 22 | $32
3521 Oak Grove Ave. (Lemmon Ave.), 214-521-1234
■ "If the name doesn't make you crow, the food will" declare patrons voting on this hospitable Oak Grove/Lemmon bastion of "excellent Southern cooking"; a "cordial owner", a "fine", "reasonably priced" wine list and "refined" rooster art are other pluses, and it's also a "great place for a group get-together", especially if you reserve the lovely room that overlooks the kitchen.

Royal Thai | 21 | 17 | 18 | $21
Old Town Shopping Ctr., 5500 Greenville Ave. (bet. Lovers Ln. & Southwestern Blvd.), 214-691-3555
■ A perennial contender for "the best Thai in Dallas", with "superb soups" and many strong entrees, this royal choice draws a "low-key, unpretentious crowd"; Lotharios add that it's also "a great date place."

Royal Toyko S | 21 | 20 | 20 | $28
7525 Greenville Ave. (bet. Meadow Rd. & Walnut Hill Ln.), 214-368-3304
■ "You'll feel like you're in Tokyo" at this multi-room Greenville Japanese stalwart with kimono-clad waitresses, a koi pond and hibachi grill room where kids love to watch the "quality steaks" sizzle; moreover, a huge menu that includes everything from shabu-shabu to the signature green tea ice cream further explains its "favorite" status.

Ruggeri's Ristorante S | 23 | 21 | 23 | $33
5348 Belt Line Rd. (Montfort Dr.), Addison, 972-726-9555
The Quadrangle, 2800 Routh St. (Howell St.), 214-871-7377
■ "Old-world charm" reigns at this classy Addison and Downtown duo whose serene settings and tinkling piano music make for "romantic" anniversary meals; "always dependable" cuisine and an experienced staff that "could teach others about service" round out the package.

www.zagat.com

Dallas

| | F | D | S | C |

RUTH'S CHRIS STEAK HOUSE S | 25 | 22 | 24 | $47 |
5922 Cedar Springs Rd. (bet. Inwood Rd. & Mockingbird Ln.), 214-902-8080
17840 Dallas Pkwy. (bet. Frankford & Trinity Mills Rds.), 972-250-2244

■ You'll "never leave hungry" after eating one of the "excellent", buttery steaks served on a "sizzling" hot platter at these North Dallas and Northwest of Downtown beef houses, which attract a "steady" stream of carnivorous "expense-accounters"; masculine decor, a business-friendly, "low noise level", a large wine list and "fast, personable service" are additional factors in this chain's success.

Sal's Pizza ● S | 20 | 12 | 14 | $13 |
2525 Wycliff Ave. (Maple Ave.), 214-522-1828

■ Never mind its "hole-in-the-wall" strip mall location in the Oak Lawn area of town, this Dallas institution is always packed with patrons enjoying its "outstanding" Sicilian and hand-tossed thin-crust pizzas as well as many Italian options from a four-page menu.

Saltgrass Steak House S | 18 | 18 | 18 | $25 |
4101 LBJ Frwy. (Midway Rd.), Farmers Branch, 972-243-9440
18680 LBJ Frwy. (Towne Ctr. Blvd.), Mesquite, 972-270-5200
3000 Dallas N. Tollway (south of Parker Rd.), Plano, 972-781-2202
See review in Fort Worth Directory.

SALVE! S | 24 | 24 | 22 | $48 |
2120 McKinney Ave. (Pearl St.), 214-220-0070

■ "A shoe-in for best newcomer" and already labeled "Dallas' most sophisticated restaurant", this "exceptional" Uptown Italian from Mi Piaci duo Phil and Janet Cobb features a "sleek", angular setting, a truly "outstanding", "diverse menu of upscale Tuscan food", an impressive all-Italian wine list and a staff led by suavely solicitous maitre d' Wayne Broadwell; N.B. opening chef Sharon Hage has moved on.

Samba Room, The ● S | 22 | 23 | 18 | $36 |
4514 Travis St. (Armstrong Ave.), 214-522-4137

■ "Beautiful people" know to "wear black" when dining at this "seductive" Knox/Henderson Latin American, a "very hip" "oasis within the Dallas BBQ culture" with a sizzling, "people-watching" bar for sipping mojitos and decor "reminiscent of '50s-style Copacabana"; the food certainly "ain't bad either" (consider the red snapper and banana 'splif' dessert), but "would someone please tell them to turn down the music?"

www.zagat.com

Dallas   F D S C

Sambuca Jazz Cafe S   21 | 22 | 18 | $31
2618 Elm St. (Good-Latimer Expwy.), 214-744-0820
15207 Addison Rd. (Belt Line Rd.), Addison, 972-385-8455
■ "The perfect way to introduce someone to Dallas" might be a visit to these Deep Ellum and Addison jazz clubs, "hot hang-out places" for "upscale yuppies" looking for "cool happy hours", hip 'n' happening decor and local and national bands; atmosphere may be the emphasis, but the Med-focused International menu can keep the beat too.

Sammy's Barbecue   25 | 16 | 20 | $14
2126 Leonard St. (bet. McKinney Ave. & Woodall Rodgers Frwy.), 214-880-9064
■ "It doesn't get any better than this" coo 'cue connoisseurs commenting on this "family-run" Downtown rib haven, which is "always packed at lunch" with happy customers chowing down on wondrous beef sausages and "fantastic potato casserole"; in short; a "real Texas" experience.

Samui Thai Cuisine S   – | – | – | I
906 W. McDermott Rd. (Hwy. 75, exit 34), Allen, 972-747-7452
Delightfully accommodating, this Allen newcomer is backed by a family with an impressive restaurant-family pedigree and offers great service, vibrant decor and delicious exotic Siamese fare; the expertly fashioned sauces and vinaigrettes make the seafood-oriented menu sing.

S & D Oyster Company   23 | 18 | 22 | $20
2701 McKinney Ave. (Boll St.), 214-880-0111
■ Operating in the same location and with the same owner for almost 25 years, this "never-changing" New Orleans–style seafooder on McKinney has been "a winner from day one" and is now a "Dallas landmark" for oysters on the half-shell, "the best gumbo" and luscious lemon pie, served by a steady group of familiar faces.

S & S Tearoom S   17 | 16 | 16 | $18
Inwood Village, 5560 W. Lovers Ln. (Inwood Ln.), 214-351-6888
■ Since 1929 women have made time for tea, sandwiches and salads at this Lovers Lane American; as it's a "permanent standby" in Dallas, there's no need to rush through the "relaxing" meal, which may also include heartier options like the rib eye steak.

San Francisco Rose ☽S   14 | 13 | 14 | $17
3024 Greenville Ave. (Marquita Ave.), 214-826-2020
■ This funky, unpretentious Lower Greenville old-timer plates up classic American fare like burgers and sizzling steaks, along with a few Tex-Mex touches like fajitas, quesadillas and vanilla flan; its cozy, casual atmosphere makes it a popular neighborhood destination for watching games on big-screen TVs.

Dallas F | D | S | C

Sea Grill S — | — | — | M
17617 Dallas Pkwy. (Trinity Mills Rd.), 972-733-4904
At press time, this former Plano seafooder was in the process of relocating to new North Dallas digs; expect a larger space, a menu with a wider range of price points and the same high standards from chef Andy Tun, who performs his piscine magic with a Pan-Asian flair.

Seventeen Seventeen ◑ S 24 | 21 | 22 | $37
Dallas Museum of Art, 1717 N. Harwood St. (Ross Ave.), 214-880-0158
◪ Drenched in sunshine at midday and boasting some of the "best museum food" around, this "elegant" brunch-and-lunch-only New American in the Dallas Museum of Art turns out "fantastic" cuisine in "great presentations" that rival what's hanging on the gallery walls; grousers grumble that the minimal portions aren't "enough for the money."

SEVY'S GRILL S 23 | 22 | 22 | $33
8201 Preston Rd. (Sherry Ln.), 214-265-7389
◼ "All the essential elements" of a successful restaurant can be found at this Park Cities New American "favorite", which features a mission-style, wood-lined interior, a martini bar that's "quite a gathering place", two hands-on entertaining owners and "impressive" food (especially "if you like roasted or wood-fired anything").

Sipango ◑ 19 | 21 | 18 | $36
4513 Travis St. (Knox St.), 214-522-2411
◪ "Cool" Knox-Henderson night crawlers still flock to this Cal-Italian for its modern, upscale look, hip atmosphere and pizzas, pastas and salads; if you don't mind a deafening noise level, head to the dance club in the back.

Snuffer's ◑ S 20 | 14 | 17 | $14
3526 Greenville Ave. (Mockingbird Ln.), 214-826-6850
14910 Midway Rd. (south of Belt Line Rd.), Addison, 972-991-8811
◼ "Now that was a hamburger" proclaim partisans of these Addison and Greenville patty emporiums where its nice to round out the "well-balanced meal" (wink, wink) with "must-try" cheese fries and a slew of margaritas; P.S. don't let their "spartan decor" deter you from stopping by for a "late-night snack."

Soho Food, Drinks & Jazz — | — | — | M
5290 Belt Line Rd. (Montford Dr.), 972-490-8686
Lively with jazz and full-flavored Eclectic dishes, this Addison nook has a cozy outdoor patio that's a nice place to share meze and a good selection of wines by the glass.

| **Dallas** | | F | D | S | C |

Sonny Bryan's Smokehouse   21 | 12 | 15 | $13
2202 Inwood Rd. (Harry Hines Blvd.), 214-357-7120 S
Macy's at Galleria Mall, 13375 Noel Rd. (bet. LBJ Frwy. & N. Dallas Tollway), 972-851-5131 S
Frankford Crossing, 4625 Frankford Rd. (bet. Dallas Pkwy. & Pear Ridge Rd.), 972-447-0102 S
302 N. Market St. (Pacific Ave.), 214-744-1610 S
Republic Towers, 325 N. St. Paul St. (bet. Bryan St. & Pacific Ave.), 214-979-0102
5519 W. Lovers Ln. (Inwood Rd.), 214-351-2024 S
■ The "funky, original" Inwood location "will always be the best" branch of this famous BBQ chain, which is still revered for its "enormous onion rings" and hickory-smoked "tender" brisket, pulled pork and ribs.

Spaghetti Warehouse S   14 | 16 | 15 | $18
1815 N. Market St. (Munger Ave.), 214-651-8475
◪ Surveyors split on this Metroplex chain of Italian pasta purveyors, located (like the name says) in souped-up warehouse settings: while some praise the "massive portions" as "competent" and a "good value" (especially the "excellent 15-layer lasagna"), others snap "save your money and buy a can of Chef Boyardee."

Spring Creek BBQ S   18 | 13 | 16 | $14
12835 Preston Rd. (LBJ Frwy.), 972-726-9002
14941 Midway Rd. (Belt Line Rd.), Addison, 972-385-0970
3335 N. George Bush Frwy. (north of Hwy. 78), Garland, 972-675-2920
3939 W. Emporium Circle (Town East Blvd.), Mesquite, 972-682-3770
270 N. Central Expwy. (Belt Line Rd.), Richardson, 972-669-0505
◪ "Can't get enough of the hot rolls and butter" drool devotees of this popular chain, whose "fast", "friendly staff" serves "consistently" "decent", "inexpensive" BBQ; tougher types find the offerings "uninspired."

STAR CANYON S   26 | 26 | 24 | $48
Centrum Bldg., 3102 Oak Lawn Ave. (Cedar Springs Rd.), 214-520-7827
■ Superstar kitchen wizard Stephan Pyles has moved on, but "executive chef Matthew Dunn [keeps things] humming" at this Oak Lawn clay, green and gold–colored destination that "sets an example for great Southwestern food", ranging from "always innovative" dishes like the "fantastic wild mushroom huitlacoche enchiladas" to classics like the "awesome bone-in rib eye"; reviewers also rave about the "Texas-perfect decor, right down to the ceiling tiles branded with town names"; P.S. best of all, it's "easier to get reservations now."

Dallas   F | D | S | C

Steak N' Ale Ⓢ   17 | 15 | 18 | $23
9323 LBJ Frwy. (Abrams Rd.), 972-690-1095
5220 Belt Line Rd. (bet. Dallas Pkwy. & Montfort Dr.),
Addison, 972-661-8299
4901 W. Camp Wisdom Rd. (Cockerell Hill Rd.),
Duncanville, 972-296-9923
1957 Northwest Hwy. (bet. I-635 & Town Gate Blvd.),
Garland, 972-864-1500
3726 Towne Crossing Blvd. (I-635), Mesquite, 972-686-1888
1900 N. Central Expwy. (Park Blvd.), Plano, 972-422-7903
◪ "Don't overindulge at the salad bar, save some room" for the prime rib is the smart advice proffered by patrons of this steakhouse chain; but while fans find it especially "reasonable" for an "early dinner", critics complain that this vet is ailing: both the "decor and the concept are tired."

St. Martin's Ⓢ   22 | 21 | 22 | $34
3020 Greenville Ave. (Monticello Ave.), 214-826-0940
■ "The best date place", this "cozy and romantic" French bistro on Lower Greenville serves "wonderful appetizers" (like the signature champagne-brie soup), "lots of specials" and "great desserts"; the attentive service and nice wine list (400 labels) help create an "elegant" evening out.

Stoneleigh P ◐Ⓢ   18 | 17 | 16 | $20
2926 Maple Ave. (Wolf St.), 214-871-2346
■ A Dallas institution, this bare-boned burger joint Uptown attracts a young crowd, which likes to mingle at the bar or grab a magazine from the rack before chowing down on "excellent *queso verde*" and other Tex-Mex snacks.

St. Pete's Dancing Marlin Ⓢ   19 | 16 | 17 | $17
2730 Commerce St. (Crowdus St.), 214-698-1511
■ It's a "great pick-up bar, but the fish is also worthwhile" at this Deep Ellum American, whose signature pasta Diablo – shrimp, pepper and salami in a marinara sauce – is so spicy it's "served with chocolate milk" (and "you'll need it").

Street's Famous Sandwiches   20 | 11 | 15 | $10
3848 Oak Lawn Ave. (Cedar Springs Rd.), 214-526-2505
14833 Midway Rd. (Belt Line Rd.), Addison, 972-404-8115
■ This Oak Lawn and Addison "kid-friendly" twosome is "perfect for sandwiches", especially those piled high with that "rarity – real turkey, not processed"; good as they are, the "soups are [even] better" say streetwise surveyors.

Sullivan's   24 | 23 | 23 | $40
17795 N. Dallas Pkwy. (Briargrove Ln.), 972-267-9393
■ "Lively and fun", this North Dallas steakhouse has a '40s-style setting (and music in its jazz bar) as well as the "best" blue cheese–covered iceberg salad and "great filet mignon"; surveyors also like the "reasonable prices" and the "well-selected wine list" but suggest that someone "hand out megaphones so you can hold a conversation."

Dallas F D S C

Sushi at the Stoneleigh S ▽ 21 | 15 | 16 | $32
Stoneleigh Hotel, 2927 Maple Ave. (Wolf St.), 214-871-7111
■ Set in a modern little nook in the regal Stoneleigh Hotel, this Japanese draws a strong crowd of regulars, who like to let the sushi chef order for them and appreciate the wide variety of native beers and sakes; N.B. monthly tastings are conducted for connoisseurs of the latter.

Sushi Masa Japanese Restaurant S ▽ 18 | 11 | 17 | $27
14902 Preston Rd. (south of Belt Line Rd.), 972-503-6888
■ "Hip", helpful chef Masa offers plenty of encouragement to first-time visitors to this North Dallas Japanese, which in addition to pristine sushi and sashimi offers "plenty of cooked food" like tempura, teriyaki and *yakiniku*; while it may not be as aesthetically pleasing as others in its genre, you'll want to return, especially for the twice-a-month sushi-making classes.

Sushi on McKinney S 22 | 15 | 19 | $28
4500 McKinney Ave. (Knox St.), 214-521-0969
■ While once a hot spot, this Uptown Japanese is "not as trendy as it used to be"; however, the "more relaxed atmosphere" only enhances the "yummy" sushi menu, which sneaks in Southwestern and other nontraditional touches, and if you're lucky, you might get a nicely sectioned orange after your meal.

SushiSake ▽ 29 | 25 | 25 | $29
220 W. Campbell Rd. (Central Expwy.), Richardson, 972-470-0722
■ "Wish you hadn't discovered it" sigh surveyors smitten with this small Richardson Japanese where chef Takashi Soda (who "has built a loyal following" from his days at Nakamoto) offers "fresh", "creative" raw fish plates that represent "the best sushi in Dallas"; "smart, soothing decor" and a friendly staff round out the "wonderful" experience.

Suze 25 | 17 | 22 | $34
Preston Hollow, 4345 W. Northwest Hwy. (Midway Rd.), 214-350-6135
■ Now under new ownership, this "great find" in North Dallas dishes up a "creative", Med-influenced Eclectic cuisine with options ranging from a "wonderful seared foie gras" to tandoori shrimp; though located in a strip mall, the "charming space" can be "very intimate"; P.S. "don't go without a reservation on the weekend."

Szechwan Pavilion S 19 | 16 | 17 | $19
8411 Preston Rd. (Northwest Hwy.), 214-368-4303
◪ Programmed into many a telephone speed-dial, this Park Cities Chinese is a weekly Big D family tradition for staples such as sesame chicken and moo shu pork; but since some might find its atmosphere "tired", consider takeout.

Dallas

| | F | D | S | C |

Taco Diner S
19 | 16 | 16 | $17

Preston Ctr. E., 4011 Villanova Dr. (Pickwick Ln.), 214-696-4944

■ As the name suggests, this popular Park Cities place is an ultra laid-back, "casual" eatery with a satisfying selection of salsas to complement its "almost greaseless Tex-Mex" fare; the "friendly atmosphere" makes it "a great spot for a quick lunch" or to take "the children at night."

Taqueria Canonita S
– | – | – | M

4001 Preston Rd. (bet. Parker Rd. & Spring Creek Pkwy.), Plano, 469-467-8655

Hotly anticipated, this Plano newcomer specializing in 'Mexico City Soul Food' has been packed since opening, with people lounging on the patio, sipping margaritas at the bar and sampling the ostensibly humble fare that tastes oh-so-rich; local wonder chef Stephan Pyles, though no longer associated, was the opening force here.

TEI TEI ROBATA BAR S
25 | 23 | 23 | $42

2906 N. Henderson Ave. (Willis Ave.), 214-828-2400

■ "Hip patrons and trendy decor" are just the appetizers at this justifiably "pricey" Knox/Henderson Japanese where the "world-class chef" creates super "fresh sushi and sashimi"; a "tremendous array" of robata (or grilled) dishes also explains why some will "travel 150 miles" to satisfy their yen here.

Teppo S
▽ 26 | 24 | 23 | $33

2014 Greenville Ave. (Oram St.), 214-826-8989

■ A sibling of Tei Tei Robata Bar, this Lower Greenville Japanese wows 'em with some of "the best" sushi in town and "to-die-for" yakitori hot off the grill; a "cool, modern" look and "upbeat atmosphere" are further pluses.

Terilli's ●S
20 | 18 | 18 | $27

2815 Greenville Ave. (bet. Belmont Ave. & Mockingbird Ln.), 214-827-3993

◪ The Italchos (or Italian nachos) are a must when dining at this "popular" Lower Greenville taste of the red, white and green, which has a solid Sunday brunch and "exciting" jazz (arrive early or it may be "difficult to get a seat").

Texadelphia S
16 | 12 | 14 | $11

Old Town Shopping Ctr., 5500 Greenville Ave. (Lovers Ln.), 214-265-8044
2312 Leonard St. (McKinney Ave.), 214-969-0905
Lakeside Mkt., 5813 Preston Rd. (Spring Creek Pkwy.), Plano, 972-378-6898
1920 N. Coit Rd. (Campbell Rd.), Richardson, 972-664-9998

◪ "Philly, eat your heart out!" say cheese steak lovers of this "no-frills" local chain whose "good, sloppy sandwiches" come with tortilla chips; "UT and Austin ex-pats" especially crave them, but those from the City of Brotherly Love claim they "don't compare" to what's available back East.

Dallas   F | D | S | C

Texas de Brazil ⑤   21 | 20 | 21 | $40
2727 Cedar Springs Rd. (Carlisle St.), 214-720-1414
15101 Addison Rd. (Belt Line Rd.), Addison, 972-385-1000
■ If you crave a "carnivorous bacchanalia", "don't eat for three days" then samba over to these Brazilian all-the-skewered-grilled-meat-you-can-eat emporiums where "great steaks" and "excellent chicken and lamb" "get a thumbs-up from Dr. Atkins" fans; service can be "A1" too, but if you come for the salad bar, "you get what you deserve."

Texas Land & Cattle Steak House ⑤   18 | 17 | 17 | $23
3130 Lemmon Ave. (McKinney Ave.), 214-526-4664
17390 Preston Rd. (bet. Campbell & Frankford Sts.), 972-248-2424
10250 Technology Blvd. W. (Loop 12/Northwest Hwy.), 214-353-8000
Stonebriar Ctr., 3191 Preston Rd. (Hwy. 121), Frisco, 972-668-2832
◪ This "casual", "midpriced steakhouse" chain's faithful cowpokes have nice things to say about its "to-die-for sweet potatoes", "creative spicy Caesar salad" and solid hamburgers ("love 'em for a hangover remedy"), but some hardcore meat eaters grouse about cuts that are either "overcooked or undercooked."

T.G.I. Friday's ⑤   15 | 16 | 15 | $17
9100 N. Central Expwy. (Park Ln.), 214-363-2217
1713 N. Market St. (Ross Ave.), 214-744-2936
9560 Skillman St. (bet. LBJ Frwy. & Plano Rd.), 214-343-0116 ☻
5100 Belt Line Rd. (N. Dallas Tollway), Addison, 972-386-4719 ☻
3700 Towne Crossing Blvd. (Town East Blvd.), Mesquite, 972-686-8485 ☻
Collin Creek Mall, 901 N. Central Expwy. (Plano Pkwy.), Plano, 972-578-1557 ☻
2444 Preston Rd. (Park Blvd.), Plano, 972-612-8422 ☻
◪ Some reviewers are thankful for the existence of this American chain and give an "A-ok to its veggie burger", "delectable" Jack Daniel's Grill Glaze and "fair prices for casual" cuisine; ingrates "eat there for convenience only", saying "the service can be slow" and the "commercial" atmosphere "too loud."

Thai Orchid ⑤   ▽ 24 | 22 | 22 | $20
4930 Belt Line Rd. (N. Dallas Tollway), Addison, 972-720-8424
■ Blossoming in Addison, this unassuming flower is still relatively unknown, but its enthusiastic clientele braves the bustling Beltline traffic for such Siamese specialties as *tom yam kung* (lemongrass-spiked shrimp soup) and a snappy red snapper with chile; a solicitous staff and subtly charming decor further argue for a look.

Dallas

| | F | D | S | C |

Thai Soon S 20 | 13 | 18 | $19
2018 Greenville Ave. (Ross Ave.), 214-821-7666
■ "Almost worth the hassle of navigating Lower Greenville", this casual "old standby" Thai offers "good service and atmosphere" as well as "traditional" fare that's "full of flavor"; N.B. speak up if you have timid taste buds and the kitchen will reduce the fire.

Thai Taste S 19 | 13 | 16 | $20
3101 N. Fitzhugh Ave. (McKinney Ave.), 214-521-3513
■ This tranquil Uptown Thai is the older sibling of Liberty on Lower Greenville; created by renowned chef Annie Wong, its "large and inexpensive menu" is strong on curry and noodle dishes; tipsters add that it makes a "great place for lunch."

Theo's Diner ⇴ ▽ 24 | 16 | 21 | $12
111 S. Hall St. (Commerce St.), 214-747-6936
■ Folks get all shook up over the "homemade fries", Greek salad and "outstanding burgers" served at this "cheap", "friendly" Deep Ellum "shrine to Elvis", which has been rockin' for over 50 years.

Thomas Ave. Beverage Co. ▽ 26 | 17 | 19 | $24
2901 Thomas Ave. (McKinney Ave.), 214-979-0452
■ "With the kitchen in full view, it's fun to watch the chefs" prepare an "always-changing menu" of "creative" International dishes at this Uptown "secret" find; located in the historic State-Thomas district, the eatery and its surroundings have "a great deal of character."

III Forks S 23 | 23 | 21 | $50
17776 Dallas Pkwy. (bet. Frankford & Trinity Mills Rds.), 972-267-1776
◪ Opinions are two-pronged about this massive North Dallas steak-and-seafood palace: some find it an "all-around delightful dining experience" with "great prime rib", a massive wine list, "attentive service" and "unique Texas atmosphere"; foes jab that it's "overpriced" ("bring a crisp $100 bill and don't expect change for two") with ornate Western decor that's a tad "bizarre."

Tia's Tex-Mex Grill S 16 | 15 | 16 | $16
2625 Old Denton Rd. (Trinity Mills Rd.), Carrollton, 972-245-2997
3817 Pavillion Ct. (Emporium Circle), Mesquite, 972-681-0118
941 Central Expwy. (15th St.), Plano, 972-881-9119
1609 Preston Rd. (Old Sheppard Rd.), Plano, 972-758-0919
327 W. Spring Valley Rd. (Hwy. 75), Richardson, 972-231-6982
◪ Amigos acclaim this moderately priced Tex-Mex chain for its "good family atmosphere" (read cheerful, casual, loud) and "great tortillas" (made in-house), but detractors get teed off by "tables that are too close together" and "food that isn't worth the wait."

Dallas F | D | S | C

Tillman's Corner Restaurant ▽ 20 | 14 | 18 | $21
Bishop Arts District, 324 W. Seventh St. (bet. Bishop & Madison Aves.), 214-942-0988
◪ For "consistently good food" head to Oak Cliff, where this New American has been dishing up the likes of cedar-plank salmon and grilled pork medallions for nearly a decade; while it's generally "great for pre-concert dinners", the "service is not always consistent" if there's a big crowd headed for Bass Hall.

Tin Star S – | – | – | I
2626 Howell St. (bet. Routh & Worthington Sts.), 214-999-0059
3301 Preston Rd. (Hwy. 121, opp. Stonebriar Ctr.), Frisco, 972-668-4610
2208 Dallas Pkwy. (Park Blvd.), Plano, 972-403-1765
This expanding Southwestern chain may soon earn its badge with surveyors; although you order at the counter then hit the condiment bar, the resemblance to fast food halts there, as the fare is relatively innovative; other arresting features include the children's menu and cowpoke decor.

Tong's House S 21 | 12 | 17 | $17
1910 Promenade Ct. (north of Belt Line Rd.), Richardson, 972-231-8858
■ The decor may be minimal, but the flavors certainly are not at this "busy" Szechuan veteran where everything is "consistently excellent" and the "specials are superlative"; Richardson regulars know to ignore the occasionally "noisy and crowded" conditions and concentrate instead on the "authentic-tasting", truly "different cooking."

Tony Roma's S 20 | 16 | 18 | $22
10310 Lombardy Ln. (Northwest Hwy.), 214-902-0443
310 N. Market St. (Ross Ave.), 214-748-6959
5000 Belt Line Rd. (Inwood Rd.), Addison, 972-661-2671
3730 Towne Crossing Blvd. (LBJ Frwy.), Mesquite, 972-686-4270
2380 N. Central Expwy. (Park Blvd.), Plano, 972-516-4988
2408 Preston Rd. (Park Blvd.), Plano, 972-612-2702
◪ "Stick to the ribs and you'll do great" say buffs of this national BBQ chain, which has a "wide variety" of offerings, even if many are partial to the "awesome babybacks"; those on the lookout for the next new thing feel the concept could use "freshening."

Traci's 22 | 21 | 21 | $31
2403 Thomas Ave. (Maple Ave.), 214-849-0007
■ Situated in a "homey" "neat old house", this Uptown New Southerner makes a "wonderful choice for a lovely dining experience" with a date or out-of-town guest; confederates "love the fresh veggies" straight from the farm and generally "innovative", "sophisticated" cuisine; a few rebels yell (ok, whisper) about the "uncomfortable chairs" but concede "where else can you find fried green tomatoes in Dallas?"

Dallas | F | D | S | C |

Trail Dust Steak House 🆂 | 17 | 18 | 17 | $23 |
10841 Composite Dr. (Walnut Hill Ln.), 214-357-3862
21717 LBJ Frwy. (Military Pkwy.), Mesquite, 972-289-5457
◪ "Watch your tie" at these determinedly dress-down steak-and-BBQ theme joints where the rafters are filled with cut-off casualties worn by previous trailblazers; while "fun" "for families" and tourists, with fairly "flavorful grilled meats and chicken breasts", romantics might find them "too damn noisy" when the band starts playing.

Tramontana | 25 | 18 | 22 | $36 |
Preston Ctr., 8220B Westchester Dr. (Lemmon Ave.), 214-368-4188
■ "A tiny, romantic hideaway", this North Dallas French bistro gets tons of accolades for its "superior" "inventive" cuisine from an often-changing menu; surveyors add that "super-nice" chef-owner James Neel is a "treasure" whose skills are "moving this storefront to the forefront."

Truluck's 🆂 | 20 | 19 | 19 | $34 |
2401 McKinney Ave. (Maple Ave.), 214-220-2401
5001 Belt Line Rd. (Quorum Dr.), Addison, 972-503-3079
◪ "All-you-can-eat stone crab night [Monday] is the perfect time to go" to this Uptown and Addison seafood duo, which also gets the thumbs-up for its impressive desserts ("don't miss their chocolate cake"); foes find it "overrated" and add that you'll feel truly lucky if someone else is paying for the claws ("expensive").

Tupinamba 🆂 | 19 | 17 | 20 | $18 |
12270 Inwood Rd. (LBJ Frwy.), 972-991-8148
■ "Service is always fast" at this blue-and-beige North Dallas Tex-Mex outlet, an "old standard" that "grandkids love" and their grandparents respect for its "very fair prices"; favorites include the fajitas, catfish and praline pie.

Two Rows ●🆂 | 17 | 16 | 15 | $17 |
Old Town Shopping Ctr., 5500 Greenville Ave. (Lovers Ln.), 214-696-2739
◪ Sudsophiles insist "it's all about the beer" at this Greenville "brewpub of the first order", however the kitchen does get nice notices for its pizzas and burgers; delicate types warn that the collegiate atmosphere can be "noisy" at times.

Uncle Julio's 🆂 | 20 | 17 | 17 | $19 |
7557 Greenville Ave. (bet. Meadow Rd. & Walnut Hill Ln.), 214-987-9900
4125 Lemmon Ave. (Douglas Ave.), 214-520-6620
16150 N. Dallas Pkwy. (Keller Springs Rd.), 972-380-0100
■ Described as "a great place to take friends from out of town", this "tried-and-true" Tex-Mex trio is revered for its "famous swirls" (frozen margaritas striped with sangria) that could "drive a teetotaler to drink"; "plentiful" portions of "fresh tortillas" and grilled meats help offset "long waits."

Dallas

| | F | D | S | C |

Uncle Tai's Hunan Yuan ⓢ   22 | 19 | 20 | $27
Galleria Mall, 13350 Dallas Pkwy. (LBJ Frwy.), 972-934-9998
■ It's fun "to eat outside and watch the ice-skating" on the rink below this ornate Chinese veteran located in a North Dallas mall; popular choices include the crispy beef, chicken with black bean sauce and venison with garlic.

Vincent's Seafood ⓢ   21 | 18 | 20 | $25
13327 Midway Rd. (LBJ Frwy.), 972-387-3690
2432 Preston Rd. (Parker St.), Plano, 972-612-6208
◪ Separately owned, these seafooders attract a slightly older clientele that appreciates that the experience is "always the same"; those looking for a "business lunch" should consider the Plano branch, a less noisy choice for "wonderful slaw", snapper and king crab legs.

VOLTAIRE   25 | 27 | 23 | $62
5150 Keller Springs Rd. (N. Dallas Tollway), 972-239-8988
◪ "Wow" declare aesthetes commenting on this "gorgeous" French–New American newcomer in North Dallas where trendsetters go to ogle the "fabulous" Dale Chihuly glass sculptures, as well as other "beautiful" patrons; while some diners delight in the "excellent", "creative" cuisine and "fantastic", "extensive" wine list, others find it "pretentious" and ask "what's the fuss?"

Watel's ⓢ   23 | 18 | 20 | $39
2719 McKinney Ave. (Worthington Rd.), 214-720-0323
■ Since it's "French right down to its organ meats", it should be no surprise that "delightful" "sweetbreads and brains are always available" at this "classy" Uptown bistro, a "high-quality" "pre-concert destination" with "excellent wines."

We Oui ❶ⓢ   19 | 22 | 19 | $36
Hotel Crescent Court, 100 Crescent Ct. (Cedar Springs Rd.), 214-220-3990
◪ "The latest hangout for the trendy crowd", this Uptown parvenu serves whimsical French fare with an American spin; its *amis* admire its "cool" decor, "fun atmosphere" and "intriguing menu", however stern traditionalists who don't get the joke counter that the "Bistro 101" cuisine is for "unsophisticated palates."

Wild About Harry's ⓢ   22 | 14 | 18 | $8
6905 Coit Rd. (Legacy Dr.), Plano, 972-398-0940
1930 N. Coit Rd. (Campbell Rd.), Plano, 214-575-5959
3113 Knox St. (bet. Cole & McKinney Aves.), 214-520-3113 ⌿
■ A daily-changing menu of "rich", "yummy" frozen custards and lots of varieties of hot dogs (from Texas chile to vegetarian) comprise the bulk of the menu at this niche trio; people-watchers recommend the Park Cities branch, where "zillionaires eat alongside boho college kids and locals."

Dallas   F | D | S | C

Yamaguchi Bar & Sushi 🖸   23 | 13 | 19 | $31
7713 Inwood Rd. (Lovers Ln.), 214-350-8660

◪ "Melt-in-your-mouth sashimi", "interesting rolls" and popular box lunches garner a strong food score for this Inwood Japanese, but its "atmosphere needs help."

Yoli's Seafood & Grill 🖸   ▽ 20 | 13 | 16 | $20
Skillman Commons, 9220 Skillman St. (north of LBJ Frwy.), 214-341-3533

■ Regulars know to order anything from the grill, including any specials, when dining at this laid-back North Dallas seafooder; its decor is nothing special, but the shrimp Orleans, blackened snapper and catfish can hold their own.

YORK ST.   25 | 20 | 24 | $47
6047 Lewis St. (Skillman St.), 214-826-0968

■ Admirers say that "every intimate restaurant should aspire" to be this "enchanting" East Dallas New American, "tucked inside an old home", where "wonderful owner" Felissa Shaw and her "superb staff" provide angelic attention and the "interesting menu" (try the rack of lamb Provençal) is a "slice of culinary heaven."

Ziziki's Restaurant & Bar 🖸   24 | 20 | 21 | $29
Travis Walk, 4514 Travis St. (Knox St.), 214-521-2233
Shops of Spanish Village, 15707 Coit Rd. (Arapaho Rd.), 972-991-4433

■ "If you want to go Greek, go here!" implore partisans of these Hellenic-Mediterranean twins where the cuisine is "yummy" (especially the "heavenly" lamb dishes) and the staff "friendly"; P.S. buffet buffs endorse the "great Sunday champagne brunch", especially on the "charming patio" of the Knox/Henderson branch.

Zodiac   22 | 20 | 22 | $23
Neiman Marcus, 1618 Main St. (bet. Akard & Ervay Sts.), 214-573-5800
Neiman Marcus at NorthPark Ctr. Mall, 400 NorthPark Ctr. (Northwest Hwy.), 214-891-1210

■ Shop-till-you-drop admirers of these "dependable" Neiman Marcus–based American tearooms hope they "never change", what with a "wonderful chicken salad", charmingly formal touches (free cups of bouillon and "great" popovers) and correct, but unintimidating, service.

ZuZu 🖸   16 | 11 | 13 | $12
6423 Hillcrest Ave. (University Ave.), 214-521-4456
4140 Abrams Rd. (Mockingbird Ln.), 214-828-2231
4886 Belt Line Rd. (bet. Addison Rd. & Quorum Dr.), Addison, 972-960-6900

◪ Offering a step up from fast food, this casual Mex chain specializes in "fresh", healthy fare, including "terrific salsas" and grilled chicken salad; admirers "wish there were more locations", but ratings suggest it hasn't quite found its niche.

Fort Worth/Mid-Cities

F	D	S	C

Abuelo's Mexican Food Embassy S 20 | 23 | 18 | $20
1041 I-20 W. (Matlock Rd.), Arlington, 817-468-2622
824 Airport Frwy. (Precinct Line Rd.), Hurst, 817-514-9355
2520 S. Stemmons Frwy. (I-35, Roundgrove Rd. exit), Lewisville, 972-315-6057
■ "Gourmet and Mexican do go together" at these "high-end" Metroplex ethnics with stately settings (classical columns, garden fountains) and food that "tastes fresher than the competition"; specialties include the beef with bacon-wrapped shrimp and the dessert nachos.

Angelo's Barbecue ≠   23 | 14 | 17 | $14
2533 White Settlement Rd. (University Dr.), Fort Worth, 817-332-0357
■ "A tattered stuffed bear still greets you at the door" of this "no-frills", mesquite smoke–filled Northwest BBQ "institution", famous for serving the "coldest beer in town" and "great chopped beef" and brisket to "lots of guys wearing cowboy hats"; P.S. "get plenty of napkins."

Angeluna S   23 | 23 | 21 | $35
215 E. Fourth St. (bet. Calhoun & Commerce Sts.), Fort Worth, 817-334-0080
☑ "Convenient" before and after Bass Hall, this "cutting-edge" entry has a global menu of "artistically presented fusion dishes" ("Texas meets Asia and the angels sing") and "cool" decor highlighted by a skylike ceiling covered with eclectic images (Marilyn Monroe, Mr. Potato Head); still, spoilers shout that it's "pricey" and "so noisy I wanted to cry."

Asia Arc-en-Ciel S   ▽ 23 | 9 | 15 | $18
Asian Mkt. Ctr., 2208 New York Ave. (Pioneer Pkwy.), Arlington, 817-469-9999
■ Located in a thriving Arlington ethnic shopping center, this great hall of dim sum is a "treat for Texas", what with a six-page, multi-language menu that offers the Asian-food lover everything from Chinese potstickers to Vietnamese fire pots; the bargain lunch specials are an especially good deal.

Babe's Chicken Dinner House S ▽   25 | 19 | 23 | $15
104 N. Oak St. (Main St.), Roanoke, 817-491-2900
■ This Roanoke American storefront not far from Texas Motor Speedway is famous for "generous portions" of "finger lickin'" fried chicken and chicken-fried steak ("only two choices") and a "fun" interior – scratched Formica tables and "mismatched" furniture – "reminiscent of many North Texas small-town cafes"; N.B. BYO beer and dessert.

Fort Worth/Mid-Cities   F | D | S | C

Bangkok Cuisine ⑤⊄   – | – | – | I
5095 Broadway Ave. (Haltom Rd.), Haltom City, 817-831-4711
"Small building, big Thai taste" is the word on this no-frills Haltom City BYO veteran, which emphasizes "value for the money", especially at lunch; dinner is less heavily trafficked, but that means even more "superb angel wings, Penang beef and catfish with spicy sauce" for you and your party.

Bavarian Bakery & Cafe   – | – | – | M
3000 SE Loop 820 (Witchita St. exit), Fort Worth, 817-551-1150
Camouflaged in a Southeast freeway business center, this stalwart dressed to the Bavarian nines sates the sweet tooth with display cases of luscious desserts; while lunchtime brings daily hot plates and freshly stacked sandwiches, it's dinner (served only on Fridays and Saturdays) that really shows off the regional German specialties.

Bayley's ⑤   ∇ 15 | 10 | 13 | $15
109 W. Harwood Rd. (Norwood Rd.), Hurst, 817-268-5779
■ "Expect long waits on weekends" at this Hurst breakfast and lunch place where the scent of bacon, pancakes, croissants and cinnamon rolls mingles with endless pots of coffee; a few of the American dishes are spiced with chorizo, so request a substitute if you don't like the flavor.

Bellagio ⑤   ∇ 19 | 18 | 17 | $21
3516 Bluebonnet Circle (Benbrook Rd.), Fort Worth, 817-921-3242
◪ While surveyors are in agreement about the "delicious" Italian food and "convenient" location of this Bluebonnet Circle trattoria, they're of mixed minds about ever-present owner 'Stormin' Norman Nazar: yeas like the way he dominates the room with gusto ("a hoot"), while nays find him a bit much.

Bella Italia   ∇ 18 | 15 | 18 | $28
5139 Camp Bowie Blvd. (Merrick Ave.), Fort Worth, 817-738-1700
◪ It's hard to miss the red, white and green striped awning out front of this West End Italian, whose menu of typical pastas and scallopini yields top billing in season to a "wide selection of wild game" (exotics like buffalo, ostrich and antelope); carpers find the interior "overly decorated", but defenders find the "cozy" digs a "nice place to dine alone."

Benito's ⑤   ∇ 20 | 15 | 19 | $13
1450 W. Magnolia Ave. (Fairmont Ave.), Fort Worth, 817-332-8633
■ "The word's out" on what was once "FW's best-kept secret", this Hospital District Mexican whose cuisine is "more authentic" – pork with squash stew, banana-wrapped chicken tamales in red mole – than any chips-and-salsa stop; filled with piñatas and multi-colored furniture, it's also a festive spot for late-night revelers to finish the evening.

Fort Worth/Mid-Cities   F | D | S | C

Big Buck Brewery & Steakhouse S   _ | _ | _ | M
Bass Pro Shops, 2501 Bass Pro Dr. (Hwy. 121), Grapevine, 214-513-2337
Planter boxes that hold fir trees and life-size game animals, stone columns and a faux-fireplace grill fuel the outdoorsman's fantasyland at this mammoth chain addition to the Bass Pro shopping complex; look for microbrews and ales with names like Wolverine Wheat and Buck Naked Light and a meat-lover's menu that leaves no doubt who the target customer is.

BISTRO LOUISE   25 | 24 | 23 | $37
Stonegate Commons, 2900 S. Hulen St. (Oak Park Ln.), Fort Worth, 817-922-9244
■ Sharing the No. 1 spot for Popularity in the FW *Survey*, chef Louise Lamendsdorf's Med destination is praised by admirers as one of the "best in the Metroplex", with "wonderful brunches", "a newly improved wine list" and a menu that "challenges the FW steak mentality"; the "casually elegant", Provençal-themed setting attracts a lot of well-heeled locals to the Southwest side, so don't be surprised if "you always see someone you know."

BKK - Narita   ▽ 20 | 14 | 18 | $16
6060 Southwest Blvd. (Bryant Irvin Rd.), Benbrook, 817-738-3175
■ Thai visitors claim this Benbrook pleaser as "a home away from home" despite the fact that its tangy satays share the limelight with entertaining Japanese hibachi tables and vegetable-laden Chinese dishes; while not well known by voters, reservations are recommended to nab a table.

Blue Mesa Grill S   20 | 20 | 18 | $21
University Park Village, 1600 S. University Dr. (I-30), Fort Worth, 817-332-6372
See review in Dallas Directory.

Bobby Valentine's ●S   ▽ 14 | 18 | 16 | $17
4301 S. Bowen Rd. (I-20), Arlington, 817-467-9922
◪ A "fun place" for strong "drinks and viewing sports" is the score on former Texas Rangers manager Bobby Valentine's Arlington eatery, which serves catchy-named American pub grub (World Series sandwiches) that doesn't win over all the bleacher bums ("don't go for the food").

Bodacious Bar-B-Q   _ | _ | _ | M
1206 E. Division St. (bet. Collins St. & Stadium Dr.), Arlington, 817-860-4248
1470 E. Hwy. 377 (Bus. 377), Granbury, 817-573-3921 S
Expect a "friendly caring staff" and "good BBQ and sides" at these cafeteria-style East Arlington and Granbury eateries whose smokehouse standards – brisket, ribs and sausages – consistently hold their own against other 'cue emporiums; in keeping with their pretension-free approach, the homey, country settings are filled with highway signs.

Fort Worth/Mid-Cities F | D | S | C

Bruno's Italian — | — | — | M
9462 N. MacArthur Blvd. (Belt Line Rd.), Irving, 972-556-2465
Owner Bruno Zeka has been pleasing Valley Ranch residents with solid Italian fare throughout the dirt-flying, road-widening construction life of this burgeoning bedroom community; his highly trafficked eatery overlooks the Mandalay canal and is home to a sports-minded clientele, which includes owners, coaches, players and fans of the major professional teams that practice nearby.

Buffet at the Kimbell, The S 22 | 22 | 18 | $14
Kimbell Art Museum, 3333 Camp Bowie Blvd. (University Dr.), Fort Worth, 817-332-8451
■ "Very cool museum digs" provide the backdrop for this Cultural District cafeteria-style Traditional American, filled with light, art and a compelling centerpiece atrium; keep it in mind for a "quick", "excellent" soup or salad and decent glass of wine between viewing blockbuster exhibitions and exceptional private holdings; N.B. dinner is served only on Fridays, but it has become a chic time to visit.

Byblos ▽ 22 | 17 | 18 | $20
1406 N. Main St. (Central St.), Fort Worth, 817-625-9667
■ "Take friends for the experience" of an "adventurous" meal at this North Side cousin of Hedary's, where the lunch buffet is a "varied array of Middle Eastern delights" and weekend dinners are punctuated with "wiggling" belly dancers, the smoking of hookahs and the sipping of Turkish coffee ("the perfect finish").

Cabo Mix-Mex Grill S ▽ 17 | 16 | 13 | $18
Sundance Sq., 115 W. Second St. (Houston St.), Fort Worth, 817-348-8226
■ "Great margaritas" and a "fun setting" with tropical-colored digs draw a mixed crowd of Sundance Square revelers to this Tex-Mex chain link; remember, even if you're not one of those who find the victuals "better than most", you can always console yourself with one of the "nice T-shirts."

CACHAREL 26 | 25 | 25 | $44
Brookhollow Two Bldg., 2221 E. Lamar Blvd. (bet. Ballpark Way & Hwy. 360), Arlington, 817-640-9981
■ An Arlington office tower surrounded by amusement parks and fast-food chains is the unusual location for this high-achieving Classic French grande dame, which offers pampered patrons an "intimate, posh" dining room with an illuminated skyline view plus a choice between a well-priced, three-course prix fixe menu and à la carte selections; either way, the "great soufflés" should be de rigueur.

www.zagat.com

Fort Worth/Mid-Cities　　　　　　　F | D | S | C

Cactus Flower Cafe S   ▽ 19 | 14 | 18 | $11
2401 Westport Pkwy. (Hwy. 35), Fort Worth, 817-491-9524
509 University Dr. (5th St.), Fort Worth, 817-332-9552
■ "Soothing comfort food" is the hallmark of this University Area and Alliance Airport Traditional American twosome, which opens early in the morning with generous country-style breakfasts that include oversize homemade biscuits; lunch and dinner bring together families and officemates for "small-town atmosphere" and the "best chicken-fried steak", pot roast and pork chops since mama went to work.

Cafe Aspen   23 | 21 | 23 | $29
Frost Bank Shopping Plaza, 6103 Camp Bowie Blvd. (Bryant Irvin Rd.), Fort Worth, 817-738-0838
■ Nothing could be more Texan than chicken-fried lobster, the signature dish of this Ridglea New American treasured for its "great martinis, imaginative dishes that never disappoint", delectable desserts (the "bread pudding is to kill for") and "terrific, friendly service" lead by an owner who "seeks to please"; live jazz and piano music in the backroom bar round out the "dependably great" experience.

Cafe Cipriani   ▽ 21 | 21 | 22 | $33
220 E. Las Colinas Blvd. (O'Connor Rd.), Irving, 972-869-0713
■ A '20s-style art deco brass elevator delivers diners to "below-ground eating" at this easygoing Las Colinas Italian, which turns out "consistently good" cuisine like the *ravioli fantasia* (pasta stuffed with lobster, shrimp and scallops in a brandy cream sauce).

Cafe 1187 S   ▽ 20 | 19 | 19 | $19
8780 FM 1187 E. (Ben Day Murrin Rd.), Fort Worth, 817-443-1473
◪ "The rural setting adds to the pleasure" of dining at this Southwest Tarrant County prairie-style BYO homestead, which is conservatively "worth one visit" to "the boonies"; open Thursday–Sunday, its "quaint" dining rooms fill up early, so it's possible they'll "run out of the specials" on the chalkboard menu if you show up late.

Cafe on the Green S   ▽ 24 | 23 | 21 | $47
Four Seasons Resort & Club, 4150 N. MacArthur Blvd. (Northgate Dr.), Irving, 972-717-2420
■ "Better than any of the private country clubs" reflects surveyors regard for this Las Colinas venue whose New American cuisine takes many forms: there are spa selections, à la carte options, a sumptuous buffet and an "absolutely divine brunch", all of which can be enjoyed in a sunny, window-filled dining room; N.B. at press time the restaurant was being remodeled, with a temporary location set up in one of the resort's ballrooms.

Fort Worth/Mid-Cities

| F | D | S | C |

California Pizza Kitchen S
| 18 | 15 | 16 | $16 |

1051 State Hwy. 114 (William D. Tate Ave.), Grapevine, 817-481-4255
See review in Dallas Directory.

Campisi's S
| 20 | 12 | 16 | $16 |

2608 Flower Mound Rd. (Long Prairie Rd.), Flower Mound, 972-691-8890
See review in Dallas Directory.

Carrabba's Italian Grill S
| 19 | 18 | 20 | $22 |

1701 Crossroads Dr. (William D. Tate Ave.), Grapevine, 817-410-8461
See review in Dallas Directory.

Carshon's Deli S∌
| 23 | 12 | 18 | $12 |

3133 Cleburne Rd. (Berry St.), Fort Worth, 817-923-1907
■ "My grandmother is Jewish and I took her here, enough said"; well, not quite: this "bustling, authentic" kosher-style deli sandwiched between a South Side locksmith and car wash may "not be as good as its NYC" counterparts, but it's still a community icon and "better than you'd think for Texas", with Rubenesque reubens and "great soups"; now that's the final word.

Cattleman's FW Steak House S
| 20 | 17 | 19 | $32 |

2458 N. Main St. (25th St.), Fort Worth, 817-624-3945
■ You'd expect the Stockyards to have a noisy, barn of a beef house, and this is it; around since 1947, with decor that is "Texas tacky" or "swank as J.R.'s ranch", depending on whom you listen to, its "great big juicy steaks" are delivered by servers trained to handle a "party of 20 efficiently."

Charleston's S
| 20 | 20 | 18 | $21 |

3020 S. Hulen St. (Bellaire Dr.), Fort Worth, 817-735-8900
■ All-American cuisine with an injection of Southwest and Cajun influences makes this "casual, high-end" South Hulen eatery a charmer; it's a "favorite for prime rib", "super grilled trout" and "buttery, flaky croissants" "drizzled with honey" and "so light they almost float."

Charley's Hamburgers S∌
| – | – | – | I |

4616 Old Granbury Rd. (I-20), Fort Worth, 817-924-8611
3520 Alta Mere Dr. (Hwy. 80), Fort Worth, 817-244-5223
A white-bodied, purple-trimmed converted trailer on the Southside and a former KFC on the West Side comprise the quirky outlets for these family-owned patty joints, which flip a wide variety of super-fresh burgers with toppings ranging from avocado to ham; hand-breaded onion rings and cooked-to-order fries fill out the menu, but since nothing is frozen, it helps to have patience.

Fort Worth/Mid-Cities F | D | S | C

Charlie's Cafe – | – | – | I
120 S. Main St. (Wall St.), Grapevine, 817-421-6256
Imagine a farm-scene painting (veggie-print tablecloths, iced tea swigged from canning jars) and you get a sense of this Main Street American cafe in Grapevine's historical district, which dispenses "terrific burgers and fries" along with stick-to-your-ribs specials; remember, if they've run out of coconut pie, ice cream cones are scooped all day.

Chili's Grill & Bar S 16 | 15 | 16 | $14
1540 University Dr. (south of Rosedale St.), Fort Worth, 817-429-2002
5288 S. Hulen St. (South Dr.), Fort Worth, 817-572-1195
3830 S. Cooper St. (Anbrook Blvd.), Arlington, 817-467-9944
924 Copeland Rd. (Collins St.), Arlington, 817-261-3891
2400 Airport Frwy. (Central Dr.), Bedford, 817-267-6991
800 W. State Hwy. 114 (Woods Ave.), Grapevine, 817-329-1030
Grapevine Mills Mall, 3000 Grapevine Mills Pkwy. (Hwy. 26), Grapevine, 972-724-2606
110 E. John Carpenter Frwy. (Hwy. 114 & O'Connor Rd.), Irving, 972-541-0582
See review in Dallas Directory.

Chipotle Mexican Grill S 16 | 13 | 15 | $10
Trinity Commons, 3050 S. Hulen St. (Bellaire Dr.), Fort Worth, 817-735-8355
North East Mall, 1312 W. Pipeline Rd. (Airport Frwy.), Hurst, 817-595-3875
See review in Dallas Directory.

Chuck E. Cheese's S 10 | 14 | 10 | $13
3903 W. Airport Frwy. (west of Irving Mall), Irving, 972-256-1600
See review in Dallas Directory.

Classic Cafe ▽ 25 | 18 | 22 | $39
504 N. Oak St. (Denton St.), Roanoke, 817-430-8185
621 E. Southlake Blvd. (Byron Nelson Pkwy.), Southlake, 817-410-9001
■ While contrasting greatly in size – the candlelit, intimate Roanoke original seats about 90, the modern Southlake outlet 300 – both of these eateries dish up "salmon at its best" and other "exceptional" American cuisine; hands-on service and "very friendly" managers who "always remember returning guests" further explain their high scores.

Cool River Cafe ● S 21 | 23 | 19 | $33
1045 Hidden Ridge Rd. (MacArthur Blvd.), Irving, 972-871-8881
■ This Rocky Mountain–themed lodge set amidst the Los Colinas/Valley Ranch sprawl is a gathering spot for dot-com aspirants, corporate climbers and "beautiful women", who make the "bar scene"; since it's fully stocked with large-screen TVs, game tables and a cigar/cognac lounge, the Southwestern food may not be the focus, but it scores well, so try the Shiner Bock rib eye, which alone is "worth the trip."

Fort Worth/Mid-Cities   F | D | S | C

Corner Bakery   18 | 16 | 15 | $12
Courtyard by Marriott Hotel, 615 Main St. (5th St.), Fort Worth, 817-870-4991
Grapevine Mills Mall, 3000 Grapevine Mills Pkwy. (Hwy. 26), Grapevine, 972-539-6400 S
Town Ctr., 100 State St. (Carroll Ave.), Southlake, 817-329-1127 S
See review in Dallas Directory.

Costa Azul S   – | – | – | I
1521 N. Main St. (Central Dr.), Fort Worth, 817-624-0506
If spicy "fresh seafood" gumbo or a bowl of seviche is what your taste buds are screaming for, then head over to this North Side Mexican hideout with a fish-oriented menu (and decor) that's "not just tacos and enchiladas."

Cousin's Pit Barbecue   ▽ 21 | 15 | 18 | $13
6264 McCart Ave. (bet. Alta Mesa Blvd. & W. Creek Dr.), Fort Worth, 817-346-2511
5125 Bryant Irvin Rd. (Oakmont Rd.), Fort Worth, 817-346-3999
■ In the never-ending 'cue competition, this two-member smokers' club in the Southwest quadrant is rated "the best" by a contingent, which also likes its "nice family atmosphere" ("my sons love the place"); though it's "known for chicken", the cafeteria-style lines also form for the ribs, brisket and sausage; N.B. don't overlook the condiment table not far from the tub of cold long necks.

Cozymel's Coastal Mexican Grill S   18 | 18 | 16 | $19
1300 E. Copeland Rd. (Collins St.), Arlington, 817-469-9595
Grapevine Mills Mall, 2655 Grapevine Mills Circle (Hwy. 26), Grapevine, 972-724-0277
■ "Another winner for Brinker International", these "cute", "tropical Mexicans" are generally "good on quality, quantity and value" and specifically prized for their "great choice of margaritas", "best salsa" and chips (to pass "the long waits") and many seafood options.

Daddy Jack's Wood Grill S   23 | 17 | 20 | $28
150 S. Denton Tap Rd. (south of Sandy Lake Rd.), Coppell, 972-393-5152
See review in Dallas Directory.

David's Barbecue   ▽ 26 | 14 | 21 | $12
2224 W. Park Row (Bowen Rd.), Arlington, 817-261-9998
■ Disciples of this fourth-generation Arlington establishment are fervent in their belief that it serves "the most consistent, best-prepared BBQ to be found"; believe it or not, the "always succulent ribs" can be made even better with an extra dousing of the "superior sauce."

Fort Worth/Mid-Cities F | D | S | C

DEL FRISCO'S DOUBLE EAGLE STEAK HOUSE   27 | 26 | 26 | $57
812 Main St. (8th St.), Fort Worth, 817-877-3999
■ Voted No. 1 for Service in the FW *Survey* (and tied for first in Popularity), this Downtown steakhouse chain link wows surveyors with "the clubbiest environs", "wonderful sides", "the best red meat you'll ever eat", a showstopper wine list and "impeccable" service; so don your sports jacket and cowboy boots, double-check that "expense-account" limit and prepare for an "elegant power dinner"; N.B. reservations are essential on weekends.

Dick Clark's American Bandstand Grill S   ▽ 17 | 21 | 17 | $16
Grapevine Mills Mall, 3000 Grapevine Mills Pkwy. (Hwy. 26), Grapevine, 972-874-1811
◪ After a shopping blitz at Grapevine Mills Mall, take in "cool rock 'n' roll memorabilia" at this '50s-inspired jitterbug joint; while the American victuals are "average", hypsters hail the "best fish and chips this side of London."

Dickey's Barbecue S   17 | 12 | 14 | $12
2469 Dalworth St. (I-25), Grand Prairie, 972-641-9044
600A W. Northwest Hwy. (Scribney Dr.), Grapevine, 817-329-0221
5330 N. MacArthur Blvd. (bet. Meadow Creek Dr. & Walnut Hill Ln.), Irving, 972-580-1917
See review in Dallas Directory.

Edelweiss   ▽ 18 | 21 | 19 | $25
3801A Southwest Blvd. (Camp Bowie Blvd. & Hwy. 377), Fort Worth, 817-738-5934
■ "Heavy", "hit-the-spot" German food like sauerbraten and kraut and a "polka band that plays everything from Willie Nelson to Cher" make this Southwest house of "pure schmaltz" a "fun place to go occasionally in cool weather."

8.0 Restaurant & Bar ●S   15 | 18 | 16 | $19
Sundance Sq., 111 E. Third St. (Commerce St.), Fort Worth, 817-336-0880
◪ This Sundance Square mainstay for the "after-five middle-management crowd" is now "more a bar than a restaurant" since paring down its American menu; while "formerly chic", it remains an "FW tradition" for dancing and live bands.

El Chico S   15 | 14 | 15 | $15
1315 N. Collins Blvd. (bet. Randol Mill Rd. & Rd. to Six Flags), Arlington, 817-265-2127
Six Flags Mall, 2911 E. Division St. (109th St.), Arlington, 817-640-3144
2305 Airport Frwy. (bet. MacArthur Blvd. & Storey Ln.), Irving, 972-659-1662
697 S. Stemmons Frwy. (I-35, Fox St. exit), Lewisville, 972-221-4884
See review in Dallas Directory.

Fort Worth/Mid-Cities | F | D | S | C |

El Fenix ⑤ | 18 | 15 | 18 | $14 |
6391 Camp Bowie Blvd. (Hilldale Rd.), Fort Worth, 817-732-5584
Ridgmar Mall, 1814 Green Oaks Rd. Ext. (I-30), Fort Worth, 817-732-5596
4608 S. Cooper St. (I-30), Arlington, 817-557-4309
401 State Hwy. 114 W. (Main St.), Grapevine, 817-421-1151
350 E. Southwest Pkwy. (Corporate Dr. & I-35E), Lewisville, 214-488-2769
See review in Dallas Directory.

Ellington's Chop House ⑤ | – | – | – | M |
(fka Ellington's Southern Table)
301 Main St. (2nd St.), Fort Worth, 817-336-4129
The usually successful M Crowd concept team is taking another crack at this Downtown location, which now has a steakhouse-focused menu at dinner (lunch is primarily soups, sandwiches and burgers) and a warmer look.

El Paseo Mexican Restaurant ⑤ ▽ | 23 | 15 | 17 | $14 |
5436 Jacksboro Hwy. (Roberts Cutoff Rd.), Fort Worth, 817-625-9755
100 W. Main St. (Stuart St.), Azle, 817-444-8811
■ These solid Mexican citizens turn out cuisine that's as sincere as their service; do-it-yourselfers will want to put together their own platters from a list of ten options (enchiladas, tacos, tamales, etc.), while lazy types will just go with the pre-set house plates.

El Rancho Grande ▽ | 21 | 19 | 21 | $16 |
1400 N. Main St. (Central Ave.), Fort Worth, 817-624-9206
■ "Beans and rice reminiscent of my grandmother's cooking" and "tamales so good that's all I ever get" reflect voters high regard for this "very cheap" North Side Mexican, a "great stop before a night in the Stockyards."

Escargot ⑤ ▽ | 26 | 24 | 23 | $37 |
Chitcosky's Shopping Ctr., 3427 W. Seventh St. (Montgomery St.), Fort Worth, 817-336-3090
■ Chef-owner Frédéric Angevin's "wonderful new" Cultural District French entry is quickly becoming a "favorite" thanks to "outstanding" food; decorated in "elegant", understated style, the narrow slice of a dining room is tended by wife Michele; yes, "prices are high" and it can get "crowded", but that's to be expected for such a classy operation; N.B. while temporarily closed at press time due to street construction, it's scheduled to reopen in the early spring.

Esparza's ⑤ | 18 | 14 | 16 | $18 |
124 E. Worth St. (Main St.), Grapevine, 817-481-4668
◪ This ramshackle old house off Main Street in Grapevine retains the original Esparza's name while its ex sibling now goes by Johnny Esparza's; locals still find it a nice source for "the absolutely best margaritas, swirls and fajitas", though malcontents claim the "food comes up short."

Fort Worth/Mid-Cities   F | D | S | C

Esperanza's Mexican Cafe & Bakery S≠   ▽ 22 | 18 | 18 | $12
1109 Hemphill St. (Rosedale St.), Fort Worth, 817-332-3848
2122 N. Main St. (bet. 21st & 22nd Sts.), Fort Worth, 817-626-5770
■ Formerly Joe T. Garcia's Bakery, these "true Mexican panaderías and restaurants" on the North and South sides of town attract blue-jean-and-T-shirt-clad patrons for their display cases filled with oven-fresh breads and sugar-coated specialties, "terrific breakfasts" and lunches with "spectacular guacamole" and the "best carnitas."

Fernandez Cafe S≠   ▽ 21 | 13 | 19 | $12
4220 W. Vickery Blvd. (Brunswick St.), Fort Worth, 817-377-2652
■ Food and service are simple and straightforward at this small South Side "mom-and-pop" stop, which dishes out "fresh Mexican" vittles "at reasonable prices"; consider ordering the "good migas" (scrambled with almost any ingredients you desire), award-winning enchiladas and made-from-scratch desserts.

Fiesta Mexican   ▽ 17 | 14 | 17 | $13
3233 Hemphill St. (Berry St.), Fort Worth, 817-923-6941
■ Turquoise, hot-pink and lime-green murals set a party mood at this rambling brick hacienda on the South Side, where generations of families and bunches of friends gather for easy-on-the-wallet lunches and combo dinners; N.B. as you wait for a table, watch the tortillas being patted, pressed and baked in the workroom in front.

Fishmonger's Seafood Grill   ▽ 18 | 13 | 15 | $16
3468 Bluebonnet Circle (University Dr.), Fort Worth, 817-924-2700
◪ 'Our fish is so fresh you have to slap it' is the motto of this Bluebonnet Circle seafood market and eatery, which serves "basic" fried, blackened and grilled preparations; granted there's "no decor", but the crab-shack-in-the-bayou feel seems right, as does the "band playing old Western swing numbers" Wednesday, Friday and Saturday nights.

Fizzi   – | – | – | M
500 Commerce St. (W. 4th St.), Fort Worth, 817-336-3499
Despite being the sibling of Ruffino's, this new ultramodern Downtown venue offers cuisine that breaks slightly from Italian tradition and turns toward contemporary Mediterranean; with champagne as the focus of the wine list (hence the name), expect this to be a bubbly destination for hipsters and the Bass Hall crowd.

Flying Saucer Draught Emporium ◐S   14 | 18 | 16 | $15
Sundance Sq., 111 E. Fourth St. (Commerce St.), Fort Worth, 817-336-7470
Lincoln Sq., 770 Rd. to Six Flags E. (Center St.), Arlington, 817-226-7468
See review in Dallas Directory.

Fort Worth/Mid-Cities | F | D | S | C |

Fox & Hound English Pub & Grill ●S | – | – | – | I |
1001 NE Green Oaks Blvd. (Collins St.), Arlington, 817-277-3591
1640 S. Stemmons Frwy. (north of Corporate Dr.),
Lewisville, 972-221-8346
See review in Dallas Directory.

Fresh Choice S | 16 | 13 | 13 | $10 |
Trinity Commons, 3010 S. Hulen St. (Bellaire Dr.), Fort Worth, 817-738-9878
See review in Dallas Directory.

Fuddruckers S | 17 | 14 | 14 | $12 |
2001 State Hwy. 121 (Bass Pro Dr.), Grapevine, 972-724-0072
Irving Mall, 3644 Irving Mall (Belt Line Rd.), Irving, 972-252-7955
See review in Dallas Directory.

Good Eats S | 17 | 14 | 15 | $15 |
1400 Airport Frwy. (Central Dr.), Bedford, 817-540-3287
5812 I-35 N. (Rte. 288), Denton, 972-219-4775
3516 W. Airport Frwy. (Belt Line Rd.), Irving, 972-313-0803
See review in Dallas Directory.

Grady's American Grill S | 17 | 18 | 18 | $19 |
650 State Hwy. 114 W. (Main St.), Grapevine, 817-329-1198
See review in Dallas Directory.

Grape Escape Wine Bar S | 20 | 22 | 21 | $26 |
500 Commerce St. (4th St.), Fort Worth, 817-336-9463
☑ Small plates of Eclectic nibbles are creatively teamed with flights of global vintages at this compact Downtown *vin* tasting bar that makes a "nice place to converse" after a concert at nearby Bass Hall; while some sour grapes whine that it's "overpriced" with "not much food", most say "we need more places like this."

Hedary's Lebanese S | 21 | 15 | 18 | $21 |
3308 Fairfield Ave. (Camp Bowie Blvd.), Fort Worth, 817-731-6961
■ Ok, "the dining room is not the prettiest" in Cowtown, but this West End Middle Eastern turns out "high-quality" edibles that are "spicy, without being overbearing"; the "great flatbread and all-vegetarian meze" list are obvious choices, but there are also lots of meat options.

Hennington's Cafe in the Nutt House S | – | – | – | M |
Nutt House Hotel, 121 E. Bridge St. (Crockett St.), Granbury, 817-573-8400
A perennial favorite of visitors to Granbury's historic town square, this landmark eatery hangs on to its turn-of-the-century heritage in decor alone (mahogany tabletops, Victorian paintings); a thoroughly modern American menu surprises with favorites like pecan-grilled Chilean sea bass and lemon pound cake bread pudding.

Fort Worth/Mid-Cities | F | D | S | C |

Hoffbrau Steaks & Brewery S | 17 | 15 | 16 | $20
1712 S. University Dr. (Riverfront Dr.), Fort Worth, 817-870-1952
1833 W. Airport Frwy. (Parkwood Dr.), Bedford, 817-267-9303
See review in Dallas Directory.

Hot Damn, Tamales! | ▽ 22 | 8 | 17 | $12
713 W. Magnolia Ave. (Hemphill St.), Fort Worth, 817-926-9909
■ "Owner Angele Stavron should be in Hollywood" and do what Wolfgang Puck did for pizzas, declare worshipers of this "bargain" Hospital District Mexican, which "reinvents tamales" and elevates them to "healthy" gourmet with combos like wild mushroom with Texas goat cheese; the SoHo-esque factory storefront consists of four, fast-turning tables, and the take-out service is lightening quick, but if you live far away there's always overnight mail order.

H³ Ranch S | ▽ 19 | 21 | 19 | $26
Stockyards Hotel, 109 E. Exchange Ave. (Main St.), Fort Worth, 817-624-1246
◪ There's a fine line between authentic Western and Texas kitsch at this American annex to the Stockyards Hotel; the fun begins with the saddle-topped barstools in the Booger Red's Saloon (which was visited by Bonnie and Clyde) then continues with branding-iron candleholders in the dining room; menuwise, look for "roasted corn still in the husk" and steaks cooked over a wall-to-wall, hickory-wood "open pit"; while atmospherics make it fun "for out-of-town guests", the kitchen can be "inconsistent."

Humperdink's ●S | 18 | 17 | 16 | $20
700 Six Flags Dr. (bet. Copeland Rd. & Rd. to Six Flags), Arlington, 817-640-8553
4959 N. O'Connor Rd. (Hwy. 114), Irving, 972-717-5515
◪ "Fun" "places to meet after work", with "pretty good" American bar food, "excellent microbrews" and lots of TVs for viewing sports, this "busy" chain may be "unmemorable" in the grand scheme of things but has enough appeal to attract everyone from "yuppies with cell phones" to seniors and families ("they make kids welcome").

I Fratelli S | ▽ 22 | 16 | 19 | $16
7750 N. MacArthur Blvd. (LBJ Frwy.), Irving, 972-501-9700
■ "Great thin-crust pizza" and "delicious toasted ravioli" are top picks at this family-oriented Irving Italian dining room whose eclectic decor includes floral tie-back curtains, faux-marble fountains, vinyl-print tabletops and a blow-up photo of the Pope offering marital blessings to one of the owners and his bride.

Fort Worth/Mid-Cities   F | D | S | C

I Love Sushi S   ▽ 20 | 15 | 17 | $26
4101 W. Green Oaks Blvd. (Pleasant Ridge Rd.), Arlington, 817-483-9090
■ Long before Japanese food became trendy, this South Arlington ethnic was preparing "enjoyable meals" from its raw fish bar, as well as dazzling patrons with knife-wielding hibachi chefs; popular choices include vegetable and shrimp tempura, bento boxes and the Sunday–Monday happy-hour sushi deals.

Italian Villa S   ▽ 22 | 16 | 20 | $26
6033 I-20 W. (Polly Webb Rd.), Arlington, 817-572-0866
■ Locals say "don't tell anyone else" about this "solid" Arlington Italian off I-20, overseen by a "helpful" owner who is always on the premises; however, truthfully, one bite of the signature angel hair pasta pescatore and it'll be hard to keep this handy trattoria under wraps.

J & J Oyster Bar S   ▽ 20 | 13 | 18 | $17
612 N. University Dr. (7th St.), Fort Worth, 817-335-2756
■ "Fresh-shucked oysters" and "fried seafood with beer" are standard orders at this piscatory classic near the Coliseum and museums, where efficient service more than compensates for the converted fast-food-joint setting.

Japanese Palace S   ▽ 24 | 22 | 23 | $27
8445 Hwy. 80 W. (Camp Bowie Blvd.), Fort Worth, 817-244-0144
■ Culinary historians think of this dinner-only West Side veteran as the "original Japanese food place in FW", and it well might be, since it passed the 25-year mark not too long ago; its reputation for the "best sushi", lively hibachi chefs and "fun hostesses" keeps its repeat-visitor index high.

Jason's Deli S   17 | 12 | 14 | $11
5443 S. Hulen St. (South Dr.), Fort Worth, 817-370-9187
780 E. Rd. to Six Flags (Collins St.), Arlington, 817-860-2888
1270 William D. Tate Blvd. (bet. Ira E. Woods Ave. & State Hwy. 114), Grapevine, 817-421-0566
500 E. FM 3040 (I-35), Lewisville, 972-459-2905
See review in Dallas Directory.

JinBeh S   ▽ 17 | 16 | 18 | $29
301 E. Las Colinas Blvd. (O'Connor Blvd.), Irving, 972-869-4011
2440A S. Stemmons Frwy. (Vista Ridge Blvd.), Lewisville, 214-488-2224
■ These Japanese entries on the main drag in Las Colinas and in Lewisville lure in loyalists who crow about "enormous sushi rolls" ("yellowtail that melts in your mouth") and recommend gathering friends at the "entertaining hibachi table", where it's "the more the merrier."

www.zagat.com

Fort Worth/Mid-Cities   F | D | S | C

Joe T. Garcia's 🆂 ⌀   20 | 22 | 20 | $18
2201 N. Commerce St. (22nd St.), Fort Worth, 817-626-4356
■ "A FW Mexican institution" that "you must take visitors to", this cash-only hacienda compound near the Stockyards is famous for its "fabulous margaritas", best slurped "at a table by the pool" in the sprawling tropical garden; don't fear, your in-laws will be having too much "fun" to notice that the "basic" kitchen offerings play a backup role.

Johnny Esparza's 🆂   – | – | – | I
1212 William D. Tate Ave. (State Hwy. 114), Grapevine, 817-481-6570
Nothing much has changed at this Grapevine strip center Mexican, which split from its Downtown elder (Esparza's) but still serves potent margaritas and solid Mexican fare in a relaxed setting.

Jons Grille 🆂   ▽ 24 | 15 | 17 | $11
3009 S. University Dr. (Berry St.), Fort Worth, 817-923-1909
■ This '60s-themed "TCU hangout" is where generations of students and professors have scrawled their names on every square inch of wall space, "ordered the original bacon burger" with cheese fries and scarfed down the "best Frito pie in town"; shorts, sweats and a baseball cap with precisely rounded bill are about as dressy as it gets.

Jubilee Cafe 🆂   ▽ 23 | 17 | 23 | $11
2736 W. Seventh St. (bet. Carroll & Foch Sts.), Fort Worth, 817-332-4568
■ The "mayor is sometimes spotted" at this standout West Side diner where breakfast and lunch are passed out by a "friendly staff" that "makes you feel at home"; the "great biscuits" are perfect for soaking up gravy or slathering with preserves, and the "best $6 lunch in town" leaves an extra buck or so for a slice of the irresistible coconut meringue pie.

Jun Su Ree   – | – | – | I
1109 Magnolia St. (Henderson St.), Fort Worth, 817-927-3220
Yet another Thai house has taken over this Hospital District space, which was formerly the home of Bangkok City; this newcomer, a bare-bones operation, features a lunch buffet and menu true to its roots: satays and a rainbow of curries plus rice and noodle dishes entice vegetarians and meat lovers alike.

Keg Steakhouse & Bar, The ◐🆂   – | – | – | E
5760 SW Loop 820 (Bryant Irvin Rd.), Fort Worth, 817-731-3534
Further fueling the beef rage in the Southwest quad is this Canadian chain outlet, which is done up in black and caramel wood that evokes a contemporary, rather than clubby, feel; expect prime cuts of meat with the typical sides and an edited selection of wines.

Fort Worth/Mid-Cities   F | D | S | C

Kincaid's Hamburgers ⌀   25 | 14 | 17 | $10
4901 Camp Bowie Blvd. (Eldridge St.), Fort Worth, 817-732-2881
■ "Excellent", "lean, juicy burgers" "dripping with mustard" and delivered in white paper sacks generate long lines at this peerless patty joint/grocery on the West Side, which draws patrons from as far as "140 miles away"; "while it's not much for decor" (just picnic tables and stand-up counters), the staff's "old-fashioned friendliness" more than compensates; N.B. this is the No. 1 Bang for the Buck in the FW *Survey*.

King Tut   ▽ 25 | 13 | 19 | $13
1512 W. Magnolia Ave. (Hurley Way), Fort Worth, 817-335-3051
■ "One of the few places in town to get hummus, couscous and falafel", this Hospital District "ethnic treat" turns out a wide range of Middle Eastern items (including Egyptian dishes), luring in everyone from business types to eccentrics.

Kirby's Steakhouse ⑤   22 | 22 | 21 | $36
3305 E. State Hwy. 114 (Southlake Blvd.), Southlake, 817-410-2221
See review in Dallas Directory.

La Familia   ▽ 24 | 13 | 23 | $13
2720 W. Seventh St. (Carroll St.), Fort Worth, 817-870-2002
■ In a city full of Tex-Mex outlets, this charmer near Trinity Park retains a devoted fan club that swears its offerings are "the best" around; the "friendly" owner is equally confident and says if you can find fresher quesadillas, enchiladas and nachos elsewhere, go and eat there; atmosphere-wise, colored lights swing from the outdoor patio, where birthday parties and family celebrations seem nonstop.

La Hacienda Ranch ⑤   22 | 23 | 19 | $22
5250 Hwy. 121 (Hall Johnson Rd.), Colleyville, 817-318-7500
See review in Dallas Directory.

La Madeleine French   19 | 18 | 15 | $15
Bakery & Cafe ⑤
6140 Camp Bowie Blvd. (Westridge Ave.), Fort Worth, 817-654-0471
Sundance Sq., 305 Main St. (2nd St.), Fort Worth, 817-332-3639
2101 N. Collins St. (north of Lamar Blvd.), Arlington, 817-461-3634
4201 S. Cooper St. (Pleasant Ridge Rd.), Arlington, 817-417-5100
900 Hwy. 114 W. (north of Dove Rd.), Grapevine, 817-251-0255
2417 S. Stemmons Frwy. (south of Garden Ridge Blvd.), Lewisville, 972-459-5900
See review in Dallas Directory.

Fort Worth/Mid-Cities F | D | S | C

LA PIAZZA S 27 | 26 | 24 | $49
University Park Village, 1600 S. University Dr. (I-30), Fort Worth, 817-334-0000

◪ Clearly "the best Italian in FW", this "expensive", "dressy" University destination is not without controversy: while a "who's who" of regulars are welcomed as warmly as arriving relatives and whisked to prime tables to enjoy "a fabulous meal" using the "freshest ingredients" (try the veal tenders with porcini mushrooms), a minority of frustrated outsiders chafes over the owner's playing favorites.

La Playa S ▽ 23 | 20 | 21 | $16
202 W. Central Ave. (Main St.), Fort Worth, 817-626-8720

La Playa Maya S
1540 N. Main St. (14th St.), Fort Worth, 817-624-8411
3200 Hemphill St. (Berry St.), Fort Worth, 817-924-0698

■ These siblings have almost single-handedly gentrified the neighborhoods they've moved into, transforming rambling residences into classy dining spaces; you'll find every south-of-the-border specialty you can dream of, but it's seafood that takes top billing.

Lauderdale's on the Lake S ▽ 16 | 23 | 16 | $23
6500 Wells Burnett Rd. (east of Hwy. 199), Fort Worth, 817-237-5800

■ As "one of the few waterfront dining spots in FW", this two-story, riverboat-style restaurant anchored near the spillway of Eagle Mountain Lake is great for kicking back on the deck; boaters and jet-skiers find "good food and nice service", though more particular eaters might find the marina fare of fried seafood and grilled sandwiches typical.

Lonesome Dove ▽ 23 | 18 | 20 | $33
2406 N. Main St. (24th St.), Fort Worth, 817-740-8810

■ Former Reata chef Tim Love has set up his camp stove in the Stockyards with this "good new addition" featuring polished ranch-style cuisine and a small, saloon-like interior of wooden-plank doors, burlap draperies and a quintessential Western sunset painting; granted, fine linens, pewter platters and stemware are not typical chuck wagon accessories, nor is the grilled quail quesadilla or BBQ duck spring rolls, but culinary cowboys will easily adapt.

Los Amigos S – | – | – | I
202 E. Northwest Hwy. (Main St.), Grapevine, 817-488-1441
746 Grapevine Hwy. (Precinct Line Rd.), Hurst, 817-656-3038

Sometimes "cheap, cheap" Mexican grub is all you want, and this Grapevine and Hurst duo obliges; look for welcoming hosts who "meet you at the door and shake your hand", as well as satisfying weekend brunches.

Fort Worth/Mid-Cities F | D | S | C

Lover's Egg Roll S 16 | 9 | 13 | $11
5330 N. MacArthur Blvd. (bet. Meadowcreek Dr. & Walnut Hill Ln.), Irving, 972-580-8006
See review in Dallas Directory.

Lucile's Stateside Bistro S 21 | 18 | 20 | $22
4700 Camp Bowie Blvd. (Hulen St.), Fort Worth, 817-738-4761
■ Brick-oven pizzas and the "best chicken-fried steak in the universe" draw friends to this "comfortable", mahogany-trimmed, lace-curtained West End American cafe where "fun and noise" abound, especially during TCU events; the extensive weekend brunch is also worth a visit.

Mac's Bar & Grill S 21 | 19 | 19 | $26
6077 I-20 W. (Little Rd.), Arlington, 817-572-0541
5120 Hwy. 121 (Glade Rd.), Colleyville, 817-318-6227
■ Loyalists say they "can't drive I-20 through Arlington and not stop" at this "very nice neighborhood bar and American grill" where "outstanding crawfish étouffée" and seafood gumbo soothe the Cajun spirit and "excellent chicken-fried steak" is a Southern charmer; N.B. there are also branches in Plano and Colleyville.

Maharaja S ▽ 24 | 15 | 18 | $19
Hulen Pt. Shopping Ctr., 6308 Hulen Bend Blvd. (Oakmont Trail), Fort Worth, 817-263-7156
■ Indian options are "few and far between" in FW, which makes it "hard to compare", but tandoori and curry enthusiasts find this lone ranger on the Southwest side "worth a visit" for its abundant lunch buffet and "excellent dinner" selections such as chicken tikka masala.

Mama's Daughters' Diner 22 | 11 | 20 | $12
2014 Irving Blvd. (bet. Oak Lawn & Wycliff Aves.), Irving, 214-742-8646
2412 W. Shady Grove Ln. (Story Rd.), Irving, 972-790-2778
1288 W. Main St. (Old Orchard Ln.), Lewisville, 972-353-5955
See review in Dallas Directory.

Mancuso's Italian Ristorante ▽ 19 | 17 | 18 | $18
9500 White Settlement Rd. (Hwy. 820), Fort Worth, 817-246-7041
■ "Order whatever the waitress recommends" from the Northern-Southern mix of Italian dishes, insist regulars at this dress-down Far West Side entry; "the value is good here" and everyone appreciates the "owner's constant presence", though catfish on the menu (even if it is "incredible") might strike some as a fish out of water.

Massey's S ▽ 20 | 12 | 19 | $14
1805 Eighth Ave. (Park Pl.), Fort Worth, 817-921-5582
■ This long-standing Hospital District diner's "chicken-fried steak the way it should be", bargain lunch specials and all-you-can-eat catfish night attract a coterie of seniors, who tend to overlook the tired paneled walls, black Naugahyde booths and hanging baskets of artificial plants.

Fort Worth/Mid-Cities | F | D | S | C |

Mayuri ⑤
| – | – | – | M |

397 E. Las Colinas Blvd. (O'Connor Blvd.), Irving, 972-910-8788
The extensive buffet makes a fast and flavorful ethnic alternative at this Indian located in a densely populated Las Colinas office corridor; if you're not in a rush to return to work, consider the house plate combinations or assemble a mix of regional dishes from the à la carte choices.

Melanzanos ⑤⌀
| – | – | – | I |

Winn Dixie Ctr., 2030 Glade Rd. (Hwy. 121), Grapevine, 817-329-0837
A Grapevine offspring of FW neighborhood favorite Prima Pasta and Pizza, this sibling is destined to garner the same homey reputation as its relative, what with an unfussy, banner-draped dining room and a straightforward menu of Northern Italian dishes; the eggplant torte and penne with spinach and mushrooms top the list of repeat performers.

Mercado Juarez ⑤
| 17 | 15 | 16 | $17 |

1651 Northside Dr. (I-35), Fort Worth, 817-838-8285
2222 Miller Rd. (Ave. J), Arlington, 817-649-3324
125 I-20 E. (Collins St.), Arlington, 817-557-9776
See review in Dallas Directory.

Mezza Mediterranean
| – | – | – | M |

1015 Cedarland Blvd. (Collins St.), Arlington, 817-794-0393
Stark white walls and cobalt accents convey an Aegean mood at this sophisticated new Mediterranean tucked away on a side street near the Ballpark at Arlington; the young owners showcase family recipes as well as new renditions; N.B. the tournedos Rossini – fried eggplant stacked with mushrooms and medallions of beef – deserves a look.

Michaels
| 23 | 21 | 20 | $36 |

Chitcosky's Shopping Ctr., 3413 W. Seventh St. (Montgomery St.), Fort Worth, 817-877-3413
◪ "Excellent" Southwestern cuisine fired with pepper and hot sauce reigns at this trendy eatery tucked in the corner of a strip mall that fringes the Cultural District; Warhol cowboy-and-Indian prints and muslin panels are "very cool" touches that accent its open dining areas, however too much "cigar smoke" and noise from the rowdy bar can be unwelcome invaders; P.S. "don't skip dessert."

Michel at the Balcony
| 21 | 21 | 21 | $35 |

(fka Balcony of Ridglea)
Ridglea Village, 6100 Camp Bowie Blvd. (bet. Westridge & Winthrop Aves.), Fort Worth, 817-731-3719
■ A transformation from a tired city legend for gray hairs to an elegant Continental supper club for thirtysomethings has "revived" this "classy" upper-level Ridglea Village enclave, now under the stewardship of chef-owner Michel Baudouin (of Grape Escape), who's turning out "really good" classics as well as grilled seafood and chops.

Fort Worth/Mid-Cities   F | D | S | C

MI COCINA ⑤   21 | 19 | 19 | $20
509 Main St. (bet. 4th & 5th Sts.), Fort Worth, 817-877-3600
1276 Main St. (Southlake Blvd.), Southlake, 817-410-6426
See review in Dallas Directory.

Midori Sushi   – | – | – | M
4020 N. MacArthur Blvd. (Northgate Dr.), Irving, 972-887-1818
Black-and-white seafood banners fly above the sushi bar of this smallish Japanese entry in the shadow of the Los Colinas Four Seasons Resort; teriyaki, tempura and udon noodles generally make a solid showing.

Mike Salerno's ⑤   ▽ 22 | 10 | 19 | $16
6651 Camp Bowie Blvd. (bet. Clayton & Lackland Rds.), Fort Worth, 817-732-3636
■ "Started by an 18-year-old high schooler", this West Sider can be "unimpressive" in the looks department (unless you're really into Formica), but it puts out "good Italian food at rock-bottom prices"; N.B. remember to BYO, since the owner is too young to get a liquor license.

Mimi's Cafe ⑤   – | – | – | I
8580 SW Loop 820 (Bryant Irvin Rd.), Fort Worth, 817-731-9644
1449 State Hwy. 114 W. (William D. Tate Ave.), Grapevine, 817-410-7270
2486 S. Stemmons Frwy. (Hwy. 121), Lewisville, 214-488-5056
Serving Traditional American food with a New Orleans twist, these cheerful newcomers offer everything from substantial sandwiches to chicken-fried steak to pasta jambalaya, but they're also family breakfast destinations where enormous omelets and French toast rule.

Mustang Cafe ⑤   ▽ 21 | 23 | 19 | $33
5205 N. O'Connor Rd. (Hwy. 114), Irving, 972-869-9942
■ While it might be a long shot to call this Southwestern-inspired Continental "at the front of the field in the restaurant horse race", it's safe to say that the word "'cafe' doesn't do its spiffy interior justice" and that its "consistently" high-quality victuals make a good bet "for a business lunch or dinner"; N.B. it gets its name from its commanding view of Las Colinas' magnificent bronze mustang sculptures.

North Main BBQ ⑤   ▽ 23 | 9 | 12 | $11
406 N. Main St. (Hwy. 183), Euless, 817-283-0884
■ Despite being "a hole-in-the-wall" with "no atmosphere" and "limited hours", this buffet-only BBQ specialist north of the Airport Freeway commands a loyal following for its selection of meats that are "the best in the land"; P.S. don't be deterred that management "always hides the babybacks."

Fort Worth/Mid-Cities   F | D | S | C

Oasis, The 🆂   – | – | – | M
Lynn Creek Marina at Joe Pool Lake, 5700 Lake Ridge Pkwy. (Webb Lynn Rd.), Grand Prairie, 817-640-7676
Few restaurants in the Metroplex come with a view of any body of water except a fountain, which makes this floating eatery on Joe Pool Lake in Grand Prairie a unique place for boathouse American favorites like burgers, fried catfish and babybacks and a mug of cold beer; N.B. ask for a table on the upper deck for a better scan of the surroundings.

Olive Garden 🆂   15 | 14 | 16 | $18
4700 SW Loop 820 (Hulen St.), Fort Worth, 817-377-8091
301 W. State Hwy. 114 (Main St.), Grapevine, 817-251-0222
4001 W. Airport Frwy. (Belt Line Rd.), Irving, 972-258-5191
2418 S. Stemmons Frwy. (Round Grove Rd.), Lewisville, 972-315-6202
See review in Dallas Directory.

On Broadway Ristorante 🆂   23 | 19 | 21 | $27
Hulen Pt. Shopping Ctr., 6306 Hulen Bend Blvd. (Hulen St.), Fort Worth, 817-346-8841
■ "Not fancy or trendy, just flat-out great-tasting Italian food" that won't pinch your wallet is how admirers describe this Southwest quadrant stop with an unrushed, "local neighborhood feel" that allows you to slowly savor the calamari with salmon ("the best dish").

On the Border 🆂   17 | 16 | 16 | $17
4411 Bryant Irvin Rd. (I-20), Fort Worth, 817-735-8620
1121 I-20 W. (bet. Cooper St. & Matlock Rd.), Arlington, 817-467-4506
1220 Market Pl. Blvd. (I-35), Irving, 214-574-8900
2400 N. Belt Line Rd. (Hwy. 183), Irving, 972-570-5032
See review in Dallas Directory.

Outback Steakhouse 🆂   20 | 17 | 19 | $24
4608 Bryant Irvin Rd. (I-20), Fort Worth, 817-370-7800
2102 N. Collins St. (Lamar Blvd.), Arlington, 817-265-9381
1031 State Hwy. 114 (Hwy. 26), Grapevine, 817-329-4949
701 Airport Frwy. (Precint Line Rd.), Hurst, 817-285-0604
3510 W. Airport Frwy. (Belt Line Rd.), Irving, 972-399-1477
2211 S. Stemmons Frwy. (Oakbend Dr.), Lewisville, 972-315-5772
See review in Dallas Directory.

Palermo's Pizza & Pasta   – | – | – | M
1000 W. Magnolia Ave. (Henderson St.), Fort Worth, 817-878-2400
Opened by the founder of a well-respected chain of pizzerias, folks are understandably expecting a lot from this serious new kid on the block near the medical hub; it occupies a space that was formerly an ice cream parlor, and early reports indicate that you'll still lick your lips over its pastas, piccata and "value lunches."

Fort Worth/Mid-Cities | F | D | S | C |

Pappadeaux Seafood Kitchen S | 22 | 19 | 19 | $26 |
2708 West Frwy. (Forest Park Blvd. & I-30), Fort Worth, 817-877-8843
1304 E. Copeland Rd. (Collins St.), Arlington, 817-543-0544
2121 W. Airport Frwy. (Central Dr.), Bedford, 817-540-2983
See review in Dallas Directory.

Pappasito's Cantina S | 21 | 20 | 19 | $21 |
2704 West Frwy. (Forest Park Blvd. & I-30), Fort Worth, 817-877-5546
See review in Dallas Directory.

Paris Coffee Shop | 22 | 14 | 20 | $11 |
704 W. Magnolia Ave. (Hemphill St.), Fort Worth, 817-335-2041
■ A bit of Mayberry in Cowtown, this Traditional American has been serving "always-good" homestyle breakfasts and lunches in its coffee shop digs for generations; so squeeze in at the counter (or snag a table from the regulars), order up a blue plate special of fried chicken and you'll be engulfed by Hospital District sass and gossip in no time.

Parthenon, The | ∇ 23 | 16 | 21 | $19 |
401 N. Henderson St. (Peach St.), Fort Worth, 817-810-0800
■ Just because it has a slightly less impressive interior than the Parthenon in Athens is no reason to miss this "interesting" Greek spot Downtown, serving dolmas, gyros, spanakopita and Hellenic wines like retsina; those who haven't caught on to the theme ask "why don't they serve California vintages?" (actually, there are two).

Pegasus, The | ∇ 24 | 25 | 22 | $35 |
2443 Forest Park Blvd. (Park Hill Dr.), Fort Worth, 817-922-0808
■ This elegant newcomer to Forest Park "shows promise out of the gate", what with "cool", minimalist decor and an "interesting" Med-influenced global menu; first-time visitors should consider ordering some meze and entrees like the sumac-crusted filet mignon, Persian-spiced osso buco and duck with a fruit mole.

Piccolo Mondo S | ∇ 23 | 19 | 24 | $33 |
829 Lamar Blvd. E. (Collins St.), Arlington, 817-265-9174
■ Called a sentimental Arlington favorite for "romance" and "intimacy", this Italian's discreet staff does its job with just "the right amount of aloofness" to protect privacy; not just for trysts, it's also recommended for power lunches and "special events" with groups; "price increases" are to be expected, but the high quality remains.

Portofino Ristorante | ∇ 24 | 19 | 20 | $35 |
Lincoln Sq., 226 Lincoln Sq. (Collins St.), Arlington, 817-861-8300
■ Sardinian recipes are the specialty of this "classy" Arlington Italian charmer, a pleasing choice to close a business deal or win over a sweetheart; expect bow-tied waiters, a romantic, dimly lit dining room with chandeliers and flowers and nightly music.

Fort Worth/Mid-Cities | F | D | S | C |

Pour House, The S ▽ 16 | 15 | 17 | $14 |
209 W. Fifth St. (Throckmorton St.), Fort Worth, 817-335-2575

■ Since some like it "loud at night", there will always be a clientele for this Downtown American, which rocks with music and televisions tuned to sports; for a quieter scene, head to the newly added balcony with its view of the city skyline; fine tasters will notice that the American fare is a cut above pub grub.

Prima Pasta & Pizza S ▽ 23 | 16 | 20 | $12 |
6108 S. Hulen St. (Granbury Rd.), Fort Worth, 817-263-7711

■ An amazing example of what a former Dairy Queen can morph into, this cozy, old South Side Italian BYO is the kind of place you bring a bottle of Barbera to leisurely enjoy with a "wonderful", modestly priced entree or Sicilian pizza.

Purple Cow S 16 | 16 | 16 | $13 |
2051 W. Airport Frwy. (Murphy Dr.), Euless, 817-858-9000
See review in Dallas Directory.

Railhead Smokehouse 25 | 18 | 19 | $13 |
2900 Montgomery St. (I-30), Fort Worth, 817-738-9808
5220 Hwy. 121 S. (Hall Johnson Rd.), Colleyville, 817-571-2525

■ Hot as the coals that smoke their meat is the "best-BBQ" rivalry between this twosome and Angelo's; loyalists say Railhead's ribs are "the final word on" the subject and add that "the brisket is out of this world" too (especially with "a tall schooner of Shiner Bock"); moreover, while the tables and patios are perpetually overflowing with patrons, the "cafeteria-style lines move quickly" and the "fun" atmosphere (T-shirts for sale read: 'Life Is Too Short To Live in Dallas') keeps the mood light.

Rainforest Cafe S 12 | 24 | 15 | $19 |
Grapevine Mills Mall, 3000 Grapevine Mills Pkwy. (Hwy. 26), Grapevine, 972-539-5001

◪ "Excellent" rain forest–themed decor, including a waterfall, animatronic figures and vine-covered walls, make parents "take the kids" once to this Grapevine Mills theme restaurant; that said, its American-style diner food is barely "ok" and the wait for a table "is long."

Ranchman's Cafe S ▽ 22 | 19 | 19 | $19 |
(aka Ponder Steak House)
110 W. Bailey St. (Hwy. 156), Ponder, 940-479-2221

■ There once was a time when this town was considered the boondocks, but urban growth now makes this BYO chophouse seem a bit closer, if still a "long drive for a steak"; it's safe to say that this longhorn-adorned, half-century-old venue serves the best (and only) T-bones, quail and chicken-fried steak in Ponder (population 432).

Fort Worth/Mid-Cities | F | D | S | C |

RANDALL'S GOURMET CHEESECAKE CO. S   26 | 24 | 23 | $35

907 Houston St. (bet. 8th & 9th Sts.), Fort Worth, 817-336-2253

■ So much more than cheesecake, this exposed-brick, white-tablecloth Eclectic "tucked away on the nontouristy side of Downtown" has a daily-changing menu of impressive preparations as well as a romantic "Paris meets New Orleans meets San Francisco meets Greenwich Village" setting; N.B. don't forget to end your meal with a creamy wedge of the eponymous dessert.

Raneri's   – | – | – | M

8604 N. MacArthur Blvd. (Valley Ranch Pkwy.), Irving, 214-574-7655

Another upscale Italian with Continental highlights and New York lineage, this Irving outpost's florals, twinkle lights and white-draped dining room may say deb ball more than ristorante, but the pastas and scaloppini leave no doubt that the family owners are serious about what goes on in the kitchen.

Razzoo's Cajun Cafe S   16 | 18 | 17 | $18

Cityview Ctr., 4700 Bryant Irvin Rd. (I-20), Fort Worth, 817-292-8584
318 Main St. (3rd St.), Fort Worth, 817-429-7009
4001 S. Cooper St. (I-20), Arlington, 817-467-6510
2504 Airport Frwy. (Central Dr.), Bedford, 817-318-0002
1990 S. Stemmons Frwy. (Corporate Dr.), Lewisville, 972-316-0326

◪ "If you want hot" Cajun cooking, lots of deep-fried dishes and "Bayou atmosphere" "without going to Louisiana", then head to these outlets where "monster drinks" are helpful in cooling the many fiery offerings; wimps would like to see "more mild dishes" ("even the corn burned my mouth") on the menu.

REATA S   24 | 27 | 25 | $36

Bank One Bldg., 500 Throckmorton St., 35th fl. (bet. 4th & 5th Sts.), Fort Worth, 817-336-1009

■ While a March 2000 tornado shut down the other tenants in its office tower, the elevator still goes up to the 35th floor and stops at this Downtown Southwestern, which continues to be No. 1 for Decor in FW and a "place to take visitors" for a "spectacular view", elegant ranch decor and stylish but "hearty" cowboy cuisine packed with smoky flavor and made-from-scratch goodness; N.B. revered chef Grady Spears has moved on.

Red Hot & Blue S   19 | 15 | 17 | $16

3000 S. Hulen Blvd. (Bellaire Dr.), Fort Worth, 817-731-8770
1350 E. Copeland Rd. (Nolan Ryan Expwy.), Arlington, 817-795-7427
2608 Long Prairie Rd. (Forest Vista Dr.), Flower Mound, 972-899-7427

See review in Dallas Directory.

Fort Worth/Mid-Cities F | D | S | C

Rick's on the Bricks S ▽ 18 | 15 | 19 | $14
3716 Camp Bowie Blvd. (Montgomery St.), Fort Worth, 817-732-2401

■ If you want to look like a regular at this "good local burger joint" and *Cheers*-like bar on the West End, come as you are, bring the kids and enter through the side door near the back; while many just order a half-pounder with a side of fries or onion rings, salads, steaks and fried anything are available, and Tuesday and Sunday are all-you-can-eat catfish night.

Riscky Rita's S ▽ 14 | 16 | 18 | $17
140 E. Exchange Ave. (Main St.), Fort Worth, 817-626-8700

◪ "Ordinary" as the Tex-Mex victuals may be at this taco and fajita cantina, unlimited refills of soda and an AYCE lunch buffet have their appeal; moreover, listening to a band out on the patio is a pleasant way to dine after traipsing around the Stockyards tourist circuit.

Riscky's B-B-Q Deli 19 | 15 | 16 | $16
300 Main St. (2nd St.), Fort Worth, 817-877-3306 S
9000 Hwy. 377 S. (north of Winscott Rd.), Benbrook, 817-249-3320 ⊅
8100 Grapevine Hwy. (north of Harwood Rd.), Grapevine, 817-581-7696 ⊅

■ "Quick service" and AYCE portions get the nod from the BBQ and sandwich hounds that breeze in and out of these chain links for on-the-run lunches and no-frills dinners, often accompanied by a giant glass of iced tea and bowl of banana pudding.

Rockfish Seafood Grill S 19 | 16 | 18 | $19
Trinity Commons, 3050 S. Hulen St. (Bellaire Dr.), Fort Worth, 817-738-3474
7400 MacArthur Blvd. (bet. Kinwest Pkwy. & Las Colinas Blvd.), Irving, 214-574-4111
9143 Grapevine Hwy. (Precinct Line Rd.), N. Richland Hills, 817-605-1313
Southlake Town Ctr., 228 State St. (Southlake Blvd.), Southlake, 817-442-0131
See review in Dallas Directory.

Romano's Macaroni Grill S 20 | 20 | 20 | $21
1505 S. University Dr. (Rosedale St.), Fort Worth, 817-336-6676
1670 I-20 W. (Cooper Rd.), Arlington, 817-784-1197
2019 Brinker Ct. (Ballpark Way), Arlington, 817-261-6676
700 Hwy. 114 (William D. Tate Ave.), Grapevine, 817-481-1339
See review in Dallas Directory.

Fort Worth/Mid-Cities | F | D | S | C |

Rough Creek Lodge S ▽ | 29 | 29 | 29 | $54 |
County Rd. 2013 (US 67 S., 9 mi. south of Glen Rose), Glen Rose, 254-918-2550

■ Low votes kept it from earning the FW *Survey*'s highest rankings, but you can still have an "incredible experience" out on the "wide open prairie" at this haute hunting resort/conference center in the shadow of Chalk Mountain; once seated in the elegant Western-accented room, saddled between a soaring, three-story limestone fireplace and an active open kitchen, you'll wax poetic over chef Gerard Thompson's intelligently stylish New American menu; P.S. "stay overnight" to avoid the long drive back.

Ruffino's Ristorante Italiano ▽ | 24 | 21 | 23 | $32 |
2455 Forest Park Blvd. (Park Hill Dr.), Fort Worth, 817-923-0522

■ Brothers Franco and Bobby Albanese express their love of wine and "great food" ("never a dull meal") at this Forest Park cucina with golden-washed walls, starched linens and a piano player who hits all the classy, "romantic" notes; favorites include grandma's lasagna and tiramisu.

SAINT-EMILION | 28 | 25 | 26 | $47 |
3617 W. Seventh St. (Montgomery Rd.), Fort Worth, 817-737-2781

■ No. 1 for Food in FW and "a French oasis in a steak and BBQ desert", owner Bernard Tronche's "romantic" bit of southwest France in a brick cottage near the Arts District showcases "first-rate" classically prepared dishes using "quality" ingredients, as well as a top-notch wine list that favors its namesake region; while the menu advises diners to pace themselves for slow food (meals are usually two hours), to accelerate the "excellent" service advise the staff you are on an American schedule.

Saltgrass Steak House S | 18 | 18 | 18 | $25 |
4601 City Lake Blvd. W. (Bryant Irvin Rd.), Fort Worth, 817-263-5577
5845 Sandshell Dr. (I-35), Fort Worth, 817-306-7900
1051 I-20 W. (Matlock Rd.), Arlington, 817-417-7171
102 State Hwy. 114 E. (Main St.), Grapevine, 817-329-1900
2484 S. Stemmons Frwy. (Hwy. 121), Lewisville, 972-316-0086

◪ A formula of "pretty tasty" steaks ("excellent prime rib") and "casual" ranch house decor true to the prairie has drawn plenty of "budget-minded" families to these chain outposts scattered throughout the Metroplex; jaded types find them "typical" of the genre.

Sapristi! S | – | – | – | M |
2418 Forest Park Blvd. (Park Hill Dr.), Fort Worth, 817-924-7231

Forest Park residents who've yearned for a local place to drop in for a select glass of wine and lighthearted French bistro meal now have their wish thanks to Bernard Tronche (of Saint-Emilion nobility), who's breathed life into a formerly jinxed location; look for golden Provençal walls, olive-print tabletops and a staff clad in long, black Parisian aprons.

Fort Worth/Mid-Cities | F | D | S | C |

Sardines Ristorante Italian ●S | 19 | 18 | 18 | $26 |
3410 Camp Bowie Blvd. (bet. Lancaster Ave. & 7th St.), Fort Worth, 817-332-9937
■ "Only a short walk from the museums", this "fun", "funky" Italian jazz cafe has "endless dark back rooms" that brim with faux "mob atmosphere" and the aroma of "delicious seafood-and-pasta combos"; it's also enough of a mainstay to fight off the expansion of the surrounding medical center and require reservations on weekends.

Scampi's | ∇ 19 | 14 | 17 | $17 |
1057 W. Magnolia Ave. (Washington Ave.), Fort Worth, 817-927-1887
■ The name evokes a seafood concept, but this Hospital District entry is solidly Mediterranean, from the dolmas to the manicotti; clothed in black-and-white-checked table-toppers and dressed up with flower stems in San Pellegrino bottles, this "cozy", "small" eatery can get "really crowded at lunchtime" despite overflow space on an outdoor patio; N.B. the wine bottles displayed on the ledge are only for show, so BYO.

Shrimpers | ∇ 19 | 15 | 18 | $17 |
215 University Dr. (bet. 7th St. & White Settlement Rd.), Fort Worth, 817-877-3255
■ "Noisy" crowds hankering for a seafood fix pack the bar and smallish dining space of this outer fringe Cultural District fish house, whose weathered crab-shack facade comes trimmed in ultra-bright Mexican colors; the menu goes south-of-the-border as well with jalapeño garlic shrimp that turns up the heat and tortas (a type of po' boy) that come slathered with chipotle mayo.

Sofio's Italian Grill S | – | – | – | M |
1900 Long Prairie Rd. (Round Grove Rd.), Flower Mound, 972-691-3474
8600 N. McArthur Blvd. (Valley Ranch Pkwy.), Irving, 972-830-9339
Convenient and dependable, these "nice neighborhood Italians" in Flower Mound and Valley Ranch attract repeaters for straightforward preparations like veal Marsala and the signature chicken Sofio (sautéed breast meat with eggplant and mozzarella finished in a marinara sauce).

Sonny Bryan's Smokehouse S | 21 | 12 | 15 | $13 |
2421 Westport Pkwy. (I-35), Fort Worth, 817-224-9191
Las Colinas Plaza, 4030 N. MacArthur Blvd. (bet. Mills Ln. & Northgate Dr.), Irving, 972-650-9564
See review in Dallas Directory.

Fort Worth/Mid-Cities   F | D | S | C |

South Prairie Oyster Bar ⊄   – | – | – | I |
651 S. Main St. (bet. College & Hudgins Sts.), Grapevine, 817-488-3909
Perched across from the Visitor's Center in old-time Grapevine, in a simple tin-roof brick cottage with wooden porch benches, this seafood shack looks like it's been around since Bonnie and Clyde breezed through town; if they *had* stopped by, they would have appreciated that despite only six booths and limited bar seating, the tables turn quickly for freshly shucked "king-size" oysters and baskets of fried seafood, french fries and hush puppies.

Spaghetti Warehouse S   14 | 16 | 15 | $18 |
Swift & Company Bldg., 600 E. Exchange Ave. (Main St.), Fort Worth, 817-625-4171
2849 W. Airport Frwy. (Belt Line Rd.), Irving, 972-258-1260
See review in Dallas Directory.

Spring Creek BBQ S   18 | 13 | 16 | $14 |
8628 Hwy. 80 W. (Las Vegas Trail), Fort Worth, 817-244-7460
3608 S. Cooper St. (bet. Arbrook Blvd. & Mayfield Rd.), Arlington, 817-465-0553
1509 Airport Frwy. (Forest Ridge Rd.), Bedford, 817-545-0184
3514 W. Airport Frwy. (Belt Line Rd.), Irving, 972-313-0987
571 E. Round Grove Rd. (Hwy. 121), Lewisville, 972-315-2755
See review in Dallas Directory.

Star of Texas Grill S   ∇ 21 | 20 | 21 | $20 |
Renaissance Worthington Hotel, 200 Main St. (2nd St.), Fort Worth, 817-870-1000
■ If you need to meet a client for a "nice breakfast" or impress your in-laws, issue an invitation to this Downtown landmark with ritzy ambiance and flavorful American food; N.B. since Reflections, the main dining salon at the hotel, is currently closed, this adjunct space is getting more attention from management.

Sunflower Shoppe Café S   ∇ 20 | 17 | 20 | $11 |
Sunflower Shoppe, 5817 Curzon Ave. (Camp Bowie Blvd.), Fort Worth, 817-738-5454
■ In a city where organic is far from mainstream, this "peaceful" cafe inside a West End health food store is a welcome relief for those looking for freshly juiced smoothies and wholesome wrap sandwiches.

Sushi Zone   – | – | – | M |
915 E. Rd. to Six Flags (Collins St.), Arlington, 817-226-4055
The chef at this Arlington Japanese has made a name for himself around the Metroplex as a builder of sushi and tempura salons that flourish; faithfuls have tracked him to this new incarnation in a tight spot that's practically hidden from the Collins Street rush; since his skills remain sharp, this will no doubt be another success story.

Fort Worth/Mid-Cities | F | D | S | C |

Szechuan Chinese ◨ | 20 | 16 | 18 | $19 |
5712 Locke Ave. (bet. Camp Bowie Blvd. & Horne St.), Fort Worth, 817-738-7300
City View, 4750 Bryant Irvin Rd. (I-20), Fort Worth, 817-346-6111
■ "Value" prices on crunchy egg rolls and "good-to-fantastic" Peking duck, and a willingness to spice things up on demand explain the popularity of these West Side and Southwest Szechuan and Hunan haunts, perennial contenders for "best in FW."

Tenaya ◨ | ▽ 15 | 20 | 15 | $30 |
525 Meadow Creek Dr. (Hwy. 114), Irving, 972-550-1122
◪ With a menu of clever-sounding (if less than authentic) Native American dishes, steakhouse choices and game offerings, this Eclectic entry near Las Colinas has a concept that some might find "confusing"; nonetheless, a visit still reveals "fantastic portions for the price" and an upscale lodge-like interior adorned with Colorado river rock, cypress timbers, antler light fixtures and leather window treatments.

Texana Grill ◨ | – | – | – | M |
1109 I-20 W. (Cooper St.), Arlington, 817-784-2772
Ample portions of "super pork chops" and medium-rare sirloins sided with potatoes and salad satiate the hungry trailblazers that turn up at this Texas hill country–themed steakhouse in Arlington, decorated with animal heads.

Texas de Brazil ◨ | ▽ 21 | 20 | 21 | $40 |
101 N. Houston St. (Weatherford St.), Fort Worth, 817-882-9500
See review in Dallas Directory.

Texas Land & Cattle Steak House ◨ | 18 | 17 | 17 | $23 |
2009 E. Copeland Dr. (Ballpark Way), Arlington, 817-461-1500
1813 Hwy. 121 (Hwy. 183), Bedford, 817-318-1811
See review in Dallas Directory.

T.G.I. Friday's ●◨ | 15 | 16 | 15 | $17 |
2505 S. Stemmons Frwy. (bet. Roundgrove Rd. & Vista Ridge Blvd.), Lewisville, 972-315-1622
See review in Dallas Directory.

Tia's Tex-Mex Grill ◨ | 16 | 15 | 16 | $16 |
1133 S. Stemmons Frwy. (Hwy. 121), Lewisville, 972-420-8508
See review in Dallas Directory.

Tony Roma's ◨ | 20 | 16 | 18 | $22 |
Vista Ridge Mall, 775 Vista Ridge Mall Dr. (I-35), Lewisville, 972-459-0986
See review in Dallas Directory.

Trail Dust Steak House ◨ | 17 | 18 | 17 | $23 |
2300 E. Lamar St. (Ballpark Way), Arlington, 817-640-6411
26501 Hwy. 380 E. (FM 428), Aubrey, 940-440-3878
See review in Dallas Directory.

Fort Worth/Mid-Cities F | D | S | C

Trevi's S – | – | – | M
(fka Cafe D'Or)
Omni Mandalay Hotel, 223 E. Las Colinas Blvd. (O'Connor Rd.), Irving, 972-869-5550
Long a classy destination for business dinners, this dining room at the Omni Mandalay Hotel recently reopened with old-world refinements and a Mediterranean-Italian menu; consider alfresco dining amid columns and trellises when temps hit the moderate range.

Via Real S ▽ 22 | 21 | 21 | $25
Las Colinas Plaza, 4020 N. MacArthur Blvd. (Mills Ln.), Irving, 972-650-9001
■ This cactus-and-ficus-tree-filled veranda room in Las Colinas regularly fills to capacity for its "upscale Mexican" and Southwestern dishes that "cover all the bases" – marvelous margs, "awesome queso", worthwhile wild mushroom quesadillas – and views of pros playing on nearby courses ("the best place to watch the Byron Nelson golf tournament").

Water Street Seafood Co. S 21 | 17 | 19 | $25
University Park Shopping Ctr., 1540 S. University Dr. (I-30), Fort Worth, 817-877-3474
■ "Cheap oysters" at happy hour and the "most tender, perfectly executed shrimp dishes" are a couple of the "very good" seafood items served at this University fish house; decorated in a Gulf Coast theme, with mounted fish and vintage boating photographs, this eatery will take you back to Corpus Christi in the '30s.

Willhoite's S ▽ 15 | 14 | 16 | $18
432 S. Main St. (Franklin St.), Grapevine, 817-481-7511
■ A converted auto center on Grapevine's thoroughfare is the home of this American eatery, which despite plenty of sandwiches and an AYCE hot and cold buffet is more a place to drink and play games with your bar buddies; N.B. the place rocks Wednesday–Saturday with live bands.

Yogi's Bagel Cafe S 21 | 13 | 14 | $10
2710 S. Hulen St. (Stonegate Blvd.), Fort Worth, 817-921-4500
■ Bodacious bagels, with-it waffles, savvy sausage-filled burritos and the "best migas" are why you "can expect a crowd" at this Eclectic Southwest cafe, "an excellent place for breakfast"; not an early-riser?; in the afternoon it turns out lunches of "great sandwiches" packed with sliced meats and cheeses.

Zodiac S 22 | 20 | 22 | $23
Neiman Marcus at Ridgmar Mall, 2100 Green Oaks Rd. (I-30), Fort Worth, 817-738-3581
See review in Dallas Directory.

Indexes to Restaurants

CUISINES*

American (New)
Abacus
Antares
Beau Nash
Bistral
Breadwinners Cafe
Bronx
Cafe Aspen/FW
Cafe Express
Cafe on the Green/FW
Cheesecake Factory
City Cafe
City Cafe to Go
Classic Cafe/FW
Dakota's
Deep Ellum Cafe
Dream Cafe
French Room
Fresh Choice
Fresh Choice/FW
Gershwin's
Grape
Green Room
Hennington's Cafe/FW
Jaxx Cafe
Landmark
Laurels
Lola
Maguire's
Martini Ranch
Marty's Wine Bar
Mercury
Nana Grill
Natalie's
Plano Cafe
Pyramid Grill
Rough Creek Lodge/FW
Seventeen Seventeen
Sevy's Grill
St. Pete's Dancing Marlin
Tillman's Corner
Voltaire
York St.

American (Regional)
Gennie's Bishop Grill
H^3 Ranch/FW
Lonesome Dove/FW
Mac's
Mac's/FW
Matt's No Place
Norma's Cafe
Texadelphia
Texana Grill/FW
Traci's

American (Traditional)
Angry Dog
Babe's Chicken/FW
Bayley's/FW
Black-eyed Pea
Bobby Valentine's/FW
Buffet at Kimbell/FW
Cactus Flower Cafe/FW
Cafe 1187/FW
Celebration
Celebrity Cafe
Champps Americana
Charleston's/FW
Charlie's Cafe/FW
Chubby's
Cowboy Chicken
Dave & Buster's
Dick Clark's/FW
Dovie's
8.0/FW
Fox & Hound
Fox & Hound/FW
Fuddruckers
Fuddruckers/FW
Good Eats
Good Eats/FW
Grady's
Grady's/FW
Hard Rock Cafe
Highland Pk. Pharmacy
Houston's
Humperdink's
Humperdink's/FW
Into My Garden
Jons Grille/FW
Kel's
Lucile's Stateside Bistro/FW
Lucky's Cafe
Mac's
Mac's/FW
Magic Time Machine
Mecca
Medieval Times
Mimi's Cafe
Mimi's Cafe/FW
Oasis/FW
Old Chicago

* FW=Fort Worth/Mid-Cities.

Original Pancake Hse.
Paris Coffee Shop/FW
Planet Hollywood
Poor Richard's Cafe
Pour House/FW
Rainforest Cafe/FW
Rick's on Bricks/FW
Rock Bottom Brewery
S & S Tearoom
San Francisco Rose
Star of Texas Grill/FW
T.G.I. Friday's
T.G.I. Friday's/FW
Two Rows
Wild About Harry's
Willhoite's/FW
York St.
Zodiac
Zodiac/FW

Asian
Arc-en-Ciel
Asia Arc-en-Ciel/FW
Chow Thai
Citizen
Fishbowl
Jimmy Lu's
Liberty

Bakery
Bavarian Bakery/FW
Breadwinners Cafe
Celebrity Cafe
Corner Bakery
Corner Bakery/FW
Empire Baking Co.
Esperanza's/FW
Henk's European Deli
Kathleen's Art Cafe
La Madeleine
La Madeleine/FW

Barbecue
Anderson's BBQ House
Angelo's BBQ/FW
Baker's Ribs
Bodacious Bar-B-Q/FW
Clark's Outpost
Cousin's Pit BBQ/FW
David's BBQ/FW
Dickey's Barbecue
Dickey's Barbecue/FW
Dick's Last Resort
First Chinese
North Main BBQ/FW
Peggy Sue BBQ
Railhead Smokehse./FW
Red Hot & Blue
Red Hot & Blue/FW
Riscky's B-B-Q Deli/FW
Sammy's BBQ
Sonny Bryan's
Sonny Bryan's/FW
Spring Creek BBQ
Spring Creek BBQ/FW
Tony Roma's
Tony Roma's/FW
Trail Dust Steak
Trail Dust Steak/FW

Brazilian
Fogo de Chao
Texas de Brazil
Texas de Brazil/FW

Cajun/Creole
Charleston's/FW
Copeland's
Crescent City Cafe
Dodie's Seafood Cafe
Johnny Orleans
Margaux's
Nate's Seafood & Steak
Pappadeaux Seafood
Pappadeaux Seafood/FW
Razzoo's Cajun Cafe
Razzoo's Cajun Cafe/FW
Rockfish Seafood
Rockfish Seafood/FW
Yoli's Seafood

Californian
Sipango

Chinese
Arc-en-Ciel
Asia Arc-en-Ciel/FW
August Moon
BKK - Narita/FW
Cafe Panda
Cathy's Wok
First Chinese
Jasmine
Lover's Egg Roll
Lover's Egg Roll/FW
May Dragon
P.F. Chang's
Szechuan Chinese/FW
Szechwan Pavilion
Tong's House
Uncle Tai's

Coffeehouse/Dessert
La Creme

Coffee Shop/Diner
Barbec's
Bubba's
Cafe Brazil
Chubby's
EZ's
Jubilee Cafe/FW
Mama's Daughters'
Mama's Daughters'/FW
Massey's/FW
Mecca
Paris Coffee Shop/FW
Purple Cow
Purple Cow/FW
Theo's Diner

Continental
Cafe Capri
Chaparral Club
Hôtel St. Germain
Huntington's
Jennivine
Michel at Balcony/FW
Mustang Cafe/FW
Old Warsaw
Raneri's/FW

Deli/Sandwich Shop
Bagel Chain
Bagelstein's
Carshon's Deli/FW
Celebrity Cafe
Cindi's Deli
Gilbert's N.Y. Deli
Henk's European Deli
Jason's Deli
Jason's Deli/FW
Mr. G's Deli
Riscky's B-B-Q Deli/FW
Street's Famous
Texadelphia
Yogi's Bagel/FW

Dim Sum
Arc-en-Ciel
Asia Arc-en-Ciel/FW

Eastern European
Cafe Athenée
Franki's Li'l Europe

Eclectic/International
Angeluna/FW
Deep Ellum Cafe
EatZi's
Enigma
Firehouse
Grape Escape/FW
Marie Gabrielle
Parigi
Pegasus/FW
Randall's/FW
Sambuca Jazz Cafe
Soho Food
Suze
Tenaya/FW
Thomas Ave. Beverage
Yogi's Bagel/FW

Egyptian
King Tut/FW

English
Fox & Hound
Fox & Hound/FW
Jennivine

Ethiopian
Queen of Sheba

Fondue
Melting Pot

French
Addison Cafe
Cacharel/FW
Charolais
Clair de Lune
Escargot/FW
La Madeleine
La Madeleine/FW
La Mirabelle
Les Saisons
Mignon
Old Warsaw
Riviera
Saint-Emilion/FW

French (Bistro)
Avanti Euro Bistro
Chez Gérard
Jeroboam
L'Ancestral
Lavendou
Le Paris Bistrot
Sapristi!/FW
St. Martin's
Tramontana
Watel's
We Oui

French (New)
French Room
Hôtel St. Germain
Voltaire

German
Bavarian Bakery/FW
Bavarian Grill
Edelweiss/FW
Flying Saucer Draught
Flying Saucer Draught/FW
Henk's European Deli
Hofstetter's Spargel
Kuby's Sausage

Greek
Kostas Cafe
Parthenon/FW
Theo's Diner
Ziziki's

Hamburger
Angry Dog
Ball's Hamburgers
Champps Americana
Charley's Hamburgers/FW
Chili's Grill & Bar
Chili's Grill & Bar/FW
Chips
EZ's
Fuddruckers
Fuddruckers/FW
Hard Rock Cafe
Jons Grille/FW
Kincaid's Hamburgers/FW
Old Chicago
Pour House/FW
Purdy's
Purple Cow
Purple Cow/FW
Rick's on Bricks/FW
San Francisco Rose
Snuffer's
Stoneleigh P
Two Rows

Health Food
(*Vegetarian)
Dream Cafe
Hot Damn, Tamales!/FW
Kalachandji's*
Sunflower Shoppe/FW

Hot Dog
Angry Dog
Purdy's
Wild About Harry's

Hungarian
Franki's Li'l Europe

Indian
Akbar
Gopal
India Palace
Maharaja/FW
Mayuri/FW

Italian
(N=Northern; S=Southern; N&S=Includes both)
Alfredo Trattoria (N&S)
Amici (N&S)
Amore Italian (N&S)
Angelo's (N&S)
Arcodoro & Pomodoro (N&S)
Avanti Rest. (N&S)
Avanti Ristorante (N&S)
Bellagio/FW (N&S)
Bella Italia/FW (N)
Bruno's/FW (N&S)
Cafe Cipriani/FW (N)
Cafe Expresso (N&S)
Carrabba's (N&S)
Carrabba's/FW (N&S)
Compari's (N&S)
Covino's (S)
Ferrari's (N&S)
Fizzi/FW (N&S)
Francesca (N)
Fresco Grill (N&S)
I Fratelli/FW (N&S)
Il Grano (S)
Il Sorrento (S)
Italian Villa/FW (N&S)
Johnny Orleans (N&S)
La Dolce Vita (S)
La Piazza/FW (N&S)
La Trattoria Lombardi (N)
Leonardo's (N&S)
Lombardi Mare (N&S)
Maggiano's (S)
Mancuso's/FW (N&S)
Melanzanos/FW (N)
Mike Salerno's/FW (N&S)
Mi Piaci (N)
Modo Mio Cucina (N)
MoMo's (N&S)
MoMo's Pasta (N&S)
Nicholini's Seafood (N&S)
Nicola's (N&S)
Olive Garden (N&S)
Olive Garden/FW (N&S)
On Broadway Rist./FW (N&S)
Palermo's Pizza/FW (N&S)
Patrizio (N&S)
Piccolo Mondo/FW (N&S)
Pietro's (N&S)
Portofino/FW (N&S)
Prima Pasta/FW (N&S)
Queen of Sheba (N&S)
Raneri's/FW (N&S)

Rodolfo's (N&S)
Romano's Macaroni (N&S)
Romano's Macaroni/FW (N&S)
Ruffino's/FW (N&S)
Ruggeri's (N)
Sal's Pizza (N&S)
Salve! (N)
Sardines/FW (N&S)
Sipango (N&S)
Sofio's Italian Grill/FW (N&S)
Spaghetti Warehse. (N&S)
Spaghetti Warehse./FW (N&S)
Terilli's (N&S)
Trevi's/FW (N&S)

Japanese
Benihana Grill
Benihana of Tokyo
BKK - Narita/FW
Blue Fish
I Love Sushi/FW
Japanese Palace/FW
JinBeh/FW
Kobe Steaks
Midori Sushi/FW
Mr. Sushi
Nakamoto
Osaka Sushi
Royal Toyko
Sushi at Stoneleigh
Sushi Masa
Sushi on McKinney
SushiSake
Sushi Zone/FW
Tei Tei Robata Bar
Teppo
Yamaguchi

Jewish
Bagelstein's
Carshon's Deli/FW
Gilbert's N.Y. Deli

Latin American
Samba Room

Lebanese
Al-Amir
Byblos/FW
Hedary's
Hedary's/FW

Mediterranean
Adelmo's
Amici
Basha Mediterranean
Bistro A
Bistro Louise/FW
Cafe Highland Park
Fizzi/FW
Il Sole
Mediterraneo
Mezza Mediterranean/FW
Palomino Euro Bistro
PoPoLos Cafe
Riviera
Sambuca Jazz Cafe
Scampi's/FW
Suze
Trevi's/FW
Ziziki's

Mexican/Tex-Mex
Abuelo's
Abuelo's/FW
A.J. Gonzales'
Avila's
Benito's/FW
Blue Goose Cantina
Cabo Mix-Mex/FW
Cantina Laredo
Casa Rosa
Chili's Grill & Bar
Chili's Grill & Bar/FW
Chipotle Mexican Grill
Chipotle Mexican Grill/FW
Chubby's
Chuy's
Ciudad
Costa Azul/FW
Cozymel's
Cozymel's/FW
Desperados Mexican
El Chico
El Chico/FW
El Fenix
El Fenix/FW
El Norte Grill
El Paseo/FW
El Rancho Grande/FW
Esparza's/FW
Esperanza's/FW
Fernandez Cafe/FW
Fiesta Mexican/FW
Gloria's
Herrera's
Hot Damn, Tamales!/FW
Javier's
Joe T. Garcia's/FW
Johnny Esparza's/FW
La Calle Doce
La Familia/FW
La Hacienda Ranch
La Hacienda Ranch/FW
La Playa Maya/FW
La Valentina de Mexico

Los Amigos/FW
Los Vaqueros
Luna de Noche
Mario & Alberto
Mario's Chiquita
Martinez Cafe
Mattito's
Matt's Rancho Martinez
Mercado Juarez
Mercado Juarez/FW
Mia's Tex-Mex
Mi Cocina
Mi Cocina/FW
Monica's Aca y Alla
Nuevo Leon
On the Border
On the Border/FW
Pappasito's Cantina
Pappasito's Cantina/FW
Primo's
Riscky Rita's/FW
San Francisco Rose
Stoneleigh P
Taco Diner
Taqueria Canonita
Tia's Tex-Mex
Tia's Tex-Mex/FW
Tupinamba
Uncle Julio's
Via Real/FW
ZuZu

Middle Eastern
Al-Amir
Ali Baba Cafe
Byblos/FW
Cafe Izmir
Hedary's
Hedary's/FW
King Tut/FW

Moroccan
Avanti Euro Bistro

Pacific Rim
Blue Fish
Jimmy Lu's
Liberty

Pizza
Al's Pizzeria
Arcodoro & Pomodoro
California Pizza Kit.
California Pizza Kit./FW
Campisi's
Campisi's/FW
Chuck E. Cheese's
Chuck E. Cheese's/FW

Fresco Grill
I Fratelli/FW
Lucile's Stateside Bistro/FW
Nicola's
Old Chicago
Palermo's Pizza/FW
Prima Pasta/FW
Sal's Pizza
Sipango
Two Rows

Salvadoran
Gloria's

Seafood
Al Biernat's
AquaKnox
Aw Shucks
Big Fish, Little Fish
Cafe Pacific
Costa Azul/FW
Daddy Jack's Lobster
Daddy Jack's Wood Grill
Daddy Jack's Wood Grill/FW
Fish
Fishmonger's/FW
J & J Oyster Bar/FW
Joe's Crab Shack
La Calle Doce
Landry's Seafood
La Playa Maya/FW
Lauderdale's on the Lake/FW
Lefty's Lobster
Lombardi Mare
Mainstream Fish
Nate's Seafood & Steak
Newport's Seafood
Nicholini's Seafood
Pappadeaux Seafood
Pappadeaux Seafood/FW
Picardy's Shrimp Shop
Randy's Steakhse.
Remington's Seafood
Rockfish Seafood
Rockfish Seafood/FW
Rodolfo's
S & D Oyster Co.
Sea Grill
Shrimpers/FW
South Prairie Oyster/FW
III Forks
Truluck's
Vincent's Seafood
Water St. Seafood/FW
Yoli's Seafood

Southern/Soul
Black-eyed Pea
Celebration

Mama's Daughters'
Mama's Daughters'/FW
Mecca
Rooster
Traci's

Southwestern
Blue Mesa Grill
Blue Mesa Grill/FW
Canyon Cafe
Cisco Grill
Cool River Cafe/FW
Kathleen's Art Cafe
Mansion on Turtle Creek
Michaels/FW
Mustang Cafe/FW
Reata/FW
Star Canyon
Tin Star
Via Real/FW

Spanish
Cafe Madrid

Steakhouse
Al Biernat's
Baby Doe's
Big Buck Brewery/FW
Bob's Steak
Capital Grille
Cattleman's/FW
Chamberlain's
Charolais
Del Frisco's
Del Frisco's/FW
Dunston's Steakhse.
Ellington's Chop Hse./FW
Fogo de Chao
Hoffbrau Steaks
Hoffbrau Steaks/FW
H^3 Ranch/FW
Keg Steakhse./FW
Kirby's Steakhse.
Kirby's Steakhse./FW
Kobe Steaks
La Hacienda Ranch
La Hacienda Ranch/FW
Lawry's
Lonesome Dove/FW
Matt's No Place
Mignon
Morton's
Nate's Seafood & Steak
Nick & Sam's
Old San Fran Steak
Outback Steakhse.
Outback Steakhse./FW
Palm Restaurant
Pappas Bros. Steakhse.
Paul's Porterhouse
Ranchman's Cafe/FW
Randy's Steakhse.
Ruth's Chris
Saltgrass Steak
Saltgrass Steak/FW
Steak N' Ale
Sullivan's
Texana Grill/FW
Texas de Brazil
Texas de Brazil/FW
Texas Land & Cattle
Texas Land & Cattle/FW
III Forks
Trail Dust Steak
Trail Dust Steak/FW

Tapas
Cafe Izmir
Cafe Madrid

Tearoom
Homemade Delights
Into My Garden
Lady Primrose's
S & S Tearoom
Zodiac
Zodiac/FW

Thai
Bangkok City
Bangkok Cuisine/FW
BKK - Narita/FW
Cathy's Wok
Chow Thai Addison
Jun Su Ree/FW
Mango Thai
Royal Thai
Samui Thai
Thai Orchid
Thai Soon
Thai Taste

Turkish
Cafe Istanbul

Vietnamese
Arc-en-Ciel
Asia Arc-en-Ciel/FW
East Wind
Mai's Vietnamese

LOCATIONS

DALLAS

Addison/Richardson/
North Dallas (North of LBJ)
Addison Cafe
August Moon
Avanti Euro Bistro
Bagelstein's
Benihana of Tokyo
Black-eyed Pea
Blue Fish
Blue Goose Cantina
Blue Mesa Grill
Cafe Athenée
Cafe Brazil
Cafe Capri
Cafe Express
California Pizza Kit.
Campisi's
Cantina Laredo
Canyon Cafe
Carrabba's
Cathy's Wok
Celebrity Cafe
Chamberlain's
Champps Americana
Chili's Grill & Bar
Chipotle Mexican Grill
Chow Thai Addison
Chuck E. Cheese's
Cindi's Deli
Copeland's
Corner Bakery
Cowboy Chicken
Del Frisco's
Dickey's Barbecue
Dovie's
El Chico
El Fenix
Empire Baking Co.
Ferrari's
First Chinese
Flying Saucer Draught
Fogo de Chao
Fox & Hound
Francesca
Fresh Choice
Gloria's
Good Eats
Gopal
Grady's
Hedary's
Herrera's
Hoffbrau Steaks
Houston's
Humperdink's
Huntington's
Jasmine
Jason's Deli
Jaxx Cafe
Jimmy Lu's
Joe's Crab Shack
Johnny Orleans
Kobe Steaks
La Madeleine
La Mirabelle
Landry's Seafood
La Valentina de Mexico
Lavendou
Lawry's
Lefty's Lobster
Lombardi Mare
Maggiano's
Magic Time Machine
Maguire's
May Dragon
Mediterraneo
Melting Pot
Mi Cocina
Mi Piaci
Modo Mio Cucina
MoMo's Pasta
Morton's
Mr. Sushi
Nate's Seafood & Steak
Nicholini's Seafood
Nicola's
Norma's Cafe
Old Chicago
Olive Garden
On the Border
Original Pancake Hse.
Osaka Sushi
Outback Steakhse.
Pappadeaux Seafood
Pappasito's Cantina
P.F. Chang's
Purdy's
Purple Cow
Razzoo's Cajun Cafe
Remington's Seafood
Rock Bottom Brewery
Rockfish Seafood

Romano's Macaroni
Ruggeri's
Ruth's Chris
Sambuca Jazz Cafe
Sea Grill
Snuffer's
Soho Food
Sonny Bryan's
Spring Creek BBQ
Steak N' Ale
Street's Famous
Sullivan's
Sushi Masa
SushiSake
Texadelphia
Texas de Brazil
Texas Land & Cattle
T.G.I. Friday's
Thai Orchid
III Forks
Tia's Tex-Mex
Tong's House
Tony Roma's
Truluck's
Tupinamba
Uncle Julio's
Uncle Tai's
Vincent's Seafood
Voltaire
Yoli's Seafood
Ziziki's
ZuZu

**Downtown/
Deep Ellum/West End**
Angry Dog
Antares
Avanti Rest.
Baker's Ribs
Bangkok City
Cafe Brazil
Campisi's
Chaparral Club
Corner Bakery
Crescent City Cafe
Daddy Jack's Wood Grill
Dakota's
Deep Ellum Cafe
Dickey's Barbecue
Dick's Last Resort
East Wind
Fish
French Room
Green Room
Hoffbrau Steaks

Jeroboam
La Madeleine
Landry's Seafood
Mai's Vietnamese
MoMo's Pasta
Monica's Aca y Alla
Morton's
Nana Grill
Newport's Seafood
On the Border
Palm Restaurant
Sambuca Jazz Cafe
Seventeen Seventeen
Sonny Bryan's
Spaghetti Warehse.
St. Pete's Dancing Marlin
T.G.I. Friday's
Theo's Diner
Tin Star
Tony Roma's
Zodiac

**East Dallas/Lakewood/
Greenville Avenue/
Garland/Mesquite**
Al-Amir
Ali Baba Cafe
Angelo's
Arc-en-Ciel
Aw Shucks
Baker's Ribs
Bangkok City
Barbec's
Basha Mediterranean
Black-eyed Pea
Blue Fish
Blue Goose Cantina
Cafe Brazil
Cafe Izmir
Campisi's
Chili's Grill & Bar
Chubby's
Chuck E. Cheese's
Daddy Jack's Lobster
Desperados Mexican
Dickey's Barbecue
Dodie's Seafood Cafe
Dunston's Steakhse.
El Chico
El Fenix
Firehouse
Flying Saucer Draught
Franki's Li'l Europe
Fuddruckers
Gloria's

Good Eats
Grady's
Grape
Henk's European Deli
Hoffbrau Steaks
Humperdink's
Jason's Deli
Kalachandji's
Kirby's Steakhse.
Kostas Cafe
La Calle Doce
La Dolce Vita
Liberty
Luna de Noche
Mama's Daughters'
Matt's No Place
Matt's Rancho Martinez
Mi Cocina
MoMo's
Nuevo Leon
Olive Garden
On the Border
Outback Steakhse.
Pietro's
Razzoo's Cajun Cafe
Royal Thai
Royal Toyko
Saltgrass Steak
San Francisco Rose
Snuffer's
Sonny Bryan's
Spring Creek BBQ
Steak N' Ale
St. Martin's
Teppo
Terilli's
Texadelphia
T.G.I. Friday's
Thai Soon
Tia's Tex-Mex
Tony Roma's
Trail Dust Steak
Two Rows
Uncle Julio's
York St.

North of Downtown (Fairmont/Maple/Routh/McKinney Ave./Quadrangle/Cedar Springs)

Abacus
A.J. Gonzales'
Arcodoro & Pomodoro
Avanti Ristorante
Avila's
Beau Nash
Bistral
Breadwinners Cafe
Cafe Express
Capital Grille
Celebrity Cafe
Chez Gérard
Chipotle Mexican Grill
Chuy's
Dream Cafe
El Fenix
Enigma
Hard Rock Cafe
Herrera's
Hôtel St. Germain
Jennivine
Johnny Orleans
Lady Primrose's
La Trattoria Lombardi
Le Paris Bistrot
Lola
Lover's Egg Roll
Mansion on Turtle Creek
Margaux's
Marie Gabrielle
Martini Ranch
Mattito's
Medieval Times
Nick & Sam's
Old Warsaw
Palomino Euro Bistro
Pappadeaux Seafood
Planet Hollywood
Primo's
Pyramid Grill
Queen of Sheba
Ruggeri's
Ruth's Chris
Salve!
Sammy's BBQ
S & D Oyster Co.
Sonny Bryan's
Stoneleigh P
Sushi at Stoneleigh
Sushi on McKinney
Texadelphia
Texas de Brazil
Thai Taste
Thomas Ave. Beverage
Traci's
Truluck's
Watel's
We Oui

Oak Cliff/South Dallas
Chubby's
Chuck E. Cheese's
El Fenix
Gennie's Bishop Grill
Gloria's
Herrera's
La Calle Doce
Mama's Daughters'
Norma's Cafe
Steak N' Ale
Tillman's Corner

Oak Lawn/Lemmon Avenue/Little Mexico
Al Biernat's
Alfredo Trattoria
Baby Doe's
Benihana Grill
Black-eyed Pea
Bob's Steak
Bronx
Cafe Brazil
Citizen
Ciudad
EatZi's
El Fenix
Empire Baking Co.
Gloria's
Good Eats
La Madeleine
Landmark
Les Saisons
Lucky's Cafe
Marty's Wine Bar
Mia's Tex-Mex
Nuevo Leon
Original Pancake Hse.
Pappadeaux Seafood
Parigi
Rooster
Sal's Pizza
Star Canyon
Street's Famous
Texas Land & Cattle
Uncle Julio's

Park Cities/Knox/ Henderson/ Highland Park Village/ Snider Plaza
Adelmo's
Amore Italian
AquaKnox
Ball's Hamburgers
Big Fish, Little Fish
Bistro A
Bubba's
Cafe Brazil
Cafe Highland Park
Cafe Madrid
Cafe Pacific
Celebrity Cafe
Chili's Grill & Bar
Chips
Cisco Grill
Dickey's Barbecue
EZ's
Fishbowl
Fresco Grill
Highland Pk. Pharmacy
Hoffbrau Steaks
Il Sole
Il Sorrento
Javier's
Kuby's Sausage
La Madeleine
L'Ancestral
Los Vaqueros
Mi Cocina
MoMo's Pasta
Old San Fran Steak
On the Border
Patrizio
Peggy Sue BBQ
Picardy's Shrimp Shop
Rockfish Seafood
Samba Room
Sevy's Grill
Sipango
Szechwan Pavilion
Taco Diner
Tei Tei Robata Bar
Wild About Harry's
Ziziki's

Plano/Suburban North
Abuelo's
Akbar
August Moon
Bavarian Grill
Black-eyed Pea
Blue Goose Cantina
California Pizza Kit.
Campisi's
Cathy's Wok
Celebrity Cafe
Cheesecake Factory
Chipotle Mexican Grill
Chow Thai

Chubby's
Chuck E. Cheese's
Compari's
Corner Bakery
Covino's
Cozymel's
Dickey's Barbecue
El Chico
El Fenix
El Norte Grill
Fresh Choice
Fuddruckers
Grady's
Hoffbrau Steaks
Homemade Delights
Humperdink's
Il Grano
Into My Garden
Jason's Deli
Kirby's Steakhse.
Kostas Cafe
La Hacienda Ranch
La Madeleine
Leonardo's
Lover's Egg Roll
Mac's
Mango Thai
Mario's Chiquita
Martinez Cafe
Mignon
Mimi's Cafe
Mr. G's Deli
Nakamoto
On the Border
Original Pancake Hse.
Outback Steakhse.
Pappadeaux Seafood
Patrizio
Plano Cafe
Poor Richard's Cafe
Purple Cow
Randy's Steakhse.
Red Hot & Blue
Rockfish Seafood
Romano's Macaroni
Saltgrass Steak
Samui Thai
Steak N' Ale
Taqueria Canonita
Texadelphia
Texas Land & Cattle
T.G.I. Friday's
Tia's Tex-Mex
Tin Star
Tony Roma's

Vincent's Seafood
Wild About Harry's

Preston Center/Inwood/ West Lovers Lane/ Love Field Area (South of LBJ)

Al's Pizzeria
Bagel Chain
Ball's Hamburgers
Black-eyed Pea
Blue Mesa Grill
Cafe Express
Cafe Expresso
Cafe Istanbul
Cafe Panda
California Pizza Kit.
Campisi's
Cantina Laredo
Casa Rosa
Celebration
Celebrity Cafe
Charolais
Cheesecake Factory
Chili's Grill & Bar
Chipotle Mexican Grill
Chips
Cindi's Deli
City Cafe
City Cafe to Go
Clair de Lune
Corner Bakery
Dave & Buster's
Dunston's Steakhse.
El Fenix
Empire Baking Co.
Gershwin's
Gilbert's N.Y. Deli
Good Eats
Herrera's
Hofstetter's Spargel
Houston's
Humperdink's
India Palace
Jason's Deli
Joe's Crab Shack
Johnny Orleans
Kathleen's Art Cafe
Kel's
La Creme
La Madeleine
Laurels
Lover's Egg Roll
Luna de Noche
Mainstream Fish

Mama's Daughters'
Mario & Alberto
Matt's Rancho Martinez
Mecca
Mercado Juarez
Mercury
Mi Cocina
MoMo's
Natalie's
Original Pancake Hse.
Pappas Bros. Steakhse.
Pappasito's Cantina
Paul's Porterhouse
P.F. Chang's
PoPoLos Cafe
Red Hot & Blue
Riviera
Rodolfo's
Romano's Macaroni
S & S Tearoom
Sonny Bryan's
Suze
Texas Land & Cattle

T.G.I. Friday's
Tin Star
Tony Roma's
Tramontana
Yamaguchi
Zodiac
ZuZu

Rural
Clark's Outpost

Suburban Northwest
Amici
Anderson's BBQ House
Black-eyed Pea
Dunston's Steakhse.
Herrera's
La Hacienda Ranch
Norma's Cafe
Nuevo Leon
Outback Steakhse.
Tia's Tex-Mex
Trail Dust Steak

FORT WORTH/MID-CITIES

Arlington/Grand Prairie
Abuelo's
Asia Arc-en-Ciel
Bobby Valentine's
Bodacious Bar-B-Q
Cacharel
Chili's Grill & Bar
Cozymel's
David's BBQ
Dickey's Barbecue
El Chico
El Fenix
Flying Saucer Draught
Fox & Hound
Humperdink's
I Love Sushi
Italian Villa
Jason's Deli
La Madeleine
Mac's
Mercado Juarez
Mezza Mediterranean
Oasis
On the Border
Outback Steakhse.
Pappadeaux Seafood
Piccolo Mondo
Portofino
Razzoo's Cajun Cafe

Red Hot & Blue
Romano's Macaroni
Saltgrass Steak
Spring Creek BBQ
Sushi Zone
Texana Grill
Texas Land & Cattle
Trail Dust Steak

Cultural District/West/Southwest
Angelo's BBQ
Bella Italia
Bistro Louise
BKK - Narita
Buffet at Kimbell
Cafe Aspen
Charleston's
Charley's Hamburgers
Chili's Grill & Bar
Chipotle Mexican Grill
Cousin's Pit BBQ
Edelweiss
El Fenix
Fresh Choice
Hedary's
J & J Oyster Bar
Japanese Palace
Jason's Deli

Jubilee Cafe
Keg Steakhse.
Kincaid's Hamburgers
La Familia
La Madeleine
Lucile's Stateside Bistro
Maharaja
Mancuso's
Michaels
Michel at Balcony
Mike Salerno's
Olive Garden
On Broadway Rist.
On the Border
Outback Steakhse.
Pappadeaux Seafood
Pappasito's Cantina
Pegasus
Prima Pasta
Railhead Smokehse.
Razzoo's Cajun Cafe
Red Hot & Blue
Rick's on Bricks
Riscky's B-B-Q Deli
Rockfish Seafood
Ruffino's
Saint-Emilion
Sapristi!
Sardines
Shrimpers
Spring Creek BBQ
Sunflower Shoppe
Szechuan Chinese
Yogi's Bagel
Zodiac

Denton County (Lewisville, Flower Mound, Trophy Club, Roanoke, The Colony, Northlake)
Abuelo's
Babe's Chicken
Campisi's
Classic Cafe
El Chico
El Fenix
Fox & Hound
Good Eats
Jason's Deli
JinBeh
La Madeleine
Mama's Daughters'
Mimi's Cafe
Olive Garden
Outback Steakhse.
Ranchman's Cafe
Razzoo's Cajun Cafe
Red Hot & Blue
Saltgrass Steak
Sofio's Italian Grill
Spring Creek BBQ
T.G.I. Friday's
Tia's Tex-Mex
Tony Roma's
Trail Dust Steak

Downtown/ Sundance Square
Angeluna
Cabo Mix-Mex
Corner Bakery
Del Frisco's
8.0
Ellington's Chop Hse.
Fizzi
Flying Saucer Draught
Grape Escape
La Madeleine
Mi Cocina
Parthenon
Pour House
Randall's
Razzoo's Cajun Cafe
Reata
Riscky's B-B-Q Deli
Star of Texas Grill
Texas de Brazil

Hospital District/ University Area/ South Side
Bavarian Bakery
Bellagio
Benito's
Blue Mesa Grill
Cactus Flower Cafe
Carshon's Deli
Chili's Grill & Bar
Esperanza's
Fernandez Cafe
Fiesta Mexican
Fishmonger's
Hoffbrau Steaks
Hot Damn, Tamales!
Jons Grille
Jun Su Ree
King Tut
La Piazza
La Playa Maya
Massey's
Mimi's Cafe
Palermo's Pizza
Paris Coffee Shop
Romano's Macaroni
Saltgrass Steak
Scampi's
Water St. Seafood

Irving/Las Colinas
Bruno's
Cafe Cipriani
Cafe on the Green
Chili's Grill & Bar
Chuck E. Cheese's
Cool River Cafe
Dickey's Barbecue
El Chico
Fuddruckers
Good Eats
Humperdink's
I Fratelli
JinBeh
Lover's Egg Roll
Mama's Daughters'
Mayuri
Midori Sushi
Mustang Cafe
Olive Garden
On the Border
Outback Steakhse.
Raneri's
Rockfish Seafood
Sofio's Italian Grill
Sonny Bryan's
Spaghetti Warehse.
Spring Creek BBQ
Tenaya
Trevi's
Via Real

Northeast Tarrant County (North Richland Hills, Haltom City, Hurst-Euless-Bedford, Grapevine, Colleyville, Southlake)
Abuelo's
Bangkok Cuisine
Bayley's
Big Buck Brewery
Cactus Flower Cafe
California Pizza Kit.
Carrabba's
Charlie's Cafe
Chili's Grill & Bar
Chipotle Mexican Grill
Classic Cafe
Corner Bakery
Cozymel's
Daddy Jack's Wood Grill
Dick Clark's
Dickey's Barbecue
El Fenix
Esparza's
Fuddruckers
Good Eats
Grady's
Hoffbrau Steaks
Jason's Deli
Johnny Esparza's
Kirby's Steakhse.
La Hacienda Ranch
La Madeleine
Los Amigos
Mac's
Melanzanos
Mi Cocina
Mimi's Cafe
North Main BBQ
Olive Garden
Outback Steakhse.
Pappadeaux Seafood
Purple Cow
Railhead Smokehse.
Rainforest Cafe
Razzoo's Cajun Cafe
Riscky's B-B-Q Deli
Rockfish Seafood
Romano's Macaroni
Saltgrass Steak
Sonny Bryan's
South Prairie Oyster
Spring Creek BBQ
Texas Land & Cattle
Willhoite's

Rural (Granbury & Outlying Areas)
Bodacious Bar-B-Q
Cafe 1187
El Paseo
Hennington's Cafe
Lauderdale's on the Lake
Romano's Macaroni
Rough Creek Lodge

Stockyards/North Side
Byblos
Cattleman's
Costa Azul
El Paseo
El Rancho Grande
Escargot
Esperanza's
H^3 Ranch
Joe T. Garcia's
La Playa Maya
Lonesome Dove
Mercado Juarez
Riscky Rita's
Spaghetti Warehse.

SPECIAL FEATURES AND APPEALS*

Breakfast
(All hotels and the following standouts)
Bagel Chain
Bagelstein's
Barbec's
Bayley's/FW
Benito's/FW
Breadwinners Cafe
Cafe Brazil
Carshon's Deli/FW
Cindi's Deli
Corner Bakery
Dream Cafe
Empire Baking Co.
Esparza's/FW
Fernandez Cafe/FW
Gilbert's N.Y. Deli
Henk's European Deli
Herrera's
Joe T. Garcia's/FW
La Familia/FW
La Madeleine
Los Amigos/FW
Lucky's Cafe
Mama's Daughters'
Mama's Daughters'/FW
Mecca
Mimi's Cafe
Mimi's Cafe/FW
Norma's Cafe
Original Pancake Hse.
Paris Coffee Shop/FW
S & S Tearoom
Theo's Diner
Yogi's Bagel/FW

Brunch
(Best of many)
Abuelo's
Abuelo's/FW
Asia Arc-en-Ciel/FW
August Moon
Benito's/FW
Bistral
Breadwinners Cafe
Bronx
Cafe Brazil
Cafe on the Green/FW
Chuy's
Cool River Cafe/FW
Cozymel's/FW
Dream Cafe
8.0/FW
Hedary's/FW
Humperdink's
Huntington's
Jennivine
La Madeleine/FW
Landmark
Lombardi Mare
Lucky's Cafe
Mac's
Mac's/FW
Mansion on Turtle Creek
Mattito's
Mustang Cafe/FW
Nana Grill
Nuevo Leon
Paris Coffee Shop/FW
Rooster
San Francisco Rose
Seventeen Seventeen
Tenaya/FW
Ziziki's

Buffet Served
(Check prices, days and times)
Angelo's
Antares
August Moon
Baby Doe's
Blue Mesa Grill
Blue Mesa Grill/FW
Buffet at Kimbell/FW
Byblos/FW
Cafe on the Green/FW
Dick's Last Resort
Fresh Choice
Gennie's Bishop Grill
Hedary's
Hennington's Cafe/FW
Il Grano
Il Sorrento
India Palace
Jasmine
Jun Su Ree/FW
Kalachandji's
Maharaja/FW
Mario & Alberto
Mattito's

* FW=Fort Worth/Mid-Cities.

Midori Sushi/FW
North Main BBQ/FW
Osaka Sushi
Queen of Sheba
Riscky Rita's/FW
Spring Creek BBQ
Spring Creek BBQ/FW
Willhoite's/FW

Business Dining
Al Biernat's
Angeluna/FW
Antares
Bistro Louise/FW
Bob's Steak
Buffet at Kimbell/FW
Cafe Cipriani/FW
Cafe on the Green/FW
Capital Grille
Chamberlain's
Chaparral Club
Citizen
Cool River Cafe/FW
Dakota's
Del Frisco's
Del Frisco's/FW
Dunston's Steakhse.
Gershwin's
Huntington's
JinBeh/FW
Kirby's Steakhse.
Kirby's Steakhse./FW
Landmark
La Piazza/FW
La Trattoria Lombardi
Laurels
La Valentina de Mexico
Lawry's
Les Saisons
Mansion on Turtle Creek
Michaels/FW
Mi Piaci
Morton's
Mustang Cafe/FW
Nick & Sam's
Old Warsaw
Palm Restaurant
Pappas Bros. Steakhse.
Paul's Porterhouse
Piccolo Mondo/FW
Portofino/FW
Pyramid Grill
Reata/FW
Riviera
Ruggeri's
Ruth's Chris
Saint-Emilion/FW
Salve!
Sammy's BBQ
Seventeen Seventeen
Sevy's Grill
Star Canyon
Tenaya/FW
Texas Land & Cattle
III Forks
Trevi's/FW
Via Real/FW
Vincent's Seafood
Voltaire

BYO
Amici
Arc-en-Ciel
Asia Arc-en-Ciel/FW
Babe's Chicken/FW
Bangkok Cuisine/FW
Bayley's/FW
Campisi's
Cathy's Wok
Covino's
Fernandez Cafe/FW
Homemade Delights
Leonardo's
Los Amigos/FW
Mai's Vietnamese
Melanzanos/FW
Mike Salerno's/FW
Natalie's
North Main BBQ/FW
Prima Pasta/FW
Ranchman's Cafe/FW
Scampi's/FW
Theo's Diner

Caters
(Best of many)
A.J. Gonzales'
Akbar
Ali Baba Cafe
Amore Italian
Anderson's BBQ House
Angelo's
Avanti Euro Bistro
Avanti Rest.
Avanti Ristorante
Avila's
Baker's Ribs
Bangkok City
Basha Mediterranean
Benihana Grill

Big Buck Brewery/FW
Bistro A
Bistro Louise/FW
Blue Fish
Blue Mesa Grill
Blue Mesa Grill/FW
Bodacious Bar-B-Q/FW
Breadwinners Cafe
Bubba's
Byblos/FW
Cactus Flower Cafe/FW
Cafe Aspen/FW
Cafe Express
Cafe Expresso
Cafe Istanbul
Cafe Izmir
Canyon Cafe
Carrabba's
Carshon's Deli/FW
Casa Rosa
Chamberlain's
Cisco Grill
City Cafe to Go
Ciudad
Classic Cafe/FW
Cousin's Pit BBQ/FW
Cowboy Chicken
Daddy Jack's Lobster
Daddy Jack's Wood Grill
David's BBQ/FW
Deep Ellum Cafe
Desperados Mexican
Dickey's Barbecue
Dickey's Barbecue/FW
EatZi's
El Chico
Esparza's/FW
Fernandez Cafe/FW
Franki's Li'l Europe
Fresco Grill
Green Room
Hennington's Cafe/FW
Hôtel St. Germain
H^3 Ranch/FW
Il Grano
Il Sole
Javier's
Jennivine
Jeroboam
Joe T. Garcia's/FW
Kathleen's Art Cafe
Kostas Cafe
Kuby's Sausage
La Madeleine
La Madeleine/FW
La Trattoria Lombardi
Lauderdale's on the Lake/FW
La Valentina de Mexico
Lavendou
Leonardo's
Lombardi Mare
Los Amigos/FW
Los Vaqueros
Luna de Noche
Mainstream Fish
Marty's Wine Bar
Mattito's
Matt's Rancho Martinez
May Dragon
Mecca
Mercado Juarez
Mia's Tex-Mex
Michaels/FW
Mi Piaci
Norma's Cafe
North Main BBQ/FW
Nuevo Leon
On the Border
Osaka Sushi
Peggy Sue BBQ
Picardy's Shrimp Shop
PoPoLos Cafe
Railhead Smokehse./FW
Rockfish Seafood
Rockfish Seafood/FW
Rodolfo's
Romano's Macaroni
Romano's Macaroni/FW
Royal Toyko
Sammy's BBQ
S & S Tearoom
Sardines/FW
Seventeen Seventeen
Sevy's Grill
Sipango
Sofio's Italian Grill/FW
Sonny Bryan's
Sonny Bryan's/FW
St. Pete's Dancing Marlin
Street's Famous
Sushi Masa
Thai Taste
Thomas Ave. Beverage
Tony Roma's
Tony Roma's/FW
Uncle Julio's
Yogi's Bagel/FW
Ziziki's
Zodiac
Zodiac/FW

Cigar Friendly
Al Biernat's
Angry Dog
Antares
Avanti Rest.
Beau Nash
Big Buck Brewery/FW
Bob's Steak
Cabo Mix-Mex/FW
Cafe Aspen/FW
Capital Grille
Chamberlain's
Charleston's/FW
Ciudad
Cool River Cafe/FW
Copeland's
Daddy Jack's Wood Grill
Del Frisco's
Del Frisco's/FW
Dick's Last Resort
Dunston's Steakhse.
Edelweiss/FW
Ellington's Chop Hse./FW
Flying Saucer Draught
Flying Saucer Draught/FW
Fox & Hound
H^3 Ranch/FW
Humperdink's
Humperdink's/FW
Il Sole
Javier's
Jeroboam
Jimmy Lu's
Joe's Crab Shack
Johnny Orleans
Kirby's Steakhse.
Kirby's Steakhse./FW
La Calle Doce
La Mirabelle
Landry's Seafood
La Trattoria Lombardi
Lauderdale's on the Lake/FW
Laurels
Lefty's Lobster
Lucile's Stateside Bistro/FW
Mac's
Maguire's
Mansion on Turtle Creek
Martini Ranch
Matt's No Place
Matt's Rancho Martinez
Mediterraneo
Mezza Mediterranean/FW
Michaels/FW
Monica's Aca y Alla
Morton's
Mustang Cafe/FW
Nana Grill
Nick & Sam's
Old San Fran Steak
Palm Restaurant
Palomino Euro Bistro
Pappas Bros. Steakhse.
Pour House/FW
Pyramid Grill
Ranchman's Cafe/FW
Razzoo's Cajun Cafe/FW
Reata/FW
Rick's on Bricks/FW
Rock Bottom Brewery
Ruth's Chris
Saltgrass Steak
Saltgrass Steak/FW
Salve!
Sambuca Jazz Cafe
San Francisco Rose
Stoneleigh P
St. Pete's Dancing Marlin
Texas de Brazil
Texas de Brazil/FW
Thomas Ave. Beverage
III Forks
Trail Dust Steak
Voltaire

Dancing/Entertainment
(Check days, times and performers for entertainment; D=dancing; best of many)
Al-Amir (belly dancer/DJ)
Avanti Euro Bistro (jazz)
Avanti Ristorante (jazz)
Baby Doe's (D/50s & 60s band)
Basha Med. (belly dancer)
Bavarian Gr. (accordion/Dixieland)
Beau Nash (jazz/piano)
Bella Italia/FW (classical guitar)
Byblos/FW (belly dancer)
Cafe Aspen/FW (jazz/piano)
Cafe Brazil (D/varies)
Cafe Capri (harp)
Cafe Cipriani/FW (piano)
Cafe Istanbul (D/belly dancer)
Cafe Izmir (guitarist)
Cafe Madrid (flamenco/guitar)
Capital Grille (piano)
Chaparral Club (D/jazz)
Cool River Cafe/FW (D/band/DJ)
Daddy Jack's Wood Grill (piano)

Dakota's (piano)
Del Frisco's (piano)
Dick's Last Resort (band)
Edelweiss/FW (D/German band)
8.0/FW (D/varies)
Fiesta Mexican/FW (varies)
Fish (piano)
Fishmong./FW (country & west.)
Flying Saucer (band)
Flying Saucer/FW (band)
Franki's Li'l Europe (varies)
French Room (D/piano/vocals)
Gershwin's (piano)
Hard Rock Cafe (band)
Hedary's (belly dancer)
Henk's (accordion)
Hoffbrau Steaks (blues)
Houston's (piano)
H³ Ranch/FW (D)
Humperdink's/FW (DJ/karaoke)
Il Sorrento (accordion/piano)
Italian Villa/FW (piano)
Jasmine (piano)
Joe T. Garcia's/FW (mariachi)
Kirby's Steakhse. (piano)
Kirby's Steakhse./FW (piano)
Kuby's Sausage (accordion)
La Calle Doce (vocals)
Lauderdale's/FW (country/reggae)
Laurels (harp/piano)
La Valentina (mariachi)
Les Saisons (piano/band)
Lombardi Mare (jazz)
Lonesome Dove/FW (piano)
Magic Time (costumed servers)
Maguire's (jazz)
Mansion/Turtle Creek (D/varies)
Marie Gabrielle (varies)
Marty's Wine Bar (jazz/vocals)
Mattito's (salsa)
Medieval Times (med. tourn.)
Mediterraneo (guitar)
Melting Pot (magician)
Mercado Juarez (mariachi)
Mezza Med./FW (swing)
Michaels/FW (varies)
Michel/Balcony/FW (jazz/piano)
Monica's (D/Latin jazz)
Nana Grill (jazz)
Nick & Sam's (piano)
Nuevo Leon (keyboard)
Oasis/FW (band)
Old San Fran Steak (D/dancers)
Old Warsaw (piano/violin)
Palermo's Pizza/FW (varies)

Pappadeaux Seafood (bands)
Pappadeaux Seafood/FW (band)
Pappas Bros. Steakhse. (piano)
Parigi (jazz/vocals)
Pegasus/FW (guitar/viola)
Piccolo Mondo/FW (piano)
Portofino/FW (piano)
Pour House/FW (varies)
Pyramid Grill (piano)
Rainforest/FW (bird training show)
Riscky Rita's/FW (band)
Rock Bottom (D/bands/DJ)
Rough Creek Lodge/FW (jazz)
Royal Toyko (piano)
Ruffino's/FW (piano)
Ruggeri's (piano)
Sambuca Jazz Cafe (D/jazz)
San Fran. Rose (guitar/vocals)
Sardines/FW (jazz)
Sipango (D/band)
Soho Food (jazz)
St. Pete's (guitar/vocals)
Sullivan's (band)
Tenaya/FW (varies)
Teppo (harp)
Terilli's (jazz)
Texana Grill/FW (Texas country)
Texas de Brazil/FW (big band)
III Forks (piano)
Trail Dust Steak (band)
Trail Dust Steak/FW (band)
Two Rows (DJ)

Delivers*/Takeout

(Nearly all Asians, coffee shops, delis, diners and pasta/pizzerias deliver or do takeout; here are some interesting possibilities; D=delivery, T=takeout; *call to check range and charges, if any)

Abuelo's/FW (T)
Avanti Euro Bistro (D,T)
Avanti Rest. (T)
Avanti Ristorante (D,T)
Babe's Chicken/FW (T)
Bayley's/FW (T)
Bellagio/FW (T)
Bella Italia/FW (T)
Big Fish, Little Fish (T)
Bistral (T)
Bistro A (T)
Bistro Louise/FW (D,T)

Bodacious Bar-B-Q/FW (T)
Breadwinners Cafe (D,T)
Byblos/FW (T)
Cabo Mix-Mex/FW (T)
Cactus Flower Cafe/FW (T)
Cafe Aspen/FW (D,T)
Cafe Athenée (T)
Cafe Cipriani/FW (T)
Cafe 1187/FW (T)
Cafe Express (T)
Cafe Izmir (D,T)
Cantina Laredo (T)
Canyon Cafe (T)
Charleston's/FW (T)
Charlie's Cafe/FW (T)
Cheesecake Factory (T)
Chili's Grill & Bar/FW (D,T)
City Cafe to Go (D,T)
Clark's Outpost (T)
Classic Cafe/FW (T)
Cozymel's (D)
Cozymel's/FW (T)
Daddy Jack's Lobster (T)
Daddy Jack's Wood Grill (T)
Daddy Jack's Wood Grill/FW (T)
Deep Ellum Cafe (T)
Desperados Mexican (D,T)
Dick Clark's/FW (T)
Dickey's Barbecue (D,T)
Dickey's Barbecue/FW (D,T)
Dovie's (T)
Dream Cafe (D,T)
EatZi's (D,T)
Edelweiss/FW (T)
El Chico (T)
El Chico/FW (T)
El Fenix (T)
El Fenix/FW (T)
El Norte Grill (D,T)
El Paseo/FW (T)
El Rancho Grande/FW (T)
Empire Baking Co. (D,T)
Esparza's/FW (T)
Esperanza's/FW (T)
Fernandez Cafe/FW (T)
Fish (T)
Fuddruckers (D,T)
Fuddruckers/FW (D,T)
Gloria's (T)
Good Eats (D,T)
Good Eats/FW (D,T)
Grady's (T)
Grady's/FW (T)
Grape (T)
Grape Escape/FW (T)

Hedary's/FW (T)
Highland Pk. Pharmacy (T)
Hot Damn, Tamales!/FW (T)
Houston's (T)
H^3 Ranch/FW (T)
I Fratelli/FW (D,T)
India Palace (D,T)
Italian Villa/FW (T)
JinBeh/FW (T)
Joe's Crab Shack (T)
Johnny Orleans (D,T)
Jons Grille/FW (D,T)
Kel's (T)
Kincaid's Hamburgers/FW (T)
Kostas Cafe (T)
Kuby's Sausage (D,T)
La Calle Doce (T)
La Dolce Vita (T)
La Hacienda Ranch (T)
La Hacienda Ranch/FW (T)
La Madeleine (T)
La Madeleine/FW (T)
Landry's Seafood (T)
La Playa Maya/FW (T)
La Trattoria Lombardi (D,T)
Lauderdale's on the Lake/FW (T)
La Valentina de Mexico (T)
Lavendou (D,T)
Lefty's Lobster (T)
Leonardo's (T)
Les Saisons (T)
Lombardi Mare (T)
Lonesome Dove/FW (D,T)
Los Amigos/FW (T)
Los Vaqueros (D,T)
Lucile's Stateside Bistro/FW (T)
Luna de Noche (T)
Mac's (T)
Mac's/FW (T)
Maggiano's (T)
Maguire's (T)
Maharaja/FW (D,T)
Mainstream Fish (T)
Mancuso's/FW (T)
Margaux's (T)
Marie Gabrielle (T)
Mario & Alberto (T)
Mario's Chiquita (T)
Marty's Wine Bar (D,T)
Mattito's (T)
Mercado Juarez (T)
Mezza Mediterranean/FW (T)
Michaels/FW (D,T)
Michel at Balcony/FW (T)
Mike Salerno's/FW (T)

Monica's Aca y Alla (T)
Mustang Cafe/FW (D,T)
Natalie's (D,T)
Nate's Seafood & Steak (T)
Newport's Seafood (T)
North Main BBQ/FW (T)
Nuevo Leon (D,T)
Oasis/FW (T)
Old Chicago (T)
On the Border/FW (T)
Pappadeaux Seafood (T)
Pappadeaux Seafood/FW (D,T)
Parthenon/FW (D,T)
Patrizio (T)
Pegasus/FW (T)
Picardy's Shrimp Shop (D,T)
Piccolo Mondo/FW (T)
Planet Hollywood (T)
Poor Richard's Cafe (T)
PoPoLos Cafe (T)
Pour House/FW (D,T)
Queen of Sheba (D,T)
Railhead Smokehse./FW (T)
Ranchman's Cafe/FW (T)
Razzoo's Cajun Cafe (T)
Razzoo's Cajun Cafe/FW (T)
Red Hot & Blue (D,T)
Red Hot & Blue/FW (D,T)
Remington's Seafood (T)
Riscky Rita's/FW (T)
Rock Bottom Brewery (T)
Rockfish Seafood (T)
Rockfish Seafood/FW (T)
Rooster (T)
Ruggeri's (D,T)
S & D Oyster Co. (T)
S & S Tearoom (D,T)
Sapristi!/FW (T)
Sardines/FW (T)
Scampi's/FW (D,T)
Sevy's Grill (T)
Shrimpers/FW (T)
Sipango (T)
St. Pete's Dancing Marlin (T)
Tenaya/FW (T)
Terilli's (T)
Texas de Brazil (T)
Thomas Ave. Beverage (T)
Tia's Tex-Mex (D,T)
Tillman's Corner (T)
Tony Roma's (D,T)
Tony Roma's/FW (D,T)
Trail Dust Steak (T)
Trail Dust Steak/FW (T)
Tupinamba (T)

Two Rows (T)
Via Real/FW (T)
Water St. Seafood/FW (T)
Willhoite's/FW (T)
Yoli's Seafood (T)

Dessert/Ice Cream
Celebrity Cafe
Charlie's Cafe/FW
City Cafe to Go
French Room
Hennington's Cafe/FW
Highland Pk. Pharmacy
Jubilee Cafe/FW
Kathleen's Art Cafe
Lady Primrose's
La Madeleine
La Madeleine/FW
Purple Cow
Randall's/FW
Wild About Harry's

Dining Alone
(Other than hotels, coffee shops, sushi bars and places with counter service)
Abuelo's/FW
A.J. Gonzales'
Alfredo Trattoria
Ali Baba Cafe
Amici
Angelo's BBQ/FW
Angry Dog
Avanti Ristorante
Avila's
Babe's Chicken/FW
Bangkok Cuisine/FW
Bistral
Bistro Louise/FW
Black-eyed Pea
Buffet at Kimbell/FW
Cafe Madrid
Campisi's
Chili's Grill & Bar
Chow Thai Addison
Chuy's
Ciudad
Cozymel's
Crescent City Cafe
Deep Ellum Cafe
Dick Clark's/FW
Dunston's Steakhse.
El Fenix/FW
Fernandez Cafe/FW
Fresco Grill

Gennie's Bishop Grill
Gilbert's N.Y. Deli
Good Eats
Grady's
Grape Escape/FW
Herrera's
Houston's
I Fratelli/FW
Il Grano
JinBeh/FW
Joe's Crab Shack
Kalachandji's
Kathleen's Art Cafe
Kel's
Kuby's Sausage
La Creme
Lady Primrose's
La Familia/FW
Landry's Seafood
Liberty
Maharaja/FW
Mainstream Fish
Mama's Daughters'
Mama's Daughters'/FW
Matt's Rancho Martinez
Mecca
Mi Cocina/FW
MoMo's
Mr. G's Deli
Nate's Seafood & Steak
Nicola's
Nuevo Leon
On the Border
Pappadeaux Seafood
Pappadeaux Seafood/FW
Pappasito's Cantina
Patrizio
Poor Richard's Cafe
PoPoLos Cafe
Pour House/FW
Primo's
Purdy's
Red Hot & Blue
Red Hot & Blue/FW
Rockfish Seafood
Sapristi!/FW
Seventeen Seventeen
Snuffer's
Steak N' Ale
Street's Famous
Taco Diner
Tia's Tex-Mex
Tillman's Corner
Tony Roma's
Tony Roma's/FW
Tramontana
Truluck's
Uncle Julio's
Vincent's Seafood
Wild About Harry's
Zodiac/FW

Expense Account
Angeluna/FW
AquaKnox
Bistro Louise/FW
Bob's Steak
Cacharel/FW
Del Frisco's/FW
Enigma
Escargot/FW
French Room
Landmark
Lawry's
Mansion on Turtle Creek
Nana Grill
Nick & Sam's
Old Warsaw
Pappas Bros. Steakhse.
Riviera
Rough Creek Lodge/FW
Ruth's Chris
Saint-Emilion/FW
Star Canyon
III Forks
Voltaire
York St.

Family Appeal
Abuelo's/FW
Al's Pizzeria
Amore Italian
Angelo's
August Moon
Aw Shucks
Babe's Chicken/FW
Baker's Ribs
Ball's Hamburgers
Bangkok Cuisine/FW
Bavarian Grill
Bayley's/FW
Benihana of Tokyo
Black-eyed Pea
Blue Goose Cantina
Bubba's
Cafe 1187/FW
Campisi's
Casa Rosa
Celebration
Charlie's Cafe/FW
Chuck E. Cheese's

Clark's Outpost
Copeland's
Cousin's Pit BBQ/FW
Cozymel's
Cozymel's/FW
David's BBQ/FW
Dick Clark's/FW
Dickey's Barbecue
Dickey's Barbecue/FW
Dodie's Seafood Cafe
Edelweiss/FW
El Paseo/FW
El Rancho Grande/FW
EZ's
Fernandez Cafe/FW
Fiesta Mexican/FW
Gilbert's N.Y. Deli
Gloria's
Herrera's
I Love Sushi/FW
India Palace
JinBeh/FW
Joe's Crab Shack
Joe T. Garcia's/FW
Jubilee Cafe/FW
Kobe Steaks
Kuby's Sausage
La Familia/FW
La Hacienda Ranch/FW
Los Vaqueros
Lover's Egg Roll
Lover's Egg Roll/FW
Lucky's Cafe
Maggiano's
Magic Time Machine
Maharaja/FW
Mai's Vietnamese
Mama's Daughters'
Mama's Daughters'/FW
Mario & Alberto
Mario's Chiquita
Massey's/FW
Medieval Times
Melting Pot
Mercado Juarez
Mia's Tex-Mex
MoMo's Pasta
Old Chicago
Olive Garden
Olive Garden/FW
On the Border
On the Border/FW
Outback Steakhse.
Outback Steakhse./FW
Pappadeaux Seafood

Pappadeaux Seafood/FW
Paris Coffee Shop/FW
Peggy Sue BBQ
Picardy's Shrimp Shop
Pietro's
Prima Pasta/FW
Railhead Smokehse./FW
Rainforest Cafe/FW
Royal Toyko
S & D Oyster Co.
Spaghetti Warehse.
Spaghetti Warehse./FW
Texas Land & Cattle
Texas Land & Cattle/FW
Tony Roma's

Fireplace
Al Biernat's
Bella Italia/FW
Blue Mesa Grill/FW
Cafe Aspen/FW
City Cafe
Compari's
Cool River Cafe/FW
Cozymel's
Dakota's
Del Frisco's
Dovie's
Dunston's Steakhse.
Edelweiss/FW
Firehouse
French Room
Hedary's
Hôtel St. Germain
Joe T. Garcia's/FW
Kirby's Steakhse.
La Calle Doce
Lauderdale's on the Lake/FW
Laurels
Mattito's
MoMo's
Nuevo Leon
Pappas Bros. Steakhse.
Patrizio
Rock Bottom Brewery
Rough Creek Lodge/FW
Ruth's Chris
Saltgrass Steak
Saltgrass Steak/FW
Star Canyon
Tenaya/FW
Texana Grill/FW
Texas Land & Cattle
Texas Land & Cattle/FW
III Forks

Via Real/FW
Voltaire

Game in Season
Abacus
Amici
Angry Dog
Aw Shucks
Bavarian Grill
Bella Italia/FW
Big Buck Brewery/FW
Bruno's/FW
Cacharel/FW
Cafe Aspen/FW
Cafe on the Green/FW
Chamberlain's
Champps Americana
Ciudad
Dakota's
Flying Saucer Draught
Flying Saucer Draught/FW
Hofstetter's Spargel
Hôtel St. Germain
Il Sole
Jennivine
Laurels
Lonesome Dove/FW
Matt's No Place
Michaels/FW
Mi Piaci
Monica's Aca y Alla
Nana Grill
Pappas Bros. Steakhse.
Paul's Porterhouse
Pegasus/FW
Railhead Smokehse./FW
Rockfish Seafood/FW
Rough Creek Lodge/FW
Salve!
Tenaya/FW
Texas de Brazil/FW
Watel's

Happy Hour
(Check hours and locations)
Angelo's BBQ/FW
Angeluna/FW
Avanti Rest.
Blue Goose Cantina
Blue Mesa Grill
Blue Mesa Grill/FW
Canyon Cafe
Citizen
Ciudad
Corner Bakery
Cozymel's/FW
Dave & Buster's
Desperados Mexican
Dick's Last Resort
El Fenix
El Paseo/FW
Firehouse
Flying Saucer Draught
Flying Saucer Draught/FW
Gloria's
Green Room
Hard Rock Cafe
Hoffbrau Steaks
Humperdink's
Humperdink's/FW
Jaxx Cafe
Joe's Crab Shack
Joe T. Garcia's/FW
La Valentina de Mexico
Mercado Juarez
Mi Cocina/FW
Monica's Aca y Alla
Nana Grill
On the Border
Palomino Euro Bistro
Patrizio
Primo's
Rock Bottom Brewery
S & D Oyster Co.
Shrimpers/FW
St. Martin's
Stoneleigh P
Sushi Masa
Terilli's
Texana Grill/FW
T.G.I. Friday's
T.G.I. Friday's/FW
Tony Roma's
Uncle Julio's
Via Real/FW

Historic Interest
(Year opened; *building)
1885 Newport's Seafood*
1889 Clark's Outpost*
1891 S & D Oyster Co.*
1893 Hennington's Cafe/FW*
1902 Spagh.Warehse./FW*
  (Exchange)
1906 Hôtel St. Germain*
1907 H^3 Ranch/FW*
1910 Sonny Bryan's (Inwood)
1912 French Room*
1918 El Fenix (McKinney)
1921 Highland Pk. Pharmacy

1924 Sushi at Stoneleigh*
1925 Fish*
1925 Mansion on Turtle Creek
1929 S & S Tearoom
1931 Dovie's*
1935 Joe T. Garcia's/FW
1947 Cattleman's/FW
1948 El Rancho Grande/FW
1948 Old Warsaw

Hotel Dining

Adam's Mark Hotel
  Chaparral Club
Courtyard by Marriott Hotel
  Corner Bakery/FW
Fairmont Hotel
  Pyramid Grill
Four Seasons Resort & Club
  Cafe on the Green/FW
Hotel Adolphus
  French Room
Hotel Crescent Court
  Beau Nash
  Lady Primrose's
  Palomino Euro Bistro
  We Oui
Hôtel St. Germain
  Hôtel St. Germain
Hyatt Regency Dallas
  Antares
Mansion on Turtle Creek
  Mansion on Turtle Creek
Melrose Hotel
  Landmark
Nutt House Hotel
  Hennington's Cafe/FW
Omni Mandalay Hotel
  Trevi's/FW
Paramount Hotel
  Fish
Renaissance Worthington Hotel
  Star of Texas Grill/FW
Rough Creek Lodge
  Rough Creek Lodge/FW
Stockyards Hotel
  H³ Ranch/FW
Stoneleigh Hotel
  Sushi at Stoneleigh
Westin Galleria Dallas
  Huntington's
Westin Park Central Hotel
  Laurels
Wyndham Anatole Hotel
  Nana Grill

"In" Places

Abacus
Angeluna/FW
AquaKnox
Avanti Rest.
Beau Nash
Bistro A
Bistro Louise/FW
Cafe Pacific
Ciudad
Cool River Cafe/FW
EatZi's
8.0/FW
Escargot/FW
Fizzi/FW
Flying Saucer Draught/FW
Green Room
La Piazza/FW
Liberty
Mansion on Turtle Creek
Mercury
Michaels/FW
Nick & Sam's
Palomino Euro Bistro
Pegasus/FW
Salve!
Samba Room
Sambuca Jazz Cafe
Sapristi!/FW
We Oui

Jacket Required

French Room
Mansion on Turtle Creek
Nana Grill
Old Warsaw
Riviera
Sipango
Star of Texas Grill/FW

Late Late – After 12:30

(All hours are AM; *check locations)
Cafe Brazil (24 hrs.)*
Cool River Cafe/FW (1)
Flying Saucer Draught (2)*
Humperdink's (1:30)*
Humperdink's/FW (1:30)
Samba Room (1)
San Francisco Rose (1)
Snuffer's (2)*
T.G.I. Friday's (1)*

Meet for a Drink
(Most top hotels and the following standouts)
Abuelo's/FW
Al Biernat's
AquaKnox
Avanti Euro Bistro
Avanti Rest.
Aw Shucks
Blue Mesa Grill
Bob's Steak
Canyon Cafe
Capital Grille
Champps Americana
Citizen
Ciudad
Daddy Jack's Lobster
Dakota's
Dave & Buster's
Del Frisco's
Desperados Mexican
Dick's Last Resort
8.0/FW
El Fenix
Firehouse
Fizzi/FW
Flying Saucer Draught
Flying Saucer Draught/FW
Gershwin's
Gloria's
Grape
Grape Escape/FW
Green Room
Humperdink's
Humperdink's/FW
I Love Sushi/FW
Joe T. Garcia's/FW
Lawry's
Liberty
Lombardi Mare
Los Vaqueros
Mac's
Mac's/FW
Maguire's
Mario & Alberto
Martini Ranch
Mattito's
Mediterraneo
Mercury
Mia's Tex-Mex
Mi Cocina
Mi Cocina/FW
Mi Piaci
Monica's Aca y Alla
Morton's
Mustang Cafe/FW
Nick & Sam's
Old Warsaw
On the Border
Palm Restaurant
Patrizio
P.F. Chang's
PoPoLos Cafe
Pour House/FW
Primo's
Reata/FW
Rock Bottom Brewery
Ruggeri's
Ruth's Chris
Salve!
Samba Room
Sambuca Jazz Cafe
Sevy's Grill
Sipango
Star Canyon
St. Martin's
Stoneleigh P
St. Pete's Dancing Marlin
Sullivan's
Terilli's
T.G.I. Friday's
Thomas Ave. Beverage
III Forks
Trail Dust Steak
Truluck's
Via Real/FW
Voltaire
Ziziki's

Noteworthy Newcomers (17)
Ciudad
Escargot/FW
Fizzi/FW
Gopal
Jeroboam
Lola
Lonesome Dove/FW
Mezza Mediterranean/FW
Mignon
Pegasus/FW
Rough Creek Lodge/FW
Salve!
Samui Thai
Sapristi!/FW
Taqueria Canonita
Voltaire
We Oui

Offbeat
Ali Baba Cafe
Angeluna/FW
Angry Dog
Basha Mediterranean
Bronx
Cafe Istanbul
Cafe Izmir
Cafe Madrid
Crescent City Cafe
East Wind
Edelweiss/FW
8.0/FW
Enigma
Fogo de Chao
Hennington's Cafe/FW
J & J Oyster Bar/FW
Kincaid's Hamburgers/FW
Matt's No Place
Poor Richard's Cafe
Rainforest Cafe/FW
San Francisco Rose
Shrimpers/FW
Sushi Masa
Texas de Brazil
Traci's
Trail Dust Steak

Outdoor Dining
(G=garden; P=patio;
S=sidewalk; T=terrace;
W=waterside; best of many)
Anderson's BBQ House (P)
Angeluna/FW (P)
AquaKnox (P,W)
Arcodoro & Pomodoro (P)
Avanti Euro Bistro (S)
Avanti Rest. (W)
Avanti Ristorante (P)
Bella Italia/FW (G,P)
Big Buck Brewery/FW (P)
Big Fish, Little Fish (P)
Bistro Louise/FW (P)
Blue Goose (Greenville) (P)
Blue Mesa Grill (P)
Blue Mesa Grill/FW (P)
Bobby Valentine's/FW (P)
Breadwinners Cafe (G,P)
Bronx (P)
Bubba's (P)
Cafe Express (G,W)
Cafe Highland Park (P)
Cafe Istanbul (P)
Cafe Izmir (P)
Cafe Madrid (P)
Cafe Pacific (T)
Canyon Cafe (P)
Champps Americana (P)
Charleston's/FW (P)
Charley's Hamburgers/FW (P)
Chez Gérard (T)
Cisco Grill (P)
Citizen (P)
Ciudad (G,P)
Clair de Lune (P)
Compari's (P)
Cozymel's (G,P)
Cozymel's/FW (G,P)
Dakota's (P,W)
Deep Ellum Cafe (P)
Desperados Mexican (P)
Dick's Last Resort (P)
Dodie's Seafood Cafe (P)
Dream Cafe (P)
EatZi's (P)
8.0/FW (P)
El Chico/FW (P)
Fishbowl (P,W)
Franki's Li'l Europe (P)
Grape Escape/FW (P,S)
Hoffbrau Steaks/FW (P)
Il Grano (P)
I Love Sushi/FW (G)
Il Sole (P)
Jennivine (G)
Jimmy Lu's (P)
Joe's Crab Shack (P)
Joe T. Garcia's/FW (P)
Kalachandji's (G)
La Calle Doce (P)
La Familia/FW (P)
La Piazza/FW (P)
La Playa Maya/FW (G,P)
La Trattoria Lombardi (P)
Lauderdale's on Lake/FW (P,W)
Liberty (P,W)
Los Vaqueros (P)
Maggiano's (P,T)
Maguire's (P)
Mansion on Turtle Creek (P,W)
Marie Gabrielle (G)
Martini Ranch (T)
Mattito's (G,P)
Matt's Rancho Martinez (P)
Mayuri/FW (P)
Michaels/FW (P,S)
Mi Cocina/FW (P)
Mi Piaci (P,W)
Monica's Aca y Alla (P)
Nuevo Leon (P)

Oasis/FW (P,W)
On the Border (P)
On the Border/FW (P)
Osaka Sushi (P)
Outback Steakhse. (P)
Pappasito's Cantina/FW (P)
Parigi (P)
Patrizio (P)
P.F. Chang's (P)
Primo's (P)
Randy's Steakhse. (P)
Razzoo's Cajun Cafe (P)
Razzoo's Cajun Cafe/FW (P)
Riscky Rita's/FW (P)
Rock Bottom Brewery (P)
Romano's Macaroni (P)
Rooster (P)
Rough Creek Lodge/FW (T)
Ruffino's/FW (P)
Ruggeri's (P)
Saltgrass Steak (P)
Saltgrass Steak/FW (P)
Salve! (G,P,W)
Samba Room (P)
Sambuca Jazz Cafe (P)
Sammy's BBQ (P)
S & S Tearoom (T)
San Francisco Rose (P)
Sapristi!/FW (P,S)
Sardines/FW (P)
Scampi's/FW (P)
Sea Grill (P)
Seventeen Seventeen (T)
Sevy's Grill (P)
Shrimpers/FW (P)
Sipango (P)
Snuffer's (P)
Soho Food (P)
Star Canyon (P)
Stoneleigh P (P)
St. Pete's Dancing Marlin (P)
Sushi on McKinney (P)
Szechuan Chinese/FW (P)
Taco Diner (P)
Taqueria Canonita (P)
Tenaya/FW (P)
Teppo (P)
Terilli's (P,S)
Texas de Brazil (P)
Thomas Ave. Beverage (P)
Traci's (P)
Trevi's/FW (P,S,T)
Two Rows (P)
Ziziki's (P)

Parties & Private Rooms

(Any nightclub or restaurant charges less at off-times;
* indicates private rooms available; best of many)
Abacus*
Al Biernat's*
Alfredo Trattoria*
Angelo's*
Antares*
AquaKnox*
Arcodoro & Pomodoro*
August Moon*
Avanti Euro Bistro*
Avanti Rest.
Avanti Ristorante*
Bangkok City*
Barbec's*
Basha Mediterranean*
Bellagio/FW
Bella Italia/FW*
Benihana of Tokyo*
Benito's/FW*
Big Buck Brewery/FW
Big Fish, Little Fish*
Bistro Louise/FW*
Blue Mesa Grill*
Blue Mesa Grill/FW*
Byblos/FW*
Cacharel/FW*
Cafe Aspen/FW*
Cafe Capri*
Cafe Cipriani/FW*
Cafe Highland Park*
Cafe Pacific
Canyon Cafe*
Capital Grille*
Carrabba's*
Casa Rosa*
Cattleman's/FW*
Chamberlain's*
Champps Americana
Chaparral Club*
City Cafe*
Ciudad*
Classic Cafe/FW
Compari's*
Cool River Cafe/FW*
Daddy Jack's Wood Grill*
Daddy Jack's Wood Grill/FW*
Dakota's*
Dave & Buster's*
Del Frisco's*
Del Frisco's/FW*
Desperados Mexican*

- Dick's Last Resort*
- Dunston's Steakhse.*
- Edelweiss/FW
- Ferrari's*
- Fogo de Chao
- Fox & Hound*
- Gershwin's*
- Grape
- Green Room*
- Hennington's Cafe/FW
- Hofstetter's Spargel*
- Hôtel St. Germain*
- H^3 Ranch/FW*
- Il Sole*
- Il Sorrento*
- Jasmine*
- Javier's*
- Jeroboam*
- Jimmy Lu's*
- Joe's Crab Shack*
- Joe T. Garcia's/FW*
- Kathleen's Art Cafe*
- Kirby's Steakhse.*
- Kostas Cafe
- La Dolce Vita*
- L'Ancestral
- Landry's Seafood*
- La Piazza/FW*
- La Trattoria Lombardi*
- Lauderdale's on the Lake/FW*
- Laurels*
- La Valentina de Mexico*
- Lavendou*
- Lawry's*
- Lombardi Mare*
- Luna de Noche*
- Maggiano's*
- Magic Time Machine*
- Maguire's*
- Mancuso's/FW
- Mansion on Turtle Creek*
- Marie Gabrielle*
- Martini Ranch*
- Mattito's*
- Matt's Rancho Martinez
- May Dragon*
- Medieval Times
- Mediterraneo*
- Mercado Juarez
- Mezza Mediterranean/FW*
- Michel at Balcony/FW*
- Mi Piaci*
- MoMo's*
- MoMo's Pasta*
- Monica's Aca y Alla
- Morton's*
- Mustang Cafe/FW*
- Nana Grill*
- Newport's Seafood*
- Nicholini's Seafood*
- Nick & Sam's*
- Norma's Cafe*
- Nuevo Leon*
- Oasis/FW*
- Old San Fran Steak*
- Old Warsaw*
- Palm Restaurant*
- Pappas Bros. Steakhse.*
- Patrizio*
- Paul's Porterhouse*
- P.F. Chang's
- Piccolo Mondo/FW*
- Planet Hollywood*
- PoPoLos Cafe*
- Portofino/FW*
- Pyramid Grill*
- Randy's Steakhse.
- Razzoo's Cajun Cafe
- Reata/FW*
- Riviera*
- Rock Bottom Brewery*
- Rockfish Seafood
- Rodolfo's*
- Rooster*
- Rough Creek Lodge/FW*
- Royal Toyko*
- Ruggeri's*
- Ruth's Chris*
- Salve!*
- Samba Room
- Sambuca Jazz Cafe*
- Sammy's BBQ
- Samui Thai*
- San Francisco Rose*
- Sardines/FW*
- Seventeen Seventeen*
- Sevy's Grill*
- Sipango*
- Star Canyon*
- St. Martin's*
- Stoneleigh P
- St. Pete's Dancing Marlin*
- Sullivan's*
- Sushi Masa*
- Szechuan Chinese/FW*
- Szechwan Pavilion*
- Taco Diner
- Taqueria Canonita
- Tenaya/FW*
- Terilli's

Texas Land & Cattle*
Texas Land & Cattle/FW*
Thai Orchid
Thai Taste*
Thomas Ave. Beverage*
III Forks*
Tillman's Corner
Tony Roma's*
Traci's*
Tramontana*
Truluck's*
Tupinamba*
Two Rows*
Uncle Julio's
Via Real/FW*
Vincent's Seafood*
Voltaire*
Yoli's Seafood
Ziziki's*
Zodiac*
Zodiac/FW
ZuZu

People-Watching
Abacus
Al Biernat's
Angeluna/FW
AquaKnox
Avanti Rest.
Beau Nash
Bistro A
Bistro Louise/FW
Bob's Steak
Cafe Highland Park
Cafe Pacific
Cheesecake Factory
Chez Gérard
Cool River Cafe/FW
Del Frisco's
EatZi's
Fishbowl
Fizzi/FW
Green Room
Il Sole
JinBeh/FW
Liberty
Mansion on Turtle Creek
Mercury
Michaels/FW
Nick & Sam's
Palm Restaurant
Patrizio
Pegasus/FW
Pyramid Grill
Rainforest Cafe/FW
Reata/FW
Riviera
Salve!
Samba Room
Sambuca Jazz Cafe
Sipango
Star Canyon
Voltaire
We Oui

Power Scene
Angeluna/FW
AquaKnox
Beau Nash
Cacharel/FW
Cafe Pacific
Capital Grille
Chaparral Club
Del Frisco's
Del Frisco's/FW
Fishbowl
La Piazza/FW
Mansion on Turtle Creek
Morton's
Palm Restaurant
Riviera
Ruth's Chris
Saint-Emilion/FW
Salve!
Samba Room
Voltaire

Pre-Theater/ Early Bird Menu
(Call to check prices, days and times)
Adelmo's
Dakota's
Dream Cafe
Grape
Newport's Seafood
On the Border
Steak N' Ale

Post-Theater/ Late Supper Menu
(Call to check prices, days and times)
Avanti Euro Bistro
Avanti Ristorante
Cafe Madrid
Cool River Cafe/FW
Grape
Grape Escape/FW

Il Sole
Kathleen's Art Cafe
Lonesome Dove/FW
Mezza Mediterranean/FW
Michaels/FW
Old San Fran Steak
Palomino Euro Bistro
Snuffer's
Star of Texas Grill/FW
We Oui

Prix Fixe Menu
(Call to check prices,
days and times)
Adelmo's
Al Biernat's
AquaKnox
Basha Mediterranean
Beau Nash
Cacharel/FW
Cafe Izmir
Cafe on the Green/FW
Celebrity Cafe
Chaparral Club
Dakota's
Fogo de Chao
Franki's Li'l Europe
French Room
Grape
Green Room
Hôtel St. Germain
India Palace
Landmark
Laurels
Lavendou
Mansion on Turtle Creek
Nana Grill
Nuevo Leon
Osaka Sushi
Palm Restaurant
Pyramid Grill
Rough Creek Lodge/FW
Saint-Emilion/FW
Seventeen Seventeen
Texas de Brazil/FW
Traci's

Pub/Bar/Microbrewery
Big Buck Brewery/FW
El Fenix
Flying Saucer Draught/FW
Hoffbrau Steaks
Hoffbrau Steaks/FW
Humperdink's
Humperdink's/FW
Pour House/FW
Rock Bottom Brewery
Stoneleigh P
Two Rows

Quiet Conversation
Addison Cafe
Adelmo's
Alfredo Trattoria
Basha Mediterranean
Bistro Louise/FW
Bob's Steak
Cacharel/FW
Chez Gérard
City Cafe
Del Frisco's/FW
Enigma
Escargot/FW
Fish
Fogo de Chao
French Room
Hofstetter's Spargel
Hôtel St. Germain
Huntington's
Il Sorrento
Kirby's Steakhse.
La Mirabelle
L'Ancestral
Landmark
La Trattoria Lombardi
Lavendou
Lawry's
Les Saisons
Lombardi Mare
Margaux's
Michel at Balcony/FW
Morton's
Natalie's
Old San Fran Steak
Old Warsaw
Plano Cafe
Pyramid Grill
Ruggeri's
Ruth's Chris
S & S Tearoom
Suze
Tei Tei Robata Bar
Tramontana
Watel's
York St.

Raw Bar
Aw Shucks
Baby Doe's
Big Fish, Little Fish
Blue Fish

Citizen
Fishbowl
I Love Sushi/FW
J & J Oyster Bar/FW
Japanese Palace/FW
Nick & Sam's
Osaka Sushi
Remington's Seafood
Rockfish Seafood
Rockfish Seafood/FW
S & D Oyster Co.
Sea Grill
South Prairie Oyster/FW
Sushi at Stoneleigh
Sushi Masa
Sushi on McKinney
Sushi Zone/FW
Water St. Seafood/FW
We Oui
Yamaguchi

Reservations Essential
Abacus
Angeluna/FW
BKK - Narita/FW
Cafe Cipriani/FW
Capital Grille
Chaparral Club
Dakota's
Del Frisco's
Del Frisco's/FW
Fogo de Chao
Hôtel St. Germain
Jeroboam
Lady Primrose's
La Mirabelle
La Piazza/FW
La Trattoria Lombardi
Nana Grill
Old Warsaw
Parigi
Queen of Sheba
Rough Creek Lodge/FW
Saint-Emilion/FW
Samba Room
Sambuca Jazz Cafe
Sipango
Star Canyon
Texas de Brazil/FW
Thomas Ave. Beverage

Romantic
Adelmo's
Angeluna/FW
Bistro Louise/FW
Bob's Steak

Cacharel/FW
Cafe Highland Park
Chez Gérard
Dakota's
Del Frisco's/FW
Escargot/FW
French Room
Grape
Hôtel St. Germain
Il Sorrento
Jennivine
La Mirabelle
Landmark
La Piazza/FW
Lavendou
Mansion on Turtle Creek
Michel at Balcony/FW
Mi Piaci
Plano Cafe
Pyramid Grill
Randall's/FW
Saint-Emilion/FW
Suze
Watel's
York St.

Senior Appeal
August Moon
Bagel Chain
Bagelstein's
Baker's Ribs
Black-eyed Pea
Celebration
Chili's Grill & Bar
Corner Bakery
Corner Bakery/FW
David's BBQ/FW
Dickey's Barbecue/FW
Dunston's Steakhse.
Edelweiss/FW
El Chico
El Chico/FW
El Paseo/FW
El Rancho Grande/FW
Fernandez Cafe/FW
Fiesta Mexican/FW
Fishmonger's/FW
Fresh Choice
Fresh Choice/FW
Good Eats
Henk's European Deli
Hennington's Cafe/FW
Highland Pk. Pharmacy
Houston's
Jason's Deli

Jubilee Cafe/FW
Kuby's Sausage
La Calle Doce
La Creme
La Dolce Vita
Lady Primrose's
La Familia/FW
La Madeleine
Landry's Seafood
Mama's Daughters'
Mancuso's/FW
Margaux's
Massey's/FW
MoMo's
MoMo's Pasta
Natalie's
North Main BBQ/FW
Old Warsaw
Olive Garden
Olive Garden/FW
On the Border
Original Pancake Hse.
Piccolo Mondo/FW
Prima Pasta/FW
Red Hot & Blue/FW
Rockfish Seafood/FW
Rodolfo's
Romano's Macaroni/FW
S & S Tearoom
Spring Creek BBQ
Spring Creek BBQ/FW
Steak N' Ale
Texas Land & Cattle
Tillman's Corner
Tony Roma's
Trail Dust Steak
Vincent's Seafood
Yogi's Bagel/FW
York St.
Zodiac

Singles Scene

Angelo's BBQ/FW
Angeluna/FW
Bistro Louise/FW
Blue Fish
Blue Goose Cantina
Breadwinners Cafe
Champps Americana
Cool River Cafe/FW
Cozymel's/FW
East Wind
8.0/FW
Firehouse
Fishbowl

Flying Saucer Draught/FW
Gloria's
Green Room
Hoffbrau Steaks
Houston's
Humperdink's
Humperdink's/FW
Jennivine
Joe's Crab Shack
Joe T. Garcia's/FW
Jons Grille/FW
La Madeleine
Liberty
Mercury
MoMo's Pasta
Monica's Aca y Alla
On the Border
On the Border/FW
Patrizio
Piccolo Mondo/FW
Pour House/FW
Prima Pasta/FW
Sambuca Jazz Cafe
Spring Creek BBQ
Spring Creek BBQ/FW
St. Pete's Dancing Marlin
Sushi on McKinney
SushiSake
Texas Land & Cattle
T.G.I. Friday's
T.G.I. Friday's/FW
Thomas Ave. Beverage
Tony Roma's
Trail Dust Steak
Two Rows
Vincent's Seafood
Yamaguchi
Ziziki's

Sleepers
(Good to excellent food, but little known)
Alfredo Trattoria
Al's Pizzeria
Amici
Anderson's BBQ House
Avanti Euro Bistro
Avanti Rest.
Avanti Ristorante
Avila's
Babe's Chicken/FW
Bangkok City
Basha Mediterranean
Benito's/FW
BKK - Narita/FW

Blue Fish
Byblos/FW
Cafe Athenée
Cafe Capri
Cafe 1187/FW
Clark's Outpost
Classic Cafe/FW
Compari's
Covino's
Dodie's Seafood Cafe
El Norte Grill
El Paseo/FW
Esperanza's/FW
Firehouse
Franki's Li'l Europe
Gennie's Bishop Grill
Hedary's
Hedary's/FW
Henk's European Deli
Hot Damn, Tamales!/FW
I Fratelli/FW
I Love Sushi/FW
Italian Villa/FW
J & J Oyster Bar/FW
Kalachandji's
King Tut/FW
La Dolce Vita
La Mirabelle
Leonardo's
Mai's Vietnamese
Margaux's
Mario's Chiquita
Mike Salerno's/FW
Mr. G's Deli
Mr. Sushi
Nakamoto
Nicola's
Norma's Cafe
Old Chicago
On Broadway Rist./FW
Parthenon/FW
Paul's Porterhouse
Piccolo Mondo/FW
Poor Richard's Cafe
Prima Pasta/FW
Sunflower Shoppe/FW
Sushi at Stoneleigh
SushiSake
Tei Tei Robata Bar
Teppo
Thai Orchid
Theo's Diner
Thomas Ave. Beverage
Tillman's Corner
Tong's House
Yamaguchi
Yogi's Bagel/FW
Yoli's Seafood

Teenagers & Other Youthful Spirits
Bubba's
Casa Rosa
Champps Americana
Chili's Grill & Bar
Chili's Grill & Bar/FW
Cozymel's/FW
El Chico
El Chico
El Rancho Grande/FW
Fiesta Mexican/FW
Fuddruckers
Herrera's
Highland Pk. Pharmacy
Humperdink's
Jason's Deli
Jons Grille/FW
La Dolce Vita
On the Border
On the Border/FW
Original Pancake Hse.
Prima Pasta/FW
Rainforest Cafe/FW
Red Hot & Blue/FW
Romano's Macaroni
Spaghetti Warehse.
Spring Creek BBQ
Spring Creek BBQ/FW
T.G.I. Friday's
T.G.I. Friday's/FW
Tia's Tex-Mex
Tony Roma's
Tony Roma's/FW
Uncle Julio's

Theme Restaurant
Big Buck Brewery/FW
Chipotle Mexican Grill
Clark's Outpost
Copeland's
Cozymel's/FW
Edelweiss/FW
Humperdink's
Humperdink's/FW
Joe's Crab Shack
La Hacienda Ranch
La Hacienda Ranch/FW
Pappasito's Cantina
Planet Hollywood
Rainforest Cafe/FW
Razzoo's Cajun Cafe/FW

Wine/Beer Only

Ali Baba Cafe
Al's Pizzeria
Anderson's BBQ House
Angelo's
Angelo's BBQ/FW
Asia Arc-en-Ciel/FW
Avila's
Aw Shucks
Baker's Ribs
Ball's Hamburgers
Bangkok City
Basha Mediterranean
Bavarian Bakery/FW
Bellagio/FW
BKK - Narita/FW
Bodacious Bar-B-Q/FW
Buffet at Kimbell/FW
Cafe Brazil
Cafe Express
Cafe Istanbul
Cafe Izmir
Cafe Madrid
California Pizza Kit./FW
Carshon's Deli/FW
Chips
Corner Bakery
Corner Bakery/FW
Cousin's Pit BBQ/FW
Daddy Jack's Lobster
David's BBQ/FW
Dodie's Seafood Cafe
Dream Cafe
EatZi's
Esperanza's/FW
Fishmonger's/FW
Flying Saucer Draught
Flying Saucer Draught/FW
Fox & Hound
Fresco Grill
Fresh Choice
Fresh Choice/FW
Fuddruckers
Fuddruckers/FW
Grape Escape/FW
Hedary's/FW
Henk's European Deli
Herrera's
I Love Sushi/FW
Jason's Deli
Jason's Deli/FW
Jons Grille/FW
Jun Su Ree/FW
Kincaid's Hamburgers/FW
Kostas Cafe
Kuby's Sausage
Lady Primrose's
La Madeleine
La Madeleine/FW
Liberty
Luna de Noche
Mancuso's/FW
Mango Thai
Margaux's
Marty's Wine Bar
Massey's/FW
Mayuri/FW
Mia's Tex-Mex
Mi Cocina/FW
Mimi's Cafe
Mimi's Cafe/FW
MoMo's Pasta
On Broadway Rist./FW
Outback Steakhse.
Outback Steakhse./FW
Palermo's Pizza/FW
Parthenon/FW
Pietro's
Plano Cafe
Purdy's
Railhead Smokehse./FW
Randall's/FW
Royal Thai
Ruffino's/FW
Sal's Pizza
Saltgrass Steak
Sammy's BBQ
Samui Thai
S & D Oyster Co.
Sapristi!/FW
Sonny Bryan's
Sonny Bryan's/FW
South Prairie Oyster/FW
Spring Creek BBQ
Spring Creek BBQ/FW
Sushi Zone/FW
Suze
Taco Diner
Teppo
Texadelphia
Thai Orchid
Thai Soon
Thai Taste
York St.
Zodiac
Zodiac/FW
ZuZu

Winning Wine List

Abacus
Al Biernat's

Angeluna/FW
Bistro Louise/FW
Cacharel/FW
Cafe Pacific
City Cafe
Dakota's
Del Frisco's/FW
French Room
Grape
Grape Escape/FW
Hôtel St. Germain
Il Sole
Jeroboam
La Piazza/FW
Mansion on Turtle Creek
Marty's Wine Bar
Nana Grill
Nick & Sam's
Pyramid Grill
Randall's/FW
Riviera
Ruth's Chris
Salve!
St. Martin's
III Forks
Voltaire
Ziziki's

Young Children

(Besides the normal fast-food places; * indicates children's menu available)

Abuelo's/FW*
Amore Italian*
Angelo's*
Babe's Chicken/FW*
Barbec's
Bellagio/FW*
Benito's/FW*
Big Buck Brewery/FW*
Big Fish, Little Fish*
Blue Mesa Grill/FW*
Breadwinners Cafe*
Cactus Flower Cafe/FW*
Cafe on the Green/FW*
Campisi's*
Cantina Laredo*
Canyon Cafe*
Cathy's Wok*
Celebration*
Chamberlain's*
Champps Americana*
Charlie's Cafe/FW*
Cheesecake Factory
Chuck E. Cheese's*
Cisco Grill*
Classic Cafe/FW*
Compari's*
Corner Bakery*
Corner Bakery/FW*
Cozymel's*
Cozymel's/FW*
Dave & Buster's*
Dick Clark's/FW*
Dick's Last Resort*
Dream Cafe*
Dunston's Steakhse.*
El Chico/FW*
El Fenix*
El Fenix/FW*
El Norte Grill*
El Rancho Grande/FW
Esperanza's/FW*
Fernandez Cafe/FW*
Fiesta Mexican/FW*
Fresco Grill
Fresh Choice/FW*
Fuddruckers*
Fuddruckers/FW*
Good Eats*
Good Eats/FW*
Grady's*
Grady's/FW*
Hard Rock Cafe*
Hoffbrau Steaks*
Hoffbrau Steaks/FW*
Hofstetter's Spargel*
Humperdink's*
Humperdink's/FW*
Il Grano*
Joe's Crab Shack*
Joe T. Garcia's/FW*
Jons Grille/FW*
Jubilee Cafe/FW*
Kostas Cafe*
Kuby's Sausage*
La Calle Doce*
La Creme*
La Familia/FW*
La Hacienda Ranch*
La Hacienda Ranch/FW*
Landry's Seafood*
Lauderdale's on the Lake/FW*
Los Vaqueros*
Luna de Noche*
Mac's*
Mac's/FW*
Magic Time Machine*
Mainstream Fish*
Mancuso's/FW*

- Mario & Alberto*
- Mario's Chiquita*
- Massey's/FW*
- Mattito's*
- Matt's Rancho Martinez*
- Mercado Juarez*
- Mia's Tex-Mex*
- Mi Cocina*
- Mi Cocina/FW*
- Mike Salerno's/FW*
- Mr. G's Deli*
- Mustang Cafe/FW*
- Natalie's*
- Nate's Seafood & Steak*
- Newport's Seafood*
- Nicholini's Seafood*
- Norma's Cafe*
- Nuevo Leon*
- Oasis/FW*
- Old Chicago*
- Old San Fran Steak*
- On the Border*
- On the Border/FW*
- Original Pancake Hse.
- Original Pancake Hse.*
- Osaka Sushi*
- Outback Steakhse.*
- Outback Steakhse./FW*
- Palermo's Pizza/FW*
- Pappadeaux Seafood*
- Pappadeaux Seafood/FW*
- Pappasito's Cantina/FW*
- Pietro's
- Planet Hollywood*
- Plano Cafe*
- Poor Richard's Cafe*
- Prima Pasta/FW*
- Purple Cow*
- Purple Cow/FW*
- Rainforest Cafe/FW*
- Razzoo's Cajun Cafe*
- Razzoo's Cajun Cafe/FW*
- Red Hot & Blue*
- Red Hot & Blue/FW*
- Rockfish Seafood*
- Rockfish Seafood/FW*
- Romano's Macaroni*
- Romano's Macaroni/FW*
- Royal Toyko*
- Sal's Pizza*
- Saltgrass Steak*
- Saltgrass Steak/FW*
- S & D Oyster Co.*
- San Francisco Rose*
- Sevy's Grill*
- Snuffer's*
- Sonny Bryan's*
- Sonny Bryan's/FW*
- Spaghetti Warehse.*
- Spaghetti Warehse./FW*
- Spring Creek BBQ*
- Spring Creek BBQ/FW*
- Street's Famous*
- Sushi Masa*
- Suze*
- Taco Diner*
- Taqueria Canonita*
- Texadelphia*
- Texana Grill/FW*
- Texas Land & Cattle*
- Texas Land & Cattle/FW*
- T.G.I. Friday's*
- Tia's Tex-Mex*
- Tia's Tex-Mex/FW*
- Tong's House*
- Tony Roma's*
- Trail Dust Steak*
- Trail Dust Steak/FW*
- Two Rows*
- Uncle Julio's*
- Vincent's Seafood
- Wild About Harry's*
- Zodiac*

Wine Vintage Chart 1985-1999

This chart is designed to help you select wine to go with your meal. It is based on the same 0 to 30 scale used throughout this *Survey.* The ratings (prepared by our friend **Howard Stravitz**, a law professor at the University of South Carolina) reflect both the quality of the vintage and the wine's readiness for present consumption. Thus, if a wine is not fully mature or is over the hill, its rating has been reduced. We do not include 1987, 1991 or 1993 vintages because they are not especially recommended for most areas.

	'85	'86	'88	'89	'90	'92	'94	'95	'96	'97	'98	'99
WHITES												
French:												
Alsace	24	19	22	28	28	23	27	25	22	23	25	22
Burgundy	23	24	19	25	21	23	22	26	28	25	24	25
Loire Valley	–	–	–	26	25	–	22	24	26	23	22	23
Champagne	28	25	24	26	29	–	–	24	27	24	24	–
Sauternes	22	28	29	25	27	–	–	22	23	24	23	–
California:												
Chardonnay	–	–	–	–	–	–	22	26	22	26	23	26
REDS												
French:												
Bordeaux	26	27	25	28	29	18	24	25	24	23	24	22
Burgundy	24	–	23	26	29	22	21	26	27	25	24	25
Rhône	25	19	25	28	27	15	23	25	22	24	27	25
Beaujolais	–	–	–	–	–	–	–	23	21	24	23	24
California:												
Cab./Merlot	26	26	–	21	28	25	27	26	25	26	23	25
Zinfandel	–	–	–	–	–	–	26	25	24	23	22	23
Italian:												
Tuscany	26	–	23	–	26	–	23	25	19	28	25	24
Piedmont	25	–	25	28	28	–	–	23	26	28	26	25

May We Quote You?

Be a part of
ZAGAT SURVEY®

If you would like to participate in one of our Surveys or be added to our mailing list, please fill out this card and send it back to us.

☐ Mr. ☐ Mrs. ☐ Ms.

Your Name

Street Address   Apt #

City   State   Zip

e-mail Address

Occupation

I'd like to be a surveyor for the following city:

or a surveyor for U.S. Hotels, Resorts & Spas ☐

The city I visit most is: ─────────────

My favorite restaurant is: ─────────────

                      City

My favorite hotel is: ─────────────

                      City

I eat roughly ─── lunches and dinners out per week.

☐ This book was a gift ☐ Bought by me ☐ Surveyor copy

The title of this book is: ─────────────

BUSINESS REPLY MAIL
FIRST-CLASS MAIL PERMIT NO 4064 NEW YORK, NY

POSTAGE WILL BE PAID BY ADDRESSEE

ZAGATSURVEY®
4 COLUMBUS CIRCLE FL 5
NEW YORK NY 10102-1374

NO POSTAGE
NECESSARY
IF MAILED
IN THE
UNITED STATES